The Summa Theologiæ ranks amor Church, and is a landmark of medieval western thought. It provides the framework for Catholic studies in systematic theology and for a classical Christian philosophy, and is regularly consulted by scholars of all faiths and none, across a range of academic disciplines. This paperback reissue of the classic Latin/English edition first published by the English Dominicans in the 1960s and 1970s, in the wake of the Second Vatican Council, has been undertaken in response to regular requests from readers and librarians around the world for the entire series of 61 volumes to be made available again. The original text is unchanged, except for the correction of a small number of typographical errors.

The original aim of this edition was not narrowly ecclesiastical. It sought to make this treasure of the Christian intellectual heritage available to theologians and philosophers of all backgrounds, including those who, without claiming to be believers themselves, appreciate a religious integrity which embodies hardbitten rationalism and who recognise in Thomas Aquinas a master of that perennial philosophy which forms the bedrock of European civilisation. Because of this the editors worked under specific instructions to bear in mind not only the professional theologian, but also the general reader with an interest in the 'reason' in Christianity. The parallel English and Latin texts can be used successfully by anybody with a basic knowledge of Latin, while the presence of the Latin text has allowed the translators a degree of freedom in adapting their English version for modern readers. Each volume contains a glossary of technical terms and is designed to be complete in itself to serve for private study or as a course text.

To my mother

NIHIL OBSTAT

THOMAS GILBY O.P.
LAURENTIUS BRIGHT O.P.
THOMAS A. MOORE O.P.

IMPRIMI POTEST

GERARDUS MEATH O.P.
Prior Provincialis Angliæ

Londinii, die 18 Julii 1963

NIHIL OBSTAT

HUBERTUS RICHARDS S.T.L., L.S.S.
Censor deputatus

IMPRIMATUR

✠ GEORGIUS L. CRAVEN
Epus. Sebastopolis, Vic. Cap.

Westmonasterii, die 21 Junii 1963

ST THOMAS AQUINAS
SUMMA THEOLOGIÆ

ST THOMAS AQUINAS

SUMMA
THEOLOGIÆ

Latin text and English translation,
Introductions, Notes, Appendices
and Glossaries

NON NISI TE

PIÆ MEMORIÆ

JOANNIS

PP. XXIII

DICATUM

ALLOCUTIO

PAULI

PP. VI

MCMLXIII

HIS HOLINESS POPE PAUL VI

WAS PLEASED to grant an audience, on 13 December 1963, to a group, representing the Dominican Editors and the combined Publishers of the new translation of the *Summa Theologiæ* of St Thomas, led by His Eminence Michael Cardinal Browne, of the Order of Preachers, and the Most Reverend Father Aniceto Fernandez, Master General of the same Order.

AT THIS AUDIENCE

THE HOLY FATHER made a cordial allocution in which he first welcomed the representatives of a project in which he found particular interest. He went on to laud the perennial value of St Thomas's doctrine as embodying universal truths in so cogent a fashion. This doctrine, he said, is a treasure belonging not only to the Dominican Order but to the whole Church, and indeed to the whole world; it is not merely medieval but valid for all times, not least of all for our own.

His Holiness therefore commended the enterprise of Dominicans from English-speaking Provinces of the Order and of their friends; they were undertaking a difficult task, less because the thought of St Thomas is complicated or his language subtle, than because the clarity of his thought and exactness of language is so difficult to translate. Yet the successful outcome of their efforts would undoubtedly contribute to the religious and cultural well-being of the English-speaking world.

What gave him great satisfaction was the notable evidence of interest in the spread of divine truth on the part of the eminent laymen concerned, members of different communions yet united in a common venture.

For these reasons the Holy Father wished it all success, and warmly encouraged and blessed all those engaged. He was happy to receive the first volume presented to him as a gesture of homage, and promised that he would follow with interest the progress of the work and look forward to the regular appearance of all the subsequent volumes.

VOLUMES

GENERAL PREFACE

BY OFFICIAL APPOINTMENT THE SUMMA PROVIDES THE FRAMEWORK for Catholic studies in systematic theology and for a classical Christian philosophy. Yet the work, which is more than a text-book for professional training, is also the witness of developing tradition and the source of living science about divine things. For faith seeks understanding in the contemplation of God's Logos, his wisdom and saving providence, running through the whole universe.

The purpose, then, of this edition is not narrowly clerical, but to share with all Christians a treasury which is part of their common heritage. Moreover, it consults the interests of many who would not claim to be believers, and yet appreciate the integrity which takes religion into hard thinking.

Accordingly the editors have kept in mind the needs of the general reader who can respond to the reasons in Christianity, as well as of technical theologians and philosophers.

Putting the Latin text alongside the English is part of the purpose. The reader with a smattering of Latin can be reassured when the translator, in order to be clear and readable, renders the thought of St Thomas into the freedom of another idiom without circumlocution or paraphrase.

There are two more reasons for the inclusion of the Latin text. First, to help the editors themselves, for the author's thought is too lissom to be uniformly and flatly transliterated; it rings with analogies, and its precision cannot be reduced to a table of terms. A rigid consistency has not been imposed on the editors of the different volumes among themselves; the original is given, and the student can judge for himself.

Next, to help those whose native tongue is not English or whose duty it is to study theology in Latin, of whom many are called to teach and preach through the medium of the most widespread language of the world, now becoming the second language of the Church.

The Latin is a sound working text, selected, paragraphed, and punctuated by the responsible editor. Important variations, in manuscripts and such major printed editions as the Piana and Leonine, are indicated. The English corresponds paragraph by paragraph and almost always sentence by sentence. Each of the sixty volumes, so far as is possible, will be complete in itself, to serve as a text for a special course or for private study.

THOMAS GILBY, O.P.

ST THOMAS AQUINAS
SUMMA THEOLOGIÆ

VOLUME 2
EXISTENCE AND NATURE OF GOD

(Ia. 2–11)

Latin text. English translation, Introduction,
Notes, Appendices & Glossary

TIMOTHY McDERMOTT O.P.

Additional Appendices by
THOMAS GILBY O.P.

NON NISI TE

To my mother

CAMBRIDGE UNIVERSITY PRESS
Cambridge, New York, Melbourne, Madrid, Cape Town, Singapore, São Paulo

Cambridge University Press
The Edinburgh Building, Cambridge CB2 2RU, UK

Published in the United States of America by Cambridge University Press, New York

www.cambridge.org
Information on this title: www.cambridge.org/9780521393492

This digitally printed first paperback version 2006

A catalogue record for this publication is available from the British Library

ISBN-13 978-0-521-39349-2 hardback
ISBN-10 0-521-39349-3 hardback

ISBN-13 978-0-521-02910-0 paperback
ISBN-10 0-521-02910-4 paperback

CONTENTS

xv

EDITORIAL NOTES

THE LATIN TEXT

There are many manuscripts of the SUMMA extant and quite a few editions. The nearest we have yet come to a critical edition of our part of the SUMMA is the so-called 'Leonine' edition, commissioned by Pope Leo XIII at the end of the previous century. Unfortunately, in the first part of the SUMMA, due to the small number of manuscripts that they consulted, the editors were extremely cautious in accepting readings variant from earlier editions; and this has since turned out to have been excessive caution. The present text has been compiled by reference to the existing editions, including the 'Leonine', and to the variant readings of the manuscripts noted by the Leonine editors in their footnotes. It cannot by any means claim to be itself a critical text, but it is likely that it is more authentic than the usual texts available.

THE TRANSLATION

It has been the aim of the translator to turn the Latin into a running English sufficiently intelligible to be read without recourse to the original text. However, he has also tried to match the translation to the text, sentence by sentence, sufficiently closely for cross-reference to be easy. Latin technical terms have as far as possible been eschewed, except when their adoption in the translation would definitely help understanding. Then they have been introduced non-technically and gradually been allowed to become technical; or, in a few cases, introduced as technical terms and explained in a footnote. Where the reader experiences difficulty and does not find an explanatory footnote, he is referred to the glossary or to the index.

FOOTNOTES

These are of three kinds. The first kind, introduced by numbers, are simple references. If such a footnote is introduced by the abbreviation 'cf', then the references are editorial. If the footnote is not introduced by the abbreviation 'cf' the reference is given by St Thomas himself. However, in these latter cases, the reference which St Thomas generally gives briefly in the text itself has been expanded according to modern practice and removed to the footnote.

The second kind of footnote, introduced by letters, is always editorial, and consists of some briefly explanatory remarks deemed necessary in order to understand St Thomas's thought at that point. Longer explanations are kept to the appendices as far as possible.

The third kind of footnote, introduced by arbitrary signs such as *, †, etc., are textual variants (with translation) considered to be of some importance.

APPENDICES

The last twelve have been written by the General Editor, who alone is responsible for the views there expressed.

REFERENCES

Biblical references are to the Vulgate, bracketed numbers to the Psalms are those of versions based on the Hebrew text. Patristic references are to Migne (PG, Greek Fathers; PL, Latin Fathers). Abbreviations to St Thomas's works are as follows:

Summa Theologiæ, without title. Part, question, article, reply; e.g. 1a. 3, 2 ad 3. 1a2æ. 17, 6. 2a2æ. 180, 10. 3a. 35, 8.

Summa Contra Gentiles, CG. Book, chapter; e.g. *CG*. 1, 28.

Scriptum in IV Libros Sententiarum, Sent. Book, distinction, question, article, solution or *quæstiuncula*, reply; e.g. III *Sent.* 25, 2, 3, ii ad 3.

Compendium Theologiæ, Compend. Theol.

Commentaries of Scripture (*lecturæ, expositiones*): Job, *In Job*; Psalms, *In Psal.*; Isaiah, *In Isa.*; Jeremiah, *In Jerem.*; Lamentations, *In Thren.*; St Matthew, *In Matt.*; St John, *In Joan.*; Epistles of St Paul, e.g. *In ad Rom.* Chapter, verse, *lectio* as required.

Philosophical commentaries: On the *Liber de Causis, In De causis.* Aristotle: *Peri Hermeneias, In Periherm.*; Posterior Analytics, *In Poster.*; Physics, *In Physic.*; *De Cælo et Mundo, In De Cæl.*; *De Generatione et Corruptione, In De gen.*; *Meteorologica, In Meteor.*; *De Anima, In De anima*; *De Sensu et Sensato, In De sensu*; *De Memoria et Reminiscentia, In De memor.*; Metaphysics, *In Meta.*; Nicomachean Ethics, *In Ethic.*, Politics, *In Pol.* Book, chapter, *lectio* as required, also for Expositions on Boëthius, *Liber de Hebdomadibus* and *Liber de Trinitate, In De hebd.* and *In De Trin.*, and on Dionysius *De Divinis Nominibus, In De div. nom.* References to Aristotle give the Bekker annotation.

Quæstiones quodlibetales (de quolibet), Quodl.

Main titles are given in full for other works, including the 10 series of *Quæstiones Disputatæ*.

INTRODUCTION

IF YOU have read St Thomas before you will know what to expect from this volume; if you are coming to him for the first time you may possibly be disappointed and even bewildered, finding his references obscure, his style unfamiliar, the climate of his thought unsympathetic. Those seeking an intellectually reputable and non-dogmatic account of why men believe in God (having heard that Aquinas is the best the Christian tradition can offer) sometimes feel themselves to have found only a medieval, make-believe world, where observation and experiment play second-fiddle to metaphysical presupposition. Those, however, who wish to understand more deeply a religious faith they already hold, often complain of excessive, rather than of meagre rationality in the proceedings. Why this massive weight of syllogism and definition, they ask, and what kinship has such work with the authentic word of God in scripture?

The notes accompanying this translation, and the appendices and glossary which follow it, try to clarify such references and implications as a modern reader may find obscure. The present introduction deals rather with the style and structure of the SUMMA, and with the kind of thinking to be found there, showing how it began and how it relates to the way we think today.

Firstly, we must see the work in its historical background. No matter why we read it, we ought to remember why it was written. For some centuries before St Thomas's time commentary on the scriptures had been feeling the influence of a growing secular culture. In the early middle ages, a gradual resurrection, firstly of classical rhetoric, then of classical logic, and finally of ancient physical science, had led the medieval lecturers on the Bible to pose new kinds of question to their text. Such 'questions' would take the form of objections drawn often from these rediscovered sciences and set over against some particular statement of the scriptural text being commented; the master would discuss the proposed solutions of the dilemma, and argue on behalf of the one he preferred. In the course of time such questions became so numerous and complex that they were separated from the running commentary on the scriptures, and became a course on their own. Gradually systematized and collected in anthologies and compendia, they came to constitute in men's eyes a separate science, the science of theology.

Now St Thomas calls the work that we are translating in this series of volumes a *Summa Theologiæ*, a comprehensive theology, and its appearance in the 1270's marked the apex of the development we have been describing. The reader will notice that the book is in fact set out as an articulated series of questions. A short prologue of sorts introduces each group of questions as they come along, and each large question is broken down into several constituent questions (called 'points of inquiry' or 'articles' in the translation). Each of these constituent questions opens with objections, drawn often from previous authors or from secular science, and immediately countered with an authoritative text, usually scriptural or ecclesiastical. For example, the famous article on 'whether God exists' (question 2, article 3, below) opens with the sentence 'It seems that there is no God, because . . .', and proceeds to give two objections against God's existence; immediately after which comes the authoritative counter-text 'On the other hand, the book of Exodus . . .' To grasp what an article is about one should read all the first half of the article as a long statement of a dilemma, to be resolved in the second half. It would be a mistake to turn to the answer before one had fully grasped the dilemma requiring that answer. It would, of course, be equally a mistake to take either the objection or the counter-text as a short statement of St Thomas's own opinions: the objections are usually contrary to or contradictory of his opinions, whilst the surface meaning of the counter-text is often qualified in some way in the body of the article. After this setting out of the dilemma, St Thomas proceeds to resolve it in the section headed 'Reply', and then finally returns to answer the objections (and if need be the counter-text) in the light of that reply. This is the general structure of each constituent question ('point of inquiry'), and these constituent questions, grouped into larger questions, which are grouped into treatises, which are grouped into volumes, make up St Thomas's SUMMA THEOLOGIÆ, his comprehensive theology.

Despite the apparent complexity of this process, St Thomas's work is a great improvement on those of his predecessors and contemporaries. He tells us himself in his initial prologue (see volume I of this series) that the book is designed for teaching purposes, and so tries to avoid repetitiveness and multiplicity of useless questions and arguments (he does, in fact, usually hold the number of objections down to three), and to adopt the order proper for learning the science rather than one determined by the exposition of some text or the prosecution of some controversy. These were all flaws that he had noticed in the theology text-books available in his own time, and which had been present in his own earlier works to some degree. Perhaps, indeed, St Thomas is half-thinking of the editions of his oral disputations when he talks of repetitiveness and multiplicity of argument, or of his commentary on the Book of Sentences of Peter Lombard when he talks of the exposition of a text, or of his *Summa contra Gentes* ('Against the people outside the Church') when he talks of prosecution of a controversy. The latter work comes nearest in structure to the work we are translating as we shall see, but the difference lies in that little phrase of St Thomas's: 'the order proper to learning a science'. In order to understand the intention and structure of the SUMMA well, we should understand this phrase.

Any science, St Thomas would say, begins from certain seminal ideas. It also begins, of course, with data, with observation and experience. But no matter how much data is amassed, the science cannot begin, the understanding of these data cannot begin without certain seminal ideas. The initial step in a modern physical science, for example, is not any particular phenomenon, nor any particular technique of mathematics or logic, but the discovery of a way of conceiving phenomena which allows a particular technique of logic or of mathematics to be applied to them for the first time. Stephen Toulmin, discussing this point very fully in his book on *The Philosophy of Science*, gives as an example the conception of light as travelling in straight lines, a conception which founded the science of geometrical optics. 'The notion of a light-ray', he writes, 'one might describe as our device for reading the straight lines of our optical diagrams into the phenomena.'[1] The notion of a light-ray, in other words, is a seminal idea so representing light that the technique of geometrical diagrams becomes applicable to it for the first time. From such a seminal idea, usually expressed in an image or model, issues that systematization of observed data which alone can be called science. The merely observed data, transformed by such a seminal idea, become significant and relevant data, for it is the seminal idea, one might say, which gives the phenomena their point. The proper order, therefore, in which to learn a science, will be to begin with its seminal idea, and from there to work out by argument the idea's implications and consequences.

At this point one must distinguish the sciences of philosophy and theology as St Thomas knew them from the modern physical sciences, at least in one respect. To adopt the concept of a light-ray is to represent already familiar phenomena, such as illumination, in a new way that opens them up to calculating techniques. But it would clearly be wrong to think that a concept which opens up phenomena to calculating techniques and to the world of modern science, therefore opens them up for the first time to man and to man's world in general. The fact that man now conceives light in such a way that he can talk about it with mathematical precision does not mean that previously he has never been able to talk about it at all. So one must not only investigate how light is conceived in order that it may enter the world of scientific calculation, but also how it is conceived in order that it may enter the world of man at all, what part it is to be

[1] op cit, p 29.

given in the community of the universe within which man lives and moves and has his being. Or as the medieval would put it, how does light enter into being? Corresponding to the models and seminal ideas which show how things behave precisely and regularly, and give clear mathematical point to experimental data, we need images and concepts which display the rôle and relevance of things in the community of the universe, which reveal the universal point of every element in experience. From this kind of concept or seminal idea spring philosophy and theology.

Of course, it is always possible to reply that things have no universal point, and that nothing is meant by them—they just are. Changes, for example, just happen, because other previous changes just happened; they are not really developments, or achievements, or evolutions, or anything having point. This is not the place to argue such a question, but we must realize what St Thomas's view is. For him 'just being' or 'just happening' is in the last analysis unintelligible. Nothing can enter into being simply as a phenomenon. To exist, as St Thomas sees it, is to have significance, to have point, to play out a rôle. Such an idea of being is indeed the seminal idea of his philosophical view of the world: an idea of being, that is, not just as an arbitrary thereness of things for sense-experience, but as a logical and significant thereness in a community of the universe revealed to man by knowledge and love. The model or image that St Thomas uses to express this idea of being is the model of an action: being is playing out a rôle, realizing a significant conception. We shall be looking later (in appendix 2) at some of the consequences and implications of this seminal idea, and we need only say here that, since action is in turn conceived as the expression and execution of some agent's desire (giving point to the action), the being of things is conceived as fulfilling a rôle desired by someone, as the expression of someone's love. So that this seminal idea of being leads almost immediately to the notion of a God whose intentions rule the world, the expression of whose intentions the world indeed is.[2] Since St Thomas's word for the community of the

---

[2] As an illustration of the different approach of modern science and medieval philosophy, one might compare the two answers to the question 'How does fire heat wood?'. Modern science would make use of the seminal idea of heat as movement or vibration of particles, and explain conduction of heat as a transference of vibrational energy until equilibrium was reached. St Thomas writes as follows: 'If one asks why wood gets hot in the presence of fire, one would answer it is the action natural to fire to heat. And this is because heat belongs to fire as its characteristic property. And this is a consequence of the nature of fire. And so on, until one is driven to God's will' (*CG* III, 97). St Thomas is seeking, so to speak, the *point* of wood getting hot, and he appeals to a series of intellectual concepts designed to reveal the sense or significance of what is happening. It is not just a happening, but an effect of an action consequent upon a property deriving from a nature that is

universe about which we have been talking is 'nature', we may say that God enters into his philosophy as the one who conceives nature, as the 'author' of nature.

If then St Thomas were setting out upon a comprehensive philosophy, a *Summa Philosophiæ*, he would start out from his seminal idea of being, and in following out the implications of this idea he would come across the author of being, he would come across God. This, philosophically speaking, would be 'the proper order of learning' about God. God would occupy the somewhat blurred and puzzling place in the exposition that he occupies in most thinking before the coming of the Christian revelation: he would be recognized, that is to say, as the origin of being, and yet would figure as a conclusion of human knowledge rather than as a seminal idea in it. St Thomas, however, is living after the revelation of God in Christ, and he is setting out upon a comprehensive theology, a *Summa Theologiæ*, a new science sprung from commentary on the Christian Bible. He is engaging himself on a discipline which starts precisely from the new seminal idea given to man by God in Christ. He believes, with the Christian Church, that God has revealed himself in Christ in a new guise: as the friend of man, with whom man can have immediate communion in knowledge and love. Philosophy is now transcended. The man who accepts the Christian revelation need no longer start with a human conception of being and let that lead him to the existence of a loving author of being; he starts now with the God-given conception of a God who loves him, and lets that reveal new depth and meaning in his previous conception of being. Indeed, he lets that theological conception of God illuminate the whole place of God in philosophy, so that theology does not displace philosophy but rather comprehends it in a new synthesis. The coming of Christ, one might say, had a sort of 'reversal' effect on philosophy, for the concept of the author of being now becomes a bridge from the personally-known God to his creation, rather than as before a bridge from created being to its creator God.

Hence the structure of the *Summa*. It is arranged in what St Thomas considers the proper order of learning theology: that is to say, it begins from the seminal idea of God given in Christian revelation, and then draws from this contemplation of God implications for the world, and especially for man. But within this order we catch glimpses of a philosophical order, but in reverse. For we not only proceed from the God of the New Testament—Father, Son and Holy Spirit—to the world of Christian history—

---

intended by a God. He is trying to locate this particular happening in an architecture of the universe built out of causes and effects, doing and being, property and accident, nature and artifice, etc.

the mysteries of Christ and the sacraments of the Church; we also proceed from the author of being to the philosophically conceived cosmos of animate and inanimate, material and spiritual. The order in both cases is theological, but the theological judgments are sometimes passed on philosophical conceptions.

A previous work of St Thomas's, the *Summa contra Gentes*, has a nearly related structure, but it seems that the demands of controversy influence it slightly. Whilst remaining a theological work in that it begins with God and proceeds to consider the world, it nevertheless deals with philosophical conceptions first before approaching the data of revelation. It begins with God the author of nature and then proceeds to discuss nature itself (subjects which presumably even those outside the Christian revelation would find profitable). It then reverts to discussing God, but this time as the Trinity revealed in Christ, and finally moves to a treatment of Christ and his Church. The *Summa Theologiæ* redistributes the four basic elements of this scheme so that the discussion of God is wholly completed before the world and the Church are discussed. But even in the *Summa Theologiæ*, interestingly, within the discussion about God, human speculation is touched on first, and only after the notion of God as author of being has been clarified, do we turn to him as the Trinitarian God of the New Testament revelation. It seems to me that historical considerations have played a part here. St Thomas is conscious of revelation as a historical event that supervened on previous human attempts to know God. It is for example noteworthy that the first question asked in his *Summa* is not 'Whether revelation is necessary to man', but 'Whether revelation WAS necessary to man': a question which involves the first, but is framed with a greater awareness of the concrete way in which revelation came. And the stages by which we come to know God in the *Summa* (the earliest of which are translated in this volume) correspond exactly to the successive approximations to the future revelation of God in heaven which St Thomas sets out in the *Contra Gentes*. In that work he moves from what is common knowledge about God in all men (frequently misconstrued as innate knowledge) (III, 38), to what can be learnt by demonstration (III, 39), and then on to what is revealed to those who believe (III, 40). Not till volumes 6 and 7 of this series will we be reaching this third stage as treated in the *Summa Theologiæ*; with our present volume 2 we are only beginning the four volumes consecrated to the first two stages.

These two stages are thus set out in the *Contra Gentes*:

'An awareness of God, though not clear nor specific, exists in practically everyone. Some people think this is because it is self-evident that God exists, just as other principles of reasoning are self-evident. Others, with more truth, think that the natural use of reason leads man straight away to some sort of knowledge of God. For when men observe the sure and ordered course that things pursue by nature, they see in most cases that somebody must be producing the order they observe, since rule cannot exist without a ruler. Such a consideration, however, is not yet specific enough for one to know immediately who this ruler of nature is, or what kind of being he is, or whether only one such ruler exists. Just so, by observing the movements and actions of a human being, we see that a cause of his behaviour must exist in him such as does not exist in other things, and we call this 'soul', though without yet knowing what the soul is (whether, perhaps, it is bodily) or how it operates. . . .

'Demonstration adds to our knowledge of God, and betters it, by enabling us to come closer to specific knowledge of him. For demonstration shows God to be unchangeable, eternal, not bodily, in no way composite, unique and so on; thus eliminating many attributes from him and so distinguishing him in our minds from other things. For not only affirmations but also denials can lead us to specific knowledge of things: thus it is specific to man not only to be a reasoning animal, but also not to be either irrational or inanimate. There is this difference, however, between the two kinds of specific knowledge thus produced: the one achieved through affirmations is knowledge both of what the thing is and of how it is set apart from other things; the other, achieved through denials, is knowledge that the thing is distinct from others, but what it is remains unknown. Now it is this latter kind of specific knowledge of God that demonstration gives. . . .'

In the section of the *Summa* we are about to read St Thomas follows this summary very exactly. We begin by questioning that knowledge of God which exists in practically everyone. Does it precede demonstrative knowledge of God as knowledge of self-evident principles precedes knowledge of any conclusions drawn from those principles (q 2, art 1), or does it precede demonstrative knowledge as natural use of reason precedes reflective use of reason? St Thomas believes the latter part of this alternative, and he proceeds in the next two articles (q 2, art 2 and 3), to set out a first reflective sketch of the natural argument for the existence of God outlined above. This argument ends up with something called 'God' (as the arguments from the behaviour of human beings end up with something called 'soul'), but is not yet as specific a knowledge of God as demonstration can make it. St Thomas therefore proceeds to the demonstration by elimination described in the above quotation. This he does in five separate stages: first, he denies composition of God (q 3), but to redress the balance he then denies that lack of composition involves lack of perfection (q 4–6). His third and fourth stages explore this denial of imperfection, expressing it first as a denial of imperfection of essence or nature (God's limitlessness, q 7–8), and secondly as a denial of imperfection of existence (God's unchangeableness, q 9–10). Finally, he assures himself that only one God exists (q 11).

For whatever reason then we read this volume, we should remember why it was written: as part of a comprehensive theology, as part of a systematic investigation of the implications of the Christian revelation. What we read is set firmly within a revealed conception of God and the world, a vision taken upon faith. But in the section which is our special concern we are locating within that larger vision what a philosopher can say about God. And the whole is done in a medieval style of question, definition and argument in itself unrelievedly rational, but assuming previous wide experience of the world and acquaintance with Scripture.

QUIA IGITUR principalis intentio hujus sacræ doctrinæ est Dei cognitionem tradere, et non solum secundum quod in se est sed secundum quod est principium rerum et finis earum et specialiter rationalis creaturæ, ut ex dictis est manifestum,[1] ad hujus doctrinæ expositionem intendentes,

> primo tractabimus de Deo,
> secundo de motu rationalis creaturæ in Deum,
> tertio de Christo, qui secundum quod homo via est nobis tendendi in Deum.

> Consideratio autem de Deo tripartita erit:
> primo namque considerabimus ea quæ pertinent ad essentiam divinam,
> secundo ea quæ pertinent ad distinctionem personarum,
> tertio ea quæ pertinent ad processum creaturarum ab ipso.

> Circa essentiam vero divinam
> primo considerandum est an Deus sit,
> secundo quomodo sit vel potius quomodo non sit,
> tertio considerandum erit de his quæ ad operationem ipsius pertinent, scilicet de scientia et voluntate et potentia.

---

[1] cf Ia. 1, 7

[a] These are the three main parts of the *Summa*, namely the *Prima Pars* or first part (vols 1-15 of this series), the *Secunda Pars* or second part (vols 16-47), and the unfinished *Tertia Pars* or third part (vols 48-60). The second part is further divided into the *Prima Secundæ* or first section of the second part (vols 16-30) and the *Secunda Secundæ* or second section of the second part (vols 31-47). For a plan of

SO BECAUSE, as we have shown,[1] the fundamental aim of holy teaching is to make God known, not only as he is in himself, but as the beginning and end of all things and of reasoning creatures especially, we now intend to set forth this divine teaching by treating,

> first, of God,
> secondly, of the journey to God of reasoning creatures,
> thirdly, of Christ, who, as man, is our road to God.[a]

> The treatment of God will fall into three parts:
> first, his nature,
> secondly, the distinction of persons in God,
> thirdly, the coming forth from him of creatures.[b]

> Concerning the nature of God we must discuss
> first, whether there is a God,
> secondly, what manner of being he is, or better, what manner of being he is not.
> thirdly, the knowledge, will and power involved in God's activity.[c]

---

the whole see vol. 1 of this series, and for comments on the *Summa's* structure see the introduction to the present volume.

[b]This is the main division of the *Prima Pars*, namely on the one God (vols 2–5), the Blessed Trinity (vols 6–7), and Creation (vols 8–15).

[c]The present volume covers the first and part of the second of these subdivisions: the second subdivision is completed by vol 3, on how we can know and name God, and the third is covered by vols 4 and 5.

Quæstio 2. de Deo, an Deus sit

Circa primum quæruntur tria:

1. utrum Deum esse sit per se notum,
2. utrum sit demonstrabile,
3. an Deus sit.

articulus 1. utrum Deum esse sit per se notum

AD PRIMUM sic proceditur:[1] 1. Videtur quod Deum esse sit per se notum. Illa enim nobis dicuntur per se nota quorum cognitio nobis naturaliter inest, sicut patet de primis principiis. Sed, sicut dicit Damascenus in principio libri sui, *omnibus cognitio existendi Deum naturaliter est inserta.*[2] Ergo Deum esse est per se notum.

2. Præterea, illa dicuntur esse per se nota quæ statim cognitis terminis cognoscuntur: quod Philosophus attribuit primis demonstrationum principiis.[3] Scito enim quid est totum et quid est pars, statim scitur quod omne totum majus est sua parte. Sed intellecto quid significet hoc nomen Deus statim habetur quod Deus est. Significatur enim hoc nomine id quo majus significari non potest. Majus autem est quod est in re et intellectu quam quod est in intellectu tantum, unde cum intellecto hoc nomine Deus statim sit in intellectu, sequitur etiam quod sit in re. Ergo Deum esse est per se notum.

3. Præterea, veritatem esse est per se notum, quia qui negat veritatem esse concedit veritatem esse. Si enim veritas non est, verum est veritatem non esse; si autem est aliquid verum oportet quod veritas sit. Deus autem est ipsa veritas; *Ego sum via, veritas et vita.*[4] Ergo Deum esse est per se notum.

SED CONTRA, nullus potest cogitare oppositum ejus quod est per se notum, ut patet per Philosophum circa prima demonstrationis principia.[5] Cogitari autem potest oppositum ejus quod est Deum esse, secundum illud *Psalmi*:

---

[1]cf Ia. 17, 3 ad 2; 85, 6; 87, 1 ad 1; 88, 3; Ia2æ. 94, 2; Ia. 12 as a whole. Also I *Sent.* 3, 1, 2. *CG* I, 10, 11; III, 38. *De veritate* X, 12. *De potentia* VII, 2 ad 11. *In psalmos* 7. *In De Trinitate* I, 8 ad 6.

[2]*De Fide Orthodoxa* I, 1. PG 94, 789. St John of Damascus, died A.D. 749, the last of the Greek Fathers and the first theological encyclopædist.

[3]*Posterior Analytics* I, 2. 72a7–8

[4]*John* 14, 6

[5]*Metaphysics* IV, 3. 1005b11. *Posterior Analytics* I, 10. 76b23–27

[a]The theory of demonstration adopted by St Thomas from Aristotle can be put briefly as follows. A true statement about some subject is 1. clearly true to begin

Question 2. whether there is a God

Under the first of these questions there are three points of inquiry:

1. is it self-evident that there is a God?
2. can it be made evident?
3. is there a God?

article 1. *is it self-evident that there is a God?*

THE FIRST POINT:[1] 1. It seems self-evident that there is a God. For things are said to be self-evident to us when we are innately aware of them, as, for example, first principles. Now as Damascene says when beginning his book, *the awareness that God exists is implanted by nature in everybody.*[2] That God exists is therefore self-evident.

2. Moreover, a proposition is self-evident if we perceive its truth immediately upon perceiving the meaning of its terms: a characteristic, according to Aristotle,[3] of first principles of demonstration.[a] For example, when we know what wholes and parts are, we know at once that wholes are always bigger than their parts. Now once we understand the meaning of the word 'God' it follows that God exists. For the word means 'that than which nothing greater can be meant'. Consequently, since existence in thought and fact is greater than existence in thought alone, and since, once we understand the word 'God', he exists in thought, he must also exist in fact.[b] It is therefore self-evident that there is a God.

3. Moreover, it is self-evident that truth exists, for even denying it would admit it. Were there no such thing as truth, then it would be true that there is no truth; something then is true, and therefore there is truth. Now God is truth itself; *I am the way, the truth and the life.*[4] That there is a God, then, is self-evident.

ON THE OTHER HAND, nobody can think the opposite of a self-evident proposition, as Aristotle's discussion of first principles makes clear.[5] But the opposite of the proposition 'God exists' can be thought, for *the fool* in the

---

with, or 2. its truth can be made clear in the light of some more fundamental statement about the subject, or 3. its truth cannot be made clear in this way at all. The statements clearly true to begin with are said to state self-evident propositions, namely the *first principles* mentioned several times in this article. The most fundamental self-evident principle is the *definition* of the subject. Any other statement the truth of which can be made evident in the light of the definition is said to be *demonstrable*. A truth which cannot be made evident in this way is indemonstrable. For further comment see Appendix 1.

[b]This is a formulation of the celebrated argument of St Anselm's *Proslogion*, the so-called 'ontological' argument. For the meaning of the word 'God' see Appendix 4.

Dixit insipiens in corde suo, non est Deus.[6] Ergo Deum esse non est per se notum.

RESPONSIO: Dicendum quod contingit aliquid esse per se notum dupliciter, uno modo secundum se et non quoad nos, alio modo secundum se et quoad nos. Ex hoc enim aliqua propositio est per se nota quod prædicatum includitur in ratione subjecti; ut homo est animal, nam animal est de ratione hominis. Si igitur notum sit omnibus et de prædicato et de subjecto quid sit, propositio illa erit omnibus per se nota; sicut patet in primis demonstrationum principiis, quorum termini sunt quædam communia quæ nullus ignorat, ut ens et non ens, totum et pars, et similia. Si autem apud aliquos notum non sit de prædicato et subiecto quid sit, propositio quidem quantum in se est erit per se nota, non tamen apud illos qui prædicatum et subjectum propositionis ignorant. Et ideo contingit, ut dicit Boëtius, quod quædam sunt *communes animi conceptiones* et per se notæ *apud sapientes tantum, ut incorporalia in loco non esse.*[7]

Dico ergo quod hæc propositio Deus est, quantum in se est per se nota est, quia prædicatum est idem subjecto; Deus enim est suum esse, ut infra patebit.[8] Sed, quia nos non scimus de Deo quid est non est nobis per se nota, sed indiget demonstrari per ea quæ sunt magis nota quoad nos et minus nota secundum naturam, scilicet per effectus.

1. Ad primum ergo dicendum quod cognoscere Deum esse in aliquo communi sub quadam confusione est nobis naturaliter insertum, inquantum scilicet Deus est hominis beatitudo. Homo enim naturaliter desiderat beatitudinem, et quod naturaliter desideratur ab homine naturaliter cognoscitur ab eodem. Sed hoc non est simpliciter cognoscere Deum esse, sicut cognoscere venientem non est cognoscere Petrum quamvis sit Petrus veniens: multi enim perfectum hominis bonum quod est beatitudo æstimant divitias, quidam voluptates, quidam aliquid aliud.

2. Ad secundum dicendum quod forte ille qui audit hoc nomen Deus non intelligit significari aliquid quo majus cogitari non possit, cum quidam crediderint Deum esse corpus. Dato autem quod quilibet intelligat hoc

---

[6]*Psalms* 13 (14), 1; 52 (53), 1
[7]*Quomodo substantiæ bonæ sint* or *De Hebdomadibus.* PL 64, 1311. Anicius Manlius Severinus Boëthius, executed A.D. 524–5. His works were one of the main channels through which Greek speculation passed to the early Latin middle ages.
[8]cf Ia. 3, 4
[c]At first sight the last two sentences seem to contradict one another: if 'God is his own existence' then it would seem that 'what it is to be God' *is* evident to us. And so, since we are 'learned' enough to know that God is his own existence, it must surely be 'self-evident and commonplace' to us that he exists. To this St

psalms *said in his heart: There is no God.*[6] That God exists is therefore not self-evident.

REPLY: A self-evident proposition, though always self-evident in itself, is sometimes self-evident to us and sometimes not. For a proposition is self-evident when the predicate forms part of what the subject means; thus it is self-evident that man is an animal, since being an animal is part of the meaning of man. If therefore it is evident to everybody what it is to be this subject and what it is to have such a predicate, the proposition itself will be self-evident to everybody. This is clearly the case with first principles of demonstration, which employ common terms evident to all, such as 'be' and 'not be', 'whole' and 'part'. But if what it is to be this subject or have such a predicate is not evident to some people, then the proposition, though self-evident in itself, will not be so to those to whom its subject and predicate are not evident. And this is why Boëthius can say that *certain notions are* self-evident and *commonplaces only to the learned, as, for example, that only bodies can occupy space.*[7]

I maintain then that the proposition 'God exists' is self-evident in itself, for, as we shall see later, its subject and predicate are identical, since God is his own existence.[8] But, because what it is to be God is not evident to us, the proposition is not self-evident to us, and needs to be made evident.[c] This is done by means of things which, though less evident in themselves, are nevertheless more evident to us, by means, namely, of God's effects.

Hence: 1. The awareness that God exists is not implanted in us by nature in any clear or specific way. Admittedly, man is by nature aware of what by nature he desires, and he desires by nature a happiness which is to be found only in God. But this is not, simply speaking, awareness that there is a God, any more than to be aware of someone approaching is to be aware of Peter, even should it be Peter approaching: many, in fact, believe the ultimate good which will make us happy to be riches, or pleasure, or some such thing.[d]

2. Someone hearing the word 'God' may very well not understand it to mean 'that than which nothing greater can be thought', indeed, some people have believed God to be a body. And even if the meaning of the

---

Thomas would answer that, though we know it to be true that God is his own existence (arguing from his effects in this world), we cannot fully comprehend what that statement means (cf 1a. 3, 4 ad 2). We can therefore *know it to be true* that the proposition 'God exists' is self-evident in itself, and yet not experience that self-evidence for ourselves. We know that the proposition is self-evident by argument, from our experience of God's effects. This is the distinction the article is making.
[d]cf 1a2æ. 2, on where happiness lies.

nomine Deus significari hoc quod dicitur, scilicet illud quo majus cogitari non potest, non tamen propter hoc sequitur quod intelligat id quod significatur per nomen esse in rerum natura, sed in apprehensione intellectus tantum. Nec potest argui quod sit in re nisi daretur quod sit in re aliquid quo majus cogitari non potest—quod non est datum a ponentibus Deum non esse.

3. Ad tertium dicendum quod veritatem esse in communi est per se notum, sed primam veritatem esse hoc non est per se notum quoad nos.

articulus 2. utrum Deum esse sit demonstrabile

AD SECUNDUM sic proceditur:[1] 1. Videtur quod Deum esse non sit demonstrabile. Deum enim esse est articulus fidei. Sed ea quæ sunt fidei non sunt demonstrabilia, quia demonstratio facit scire, fides autem de *non apparentibus* est, ut patet per Apostolum.[2] Ergo Deum esse non est demonstrabile.

2. Præterea, medium demonstrationis est quod quid est. Sed de Deo non possumus scire quid est sed solum quid non est, ut dicit Damascenus.[3] Ergo non possumus demonstrare Deum esse.

3. Præterea, si demonstraretur Deum esse, hoc non esset nisi ex effectibus ejus. Sed effectus ejus non sunt proportionati ei, cum ipse sit infinitus et effectus finiti, finiti autem ad infinitum non est proportio. Cum ergo causa non possit demonstrari per effectum sibi non proportionatum, videtur quod Deum esse non possit demonstrari.

SED CONTRA est quod Apostolus dicit, *invisibilia Dei per ea quæ facta sunt intellecta conspiciuntur.*[4] Sed hoc non esset nisi per ea quæ facta sunt posset demonstrari Deum esse, primum enim quod oportet intelligi de aliquo est an sit.

RESPONSIO: Dicendum quod duplex est demonstratio. Una quæ est per causam et dicitur propter quid, et hæc est per priora simpliciter; alia est per effectum et dicitur demonstratio quia, et hæc est per ea quæ sunt priora quoad nos (cum enim effectus aliquis nobis est manifestior quam sua causa,

---

[1]cf Ia. 3, 5; 12, 12; 32, 1. III *Sent.* 24, 1, 2 (ii). *CG* I, 12. *De potentia* VII, 3. *In De Trinitate* I, 8

[2]*Hebrews* 11, 1

[3]*De Fide Orthodoxa* I, 4. PG 94, 800

[4]*Romans* I, 20

[a]For the general notion of demonstration see note *a* to previous article. In the statement of a definition, the predicate of the statement is clearly seen to be the very meaning of the subject of the statement. In any statement which is yet to be

word 'God' were generally recognized to be 'that than which nothing greater can be thought', nothing thus defined would thereby be granted existence in the world of fact, but merely as thought about. Unless one is given that something in fact exists than which nothing greater can be thought—and this nobody denying the existence of God would grant—the conclusion that God in fact exists does not follow.

3. It is self-evident that there exists truth in general, but it is not self-evident to us that there exists a First Truth.

article 2. can it be made evident?

THE SECOND POINT:[1] 1. That God exists cannot, it seems, be made evident. For that God exists is an article of faith, and since, as St Paul says, faith is concerned with *the unseen*,[2] its propositions cannot be demonstrated, that is made evident. It is therefore impossible to demonstrate that God exists.

2. Moreover, the central link of demonstration is a definition.[a] But Damascene[3] tells us that we cannot define what God is, but only what he is not. Hence we cannot demonstrate that God exists.

3. Moreover, if demonstration of God's existence were possible, this could only be by arguing from his effects. Now God and his effects are incommensurable; for God is infinite and his effects finite, and the finite cannot measure the infinite. Consequently, since effects incommensurate with their cause cannot make it evident, it does not seem possible to demonstrate that God exists.

ON THE OTHER HAND, St Paul tells us that *the hidden things of God can be clearly understood from the things that he has made*.[4] If so, one must be able to demonstrate that God exists from the things that he has made, for knowing whether a thing exists is the first step towards understanding it.

REPLY: There are two types of demonstration. One, showing 'why', follows the natural order of things among themselves, arguing from cause to effect; the other, showing 'that', follows the order in which we know things, arguing from effect to cause (for when an effect is more apparent

---

demonstrated, this is not so. But suppose the predicate of such a statement can be seen to be necessarily connected with the predicate of the definition of the statement's subject. Then, through or by means of the definition, the predicate and subject of the statement can now be seen to be necessarily connected. This is what is meant by saying that a definition acts as a 'link' in demonstration; for the predicate of the definitional statement acts as a bridge or 'central term' between the subject and predicate of the statement to be demonstrated.

per effectum procedimus ad cognitionem causæ). Ex quolibet autem effectu potest demonstrari propriam causam ejus esse, si tamen ejus effectus sint magis noti quoad nos, quia, cum effectus dependeant a causa, posito effectu necesse est causam præexistere. Unde Deum esse, secundum quod non est per se notum quoad nos, demonstrabile est per effectus nobis notos.

1. Ad primum ergo dicendum quod Deum esse et alia hujusmodi quæ per rationem naturalem nota possunt esse de Deo, ut dicitur Rom.[5] non sunt articuli fidei sed præambula ad articulos. Sic enim fides præsupponit cognitionem naturalem sicut gratia naturam et ut perfectio perfectibile. Nihil tamen prohibet illud quod per se demonstrabile est et scibile, ab aliquo accipi ut credibile qui demonstrationem non capit.

2. Ad secundum dicendum quod cum demonstratur causa per effectum necesse est uti effectu loco definitionis causæ ad probandum causam esse, et hoc maxime contingit in Deo. Quia ad probandum aliquid esse necesse est accipere pro medio quid significet nomen, non autem quod quid est (quia quæstio quid est sequitur ad quæstionem an est). Nomina autem Dei imponuntur ab effectibus, ut postea ostendetur;[6] unde demonstrando Deum esse per effectum accipere possumus pro medio quid significet hoc nomen Deus.

3. Ad tertium dicendum quod per effectus non proportionatos causæ non potest perfecta cognitio de causa haberi: sed tamen ex quocumque effectu manifeste nobis potest demonstrari causam esse, ut dictum est. Et sic ex effectibus Dei potest demonstrari Deum esse, licet per eos non perfecte possimus ipsum cognoscere secundum suam essentiam.

---

[5]*Romans* I, 19–20   [6]cf Ia. 13, 1 ff

[b]Demonstration so far described in the notes is only one type of demonstration: arguing from a thing's essential nature to its properties (or from a cause to effects). Such demonstration not only shows a certain fact to be true (the existence of a property or of an effect), but also shows why it is true (because of the thing's nature, or because of the cause). But it is possible to argue the other way round, and demonstrate the existence of a cause from the existence of an effect. Then, however, one can only show a certain fact to be true (the existence of the cause); one cannot show why it is true, although one can show *why one knows it to be true* (namely because of the existence of the effect). It is because the reasons for knowing a fact and the reasons for the existence of that fact do not always coincide, that one can have demonstrations *that* which are not demonstrations *why*.

[c]The objector thinks God's existence indemonstrable because God's essence is indefinable. But St Thomas points out that demonstration of existence cannot

to us than its cause, we come to know the cause through the effect).[b] Now any effect of a cause demonstrates that that cause exists, in cases where the effect is better known to us, since effects are dependent upon causes, and can only occur if the causes already exist. From effects evident to us, therefore, we can demonstrate what in itself is not evident to us, namely, that God exists.

Hence: 1. The truths about God which St Paul says we can know by our natural powers of reasoning[5]—that God exists, for example—are not numbered among the articles of faith, but are presupposed to them. For faith presupposes natural knowledge, just as grace does nature and all perfections that which they perfect. However, there is nothing to stop a man accepting on faith some truth which he personally cannot demonstrate, even if that truth in itself is such that demonstration could make it evident.

2. When we argue from effect to cause, the effect will take the place of a definition of the cause in the proof that the cause exists; and this especially if the cause is God. For when proving anything to exist, the central link is not what that thing is (we cannot even ask what it is until we know that it exists), but rather what we are using the name of the thing to mean.[c] Now when demonstrating from effects that God exists, we are able to start from what the word 'God' means, for, as we shall see,[6] the names of God are derived from these effects.

3. Effects can give comprehensive knowledge of their cause only when commensurate with it: but, as we have said, any effect whatever can make it clear that a cause exists. God's effects, therefore, can serve to demonstrate that God exists, even though they cannot help us to know him comprehensively for what he is.

---

depend on definition anyway, since definition presupposes existence of the thing defined. (Definition states how the word 'x' must be used if it is to name x. cf note a to 1a. 3, 6.) St Thomas sketches the following order of events: first, we know y to exist; secondly, we use the word 'x' to mean *cause of* y; thirdly, we demonstrate that x exists (cf note b); fourthly, we define x (i.e. present how the word 'x' is used as a declaration of what x is); fifthly, we then demonstrate why certain other truths hold of x (cf note a). So 'demonstrations that', unlike 'demonstrations why', do not presuppose a definition; instead they presuppose the existence of an effect, and of a word to describe the cause of that effect. The objector's point about the indefinability of God is thus irrelevant; what we need rather to know is that things exist which require the kind of cause we use the word 'God' to describe. cf 1a. 1, 7 ad 1; 13, 8. For further discussion see Appendix 1.

articulus 3. *utrum Deus sit*

AD TERTIUM sic proceditur:[1] 1. Videtur quod Deus non sit. Quia si unum contrariorum fuerit infinitum totaliter destruetur aliud. Sed hoc intelligitur in hoc nomine Deus quod sit quoddam bonum infinitum. Si ergo Deus esset, nullum malum inveniretur. Invenitur autem malum in mundo. Ergo Deus non est.

2. Præterea, quod potest compleri per pauciora principia non fit per plura. Sed videtur quod omnia quæ apparent in mundo possunt compleri per alia principia supposito quod Deus non sit, quia ea quæ sunt naturalia reducuntur in principium quod est natura, ea vero quæ sunt a proposito reducuntur in principium quod est ratio humana vel voluntas. Nulla igitur necessitas est ponere Deum esse.

SED CONTRA est quod dicitur *Exod.* ex persona Dei, *Ego sum qui sum.*[2]

RESPONSIO: Dicendum quod Deum esse quinque viis probari potest.

Prima autem et manifestior via est quæ sumitur ex parte motus. Certum est enim et sensu constat aliqua moveri in hoc mundo. Omne autem quod movetur ab alio movetur. Nihil enim movetur nisi secundum quod est in potentia ad illud ad quod movetur. Movet autem aliquid secundum quod est actu; movere enim nihil aliud est quam educere aliquid de potentia in actum, de potentia autem non potest aliquid reduci in actum nisi per aliquid ens actu: sicut calidum in actu ut ignis facit lignum quod est calidum in potentia esse calidum in actu et per hoc movet et alterat ipsum. Non autem est possibile quod idem sit simul in actu et in potentia secundum idem sed solum secundum diversa: quod enim est calidum in actu non potest simul esse calidum in potentia sed est simul frigidum in potentia. Impossibile est ergo quod idem et eodem motu* aliquid sit movens et motum vel quod moveat seipsum. Oportet ergo omne quod movetur ab

---

*Piana, Leonine: *secundum idem et eodem modo,* cannot in the same respect and in the same manner also be a cause of change.

[1]cf for general notions Ia. 7, 4; 13, 8; 44, 1–4; 46, 2 ad 7; 105, 5. For first way Ia. 75, 1 ad 1; 1a2æ. 9, 6; 109, 1. For second way Ia. 104, 2. For third way Ia. 9, 2; 46, 1–2; 48, 2 ad 3. For fourth way Ia. 3, 5 ad 2; 4, 3 ad 2; 6, 2 ad 3; 44, 1; 61, 1; 65, 1. For fifth way Ia. 44, 4; 103, 1; 1a2æ. 1, 2; 12, 5. For the problem of evil cf Ia. 49 as a whole. Other works—*De veritate* V, 2. *CG* I, 13, 15–16; II, 15. *De potentia* III, 5. *In Physic.* VII, *lect.* 2; VIII, *lect.* 9. *In Meta.* XII, *lect.* 5. *Compendium Theol.* 3

[2]*Exodus* 3, 14

[a]Appendices 3 and 4 supply for explanatory footnotes to the arguments that follow.

[b]St Thomas does not use examples in the modern way, as experimental proof of what he is saying; but in the way modern authors use diagrams, as imaginative illustration of already demonstrated truth. Thus, the example of 'fire' in this

article 3. is there a God?

THE THIRD POINT:[1] I. It seems that there is no God. For if, of two mutually exclusive things, one were to exist without limit, the other would cease to exist. But by the word 'God' is implied some limitless good. If God then existed, nobody would ever encounter evil. But evil is encountered in the world. God therefore does not exist.

2. Moreover, if a few causes fully account for some effect, one does not seek more. Now it seems that everything we observe in this world can be fully accounted for by other causes, without assuming a God. Thus natural effects are explained by natural causes, and contrived effects by human reasoning and will. There is therefore no need to suppose that a God exists.

ON THE OTHER HAND, the book of *Exodus* represents God as saying, *I am who am.*[2]

REPLY: There are five ways in which one can prove that there is a God.[a]

The first and most obvious way is based on change. Some things in the world are certainly in process of change: this we plainly see. Now anything in process of change is being changed by something else. This is so because it is characteristic of things in process of change that they do not yet have the perfection towards which they move, though able to have it; whereas it is characteristic of something causing change to have that perfection already. For to cause change is to bring into being what was previously only able to be, and this can only be done by something that already is: thus fire, which is actually hot, causes wood, which is able to be hot, to become actually hot, and in this way causes change in the wood.[b] Now the same thing cannot at the same time be both actually *x* and potentially *x*, though it can be actually *x* and potentially *y*: the actually hot cannot at the same time be potentially hot, though it can be potentially cold. Consequently, a thing in process of change cannot itself cause that same change; it cannot change itself. Of necessity therefore anything in process of change is being changed by something else. Moreover, this something else, if in

---

argument is not meant to support a previous analysis by appeal to empirical fact, but to show how such an analysis works out when applied to the interpretation of ordinary events. This is why St Thomas can content himself with a very limited number of examples, so that the illustration of 'fire' returns again and again in the following pages. At a time when everyone believed it to be one of the four constituent elements of all matter, fire provided a vivid illustration of the metaphysical thesis that causes are both sources of active energy and substances. Whether nowadays the thesis is equally capable of vivid illustration, and whether, if not, the metaphysical thesis fails, is discussed in Appendix 3.

alio moveri. Si ergo id a quo movetur moveatur, oportet et ipsum ab alio moveri, et illud ab alio. Hoc autem non est procedere in infinitum, quia sic non esset aliquod primum movens et per consequens nec aliquod aliud movens, quia moventia secunda non movent nisi per hoc quod sunt mota a primo movente, sicut baculus non movet nisi per hoc quod est motus a manu. Ergo necesse est devenire ad aliquod primum movens quod a nullo movetur, et hoc omnes intelligunt Deum.

Secunda via est ex ratione causæ efficientis. Invenimus enim in istis sensibilibus esse ordinem causarum efficientium; nec tamen invenitur nec est possibile quod aliquid sit causa efficiens sui ipsius, quia sic esset prius seipso quod est impossibile. Non autem est possibile quod in causis efficientibus procedatur in infinitum. Quia in omnibus causis efficientibus ordinatis primum est causa medii et medium est causa ultimi (sive media sint plura sive unum tantum), remota autem causa removetur effectus. Ergo si non fuerit primum in causis efficientibus non erit ultimum nec medium. Sed si procedatur in infinitum in causis efficientibus non erit prima causa efficiens, et sic non erit nec effectus ultimus nec causæ efficientes mediæ, quod patet esse falsum. Ergo necesse est ponere aliquam causam efficientem primam, quam omnes Deum nominant.

Tertia via est sumpta ex possibili et necessario, quæ talis est. Invenimus enim in rebus quædam quæ sunt possibilia esse et non esse, cum quædam inveniantur generari et corrumpi et per consequens* esse et non esse. Impossibile est autem omnia quæ sunt, talia† esse, quia quod possibile est non esse quandoque non est. Si igitur omnia sunt possibilia non esse aliquando nihil fuit in rebus. Sed si hoc est verum etiam nunc nihil esset, quia quod non est non incipit esse nisi per aliquid quod est. Si igitur nihil fuit ens, impossibile fuit quod aliquid inciperet esse, et sic modo nihil esset, quod patet esse falsum. Non ergo omnia entia sunt possibilia sed oportet aliquid esse necessarium in rebus. Omne autem necessarium vel habet causam suæ necessitatis aliunde vel non habet. Non est autem possibile quod procedatur in infinitum in necessariis quæ habent causam suæ necessitatis, sicut nec in causis efficientibus, ut probatum est. Ergo necesse est ponere aliquid quod est per se necessarium non habens causam suæ necessitatis aliunde, sed quod est causa necessitatis aliis.‡

Quarta via sumitur ex gradibus qui in rebus inveniuntur. Invenitur enim in rebus aliquid magis et minus bonum et verum et nobile, et sic

---

*Leonine adds *possibilia*, thus able to be and able not to be.
†Piana, Leonine add *semper*, now nothing of this sort can exist for ever.
‡Piana, Leonine, Pègues add *quod omnes dicunt Deum*, and this everyone calls God.
ᶜIn the first way we have been arguing to a first cause from the element of passivity to be found in all inferior causes; in the second way we argue to a first cause from

process of change, is itself being changed by yet another thing; and this last by another. Now we must stop somewhere, otherwise there will be no first cause of the change, and, as a result, no subsequent causes. For it is only when acted upon by the first cause that the intermediate causes will produce the change: if the hand does not move the stick, the stick will not move anything else. Hence one is bound to arrive at some first cause of change not itself being changed by anything, and this is what everybody understands by God.

The second way is based on the nature of causation.[c] In the observable world causes are found to be ordered in series; we never observe, nor ever could, something causing itself, for this would mean it preceded itself, and this is not possible. Such a series of causes must however stop somewhere; for in it an earlier member causes an intermediate and the intermediate a last (whether the intermediate be one or many). Now if you eliminate a cause you also eliminate its effects, so that you cannot have a last cause, nor an intermediate one, unless you have a first. Given therefore no stop in the series of causes, and hence no first cause, there would be no intermediate causes either, and no last effect, and this would be an open mistake. One is therefore forced to suppose some first cause, to which everyone gives the name 'God'.

The third way is based on what need not be and on what must be, and runs as follows. Some of the things we come across can be but need not be, for we find them springing up and dying away, thus sometimes in being and sometimes not. Now everything cannot be like this, for a thing that need not be, once was not; and if everything need not be, once upon a time there was nothing.[d] But if that were true there would be nothing even now, because something that does not exist can only be brought into being by something already existing. So that if nothing was in being nothing could be brought into being, and nothing would be in being now, which contradicts observation. Not everything therefore is the sort of thing that need not be; there has got to be something that must be. Now a thing that must be, may or may not owe this necessity to something else. But just as we must stop somewhere in a series of causes, so also in the series of things which must be and owe this to other things. One is forced therefore to suppose something which must be, and owes this to no other thing than itself; indeed it itself is the cause that other things must be.

The fourth way is based on the gradation observed in things. Some things are found to be more good, more true, more noble, and so on, and

---

the very activity of inferior causes. The difference between the two ways is more fully discussed in Appendices 7 & 11.

[d]This sentence, which has been a source of difficulty to commentators, is touched on in Appendix 8.

15

de aliis hujusmodi. Sed magis et minus dicitur de diversis secundum quod appropinquant diversimode ad aliquid quod maxime est; sicut magis calidum est quod magis appropinquat maxime calido. Est igitur aliquid quod est verissimum et optimum et nobilissimum et per consequens maxime ens; nam quæ sunt maxime vera sunt maxime entia, ut dicitur II *Metaph*.[3] *Quod autem dicitur maxime in aliquo genere est causa omnium quæ sunt illius generis*, sicut *ignis qui est maxime calidus est causa omnium calidorum*, ut in eodem libro dicitur.[4] Ergo est aliquid quod est causa esse et bonitatis et cujuslibet perfectionis in omnibus rebus, et hoc dicimus Deum.

Quinta via sumitur ex gubernatione rerum. Videmus enim quod aliqua quæ cognitione carent, scilicet corpora naturalia, operantur propter finem, quod apparet ex hoc quod semper aut frequentius eodem modo operantur et consequuntur★ id quod est optimum, unde patet quod non a casu sed ex intentione perveniunt ad finem. Ea autem quæ non habent cognitionem non tendunt in finem nisi directa ab aliquo cognoscente et intelligente, sicut sagitta a sagittatore. Ergo est aliquis† intelligens a quo omnes res naturales ordinantur ad finem, et hoc dicimus Deum.

1. Ad primum ergo dicendum quod sicut dicit Augustinus in *Enchiridio*, *Deus cum sit summe bonus nullo modo sineret aliquid mali esse in operibus suis nisi esset adeo omnipotens et bonus ut bene faceret etiam de malo*.[5] Hoc ergo ad infinitam Dei bonitatem pertinet ut esse permittat mala et ex eis eliciat bona.

2. Ad secundum dicendum quod cum natura propter determinatum finem operetur ex directione alicujus superioris agentis, necesse est ea quæ a natura fiunt etiam in Deum reducere sicut in primam causam. Similiter etiam quæ ex proposito fiunt oportet reducere in aliquam altiorem causam quæ non sit ratio et voluntas humana, quia hæc mutabilia sunt et defectibilia, oportet autem omnia mobilia et deficere possibilia reduci in aliquod primum principium immobile et per se necessarium, sicut ostensum est.

★Piana, Leonine *ut consequantur*, they behave practically always in the way which will obtain the best result.

†Piana, Leonine, *aliquid*, something with understanding.

[3]*Metaphysics* II, I. 993b30

[4]*Metaphysics* II, I. 993b25

[5]*Enchiridion* II. PL 40, 236. St Augustine of Hippo, died 430

[e]The word 'hottest' is susceptible of two interpretations. Either St Thomas means

other things less. But such comparative terms describe varying degrees of approximation to a superlative; for example, things are hotter and hotter the nearer they approach what is hottest.[e] Something therefore is the truest and best and most noble of things, and hence the most fully in being; for Aristotle says that the truest things are the things most fully in being.[3] Now *when many things possess some property in common, the one most fully possessing it causes it in the others: fire*, to use Aristotle's example, *the hottest of all things, causes all other things to be hot*.[4] [f] There is something therefore which causes in all other things their being, their goodness, and whatever other perfection they have. And this we call 'God'.

The fifth way is based on the guidedness of nature. An orderedness of actions to an end is observed in all bodies obeying natural laws, even when they lack awareness. For their behaviour hardly ever varies, and will practically always turn out well; which shows that they truly tend to a goal, and do not merely hit it by accident. Nothing however that lacks awareness tends to a goal, except under the direction of someone with awareness and with understanding; the arrow, for example, requires an archer. Everything in nature, therefore, is directed to its goal by someone with understanding,[g] and this we call 'God'.

Hence: 1. As Augustine says, *Since God is supremely good, he would not permit any evil at all in his works, unless he were sufficiently almighty and good to bring good even from evil*.[5] It is therefore a mark of the limitless goodness of God that he permits evils to exist, and draws from them good.

2. Natural causes act for definite purposes under the direction of some higher cause, so that their effects must also be referred to God as the first of all causes. In the same manner contrived effects must likewise be referred back to a higher cause than human reasoning and will, for these are changeable and can cease to be, and, as we have seen, all changeable things and things that can cease to be require some first cause which cannot change and of itself must be.

'empirically hottest', 'the hottest thing in fact'; or he means 'hottest possible', 'the fulfilment of the ideal of heat'. Either interpretation will do in the argument as it stands; but for further discussion see Appendix 9.

[f]At first sight this argument seems to depend on a Platonic view of the world not adopted by St Thomas, see Appendix 9.

[g]See Appendix 10.

17

COGNITO de aliquo an sit inquirendum restat quomodo sit ut sciatur de eo quid sit. Sed quia de Deo scire non possumus quid sit sed quid non sit, non possumus considerare de Deo quomodo sit sed potius quomodo non sit.

Primo ergo considerandum est quomodo non sit,
secundo quomodo a nobis cognoscatur,
tertio quomodo nominetur.

Potest autem ostendi de Deo quomodo non sit, removendo ab eo ea quæ ei non conveniunt, utpote compositionem, motum, et alia hujusmodi.
 Primo ergo inquiretur de simplicitate ipsius, per quam removetur ab eo compositio. Et quia simplicia in rebus corporalibus sunt imperfecta et partes,
 secundo inquiretur de perfectione ipsius,
 tertio de infinitate ejus,
 quarto de immutabilitate,
 quinto de unitate.

Quæstio 3. de Dei simplicitate

Circa primum quæruntur octo:

1. utrum Deus sit corpus quasi compositionem habens ex partibus quantitativis,
2. utrum sit in eo compositio formæ et materiæ,
3. utrum sit in eo compositio quidditatis sive essentiæ vel naturæ et subjecti,
4. utrum sit in eo compositio quæ est ex essentia et esse,
5. utrum sit in eo compositio generis et differentiæ,
6. utrum sit in eo compositio subjecti et accidentis,
7. utrum sit quocumque modo compositus vel totaliter simplex,
8. utrum veniat in compositionem cum aliis.

---

[a] St Thomas' reasons for saying that we cannot know what God is are made clear in Ia. 12. They resemble the reasons given, for example, by Kant for his agnosticism: namely, that human knowledge is limited in some way by the senses. But because St Thomas maintains that, even though God's nature remains unknown, his existence can be proved (cf Ia. 2, 2 ad 3), our very inability to know God

HAVING RECOGNIZED that a certain thing exists, we have still to investigate the way in which it exists, that we may come to understand what it is that exists. Now we cannot know what God is, but only what he is not;[a] we must therefore consider the ways in which God does not exist, rather than the ways in which he does. We treat then

> first, of the ways in which God does not exist,
> secondly, of the ways in which we know him,
> thirdly, of the ways in which we describe him.[b]

The ways in which God does not exist will become apparent if we rule out from him everything inappropriate, such as compositeness, change and the like. Let us inquire then

> First, about God's simpleness, thus ruling out composite-
> ness. And then, because in the material world simple-
> ness implies imperfection and incompleteness, let us ask
> secondly, about God's perfection,
> thirdly, about his limitlessness,
> fourthly, about his unchangeableness,
> fifthly, about his oneness.

Question 3. God's simpleness

About the first of these questions there are eight points of inquiry:[c]

> 1. is God a body? Is he, that is to say, composed of ex-
>   tended parts?
> 2. is he composed of 'form' and 'matter'?
> 3. is God to be identified with his own essence or nature,
>   with that which makes him what he is?
> 4. can one distinguish in God nature and existence?
> 5. can one distinguish in him genus and difference?
> 6. is he composed of substance and accidents?
> 7. is there any way in which he is composite, or is he alto-
>   gether simple?
> 8. does he enter into composition with other things?

becomes for St Thomas a fruitful piece of information about him. See further discussion in Appendix 12.
[b]The present volume deals with only the first of these three points. The second and the third are dealt with in volume 3 of this series.
[c]See Appendix 12 (3–9).

articulus I. *utrum Deus sit corpus quasi compositionem habens ex partibus quantitativis*

AD PRIMUM sic proceditur:[1] I. Videtur quod Deus sit corpus. Corpus enim est quod habet trinam dimensionem. Sed sacra Scriptura attribuit Deo trinam dimensionem: dicitur enim *Job*:[2] *Excelsior cælo est et quid facies? profundior inferno et unde cognosces? longior terra mensura ejus et latior mari.* Ergo Deus est corpus.

2. Præterea, omne figuratum est corpus, cum figura sit qualitas circa quantitatem. Sed Deus videtur esse figuratus, cum scriptum sit *Gen. Faciamus hominem ad imaginem et similitudinem nostram,*[3] figura enim imago dicitur secundum illud *Hebr. cum sit splendor gloriæ et figura substantiæ ejus,*[4] idest imago. Ergo Deus est corpus.

3. Præterea, omne quod habet partes corporeas est corpus. Sed Scriptura attribuit Deo partes corporeas. Dicitur enim *Job, si habes brachium ut Deus,*[5] et in psalmo, *oculi Domini super iustos,*[6] et *dextera Domini fecit virtutem.*[7] Ergo Deus est corpus.

4. Præterea, situs non competit nisi corpori. Sed ea quæ ad situm pertinent in Scripturis dicuntur de Deo, dicitur enim I *Isaiæ, vidi Dominum sedentem,*[8] et *stat ad judicandum Dominus.*[9] Ergo Deus est corpus.

5. Præterea, nihil potest esse terminus localis a quo vel ad quem nisi sit corpus vel aliquod corporeum. Sed Deus in Scriptura dicitur esse terminus localis ut ad quem secundum illud *Psalmi, accedite ad eum et illuminamini*;[10] et ut a quo secundum illud *Hierem., recedentes a te in terra scribentur.*[11] Ergo Deus est corpus.

SED CONTRA est quod dicitur Ioan. *Spiritus est Deus.*[12]

RESPONSIO: Dicendum absolute Deum non esse corpus, quod quidem tripliciter ostendi potest.

Primo quidem quia nullum corpus movet non motum, ut patet inducendo per singula. Ostensum est autem supra quod Deus est primum movens immobile.[13] Unde manifestum est quod Deus non est corpus.

Secundo vero modo quia necesse est id quod est primum ens esse in actu et nullo modo in potentia. Licet enim in uno et eodem quod exit de potentia in actum prius sit potentia quam actus, simpliciter tamen actus prior est potentia, quia quod est in potentia non reducitur in actum nisi per ens actu. Ostensum est autem quod Deus est primum ens.[14] Impossibile est igitur quod in Deo sit aliquid in potentia. Omne autem corpus est in

---

[1]cf Ia. 75, I. *CG* I, 20; *In Meta.* XII lect. 8. *Compendium Theol.* 16
[2]*Job* II, 8–9   [3]*Genesis* I, 26   [4]*Hebrews* I, 3
[5]*Job* 40, 4 (9)   [6]*Psalms* 33 (34), 16   [7]*Psalms* 117 (118), 16
[8]*Isaiah* 6, I   [9]*Isaiah* 3, 13

article 1. is God a body composed of extended parts?

THE FIRST POINT:[1] 1. God, it would seem, is a body. For anything having three dimensions is a body, and the Scriptures[2] ascribe three dimensions to God: *He is higher than the heaven and what wilt thou do? he is deeper than hell and how wilt thou know? the measure of him is longer than the earth and broader than the sea.* God then is a body.

2. Moreover, only bodies have shape, for shape is characteristic of extended things as such. God however seems to have a shape, for in *Genesis* we read: *Let us make man to our image and likeness,*[3] where image means figure or shape as in *Hebrews: who being the brightness of his glory, and the figure* (that is to say, image) *of his substance.*[4] Therefore God is a body.

3. Moreover, the parts of the body can belong only to a body. But Scripture ascribes parts of the body to God, saying in *Job, Have you an arm like God?*[5] and in the psalms, *The eyes of the Lord are toward the righteous,*[6] and *the right hand of the Lord does valiantly.*[7] Therefore God is a body.

4. Only bodies can assume postures. But Scripture ascribes certain postures to God: thus Isaiah *saw the Lord sitting,*[8] and says that *the Lord stands to judge.*[9] Therefore God is a body.

5. Moreover, nothing can act as starting-point or finishing-point of a movement unless it be body or bodily. Now God is referred to in Scripture as the finishing-point of a movement, *Come ye to him and be enlightened;*[10] and again as a starting-point, *They that depart from thee shall be written in the earth.*[11] Therefore God is a body.

ON THE OTHER HAND, John writes: *God is spirit.*[12]

REPLY: In no sense is God a body, and this may be shown in three ways.

First, experience can offer no example of a body causing change without itself being changed. Now God has been shown above to be the unchanging first cause of change.[13] Clearly then God is not a body.

Secondly, in the first existent thing everything must be actual; there can be no potentiality whatsoever. For although, when we consider things coming to exist, potential existence precedes actual existence in those particular things; nevertheless, absolutely speaking, actual existence takes precedence of potential existence. For what is able to exist is brought into existence only by what already exists. Now we have seen that the first existent is God.[14] In God then there can be no potentiality. In bodies,

---

potentia, quia continuum inquantum hujusmodi divisibile est. Impossibile est igitur Deum esse corpus.

Tertio quia Deus est id quod est nobilissimum in entibus, ut ex dictis[15] patet. Impossibile est autem aliquod corpus esse nobilissimum in entibus. Quia corpus aut est vivum aut non vivum, corpus autem vivum manifestum est quod est nobilius corpore non vivo; corpus autem vivum non vivit inquantum corpus quia sic omne corpus viveret, oportet igitur quod vivat per aliquid aliud, sicut corpus nostrum vivit per animam. Illud autem per quod vivit corpus est nobilius quam corpus. Impossibile est igitur Deum esse corpus.

1. Ad primum ergo dicendum quod sicut supra dictum est sacra Scriptura tradit nobis spiritualia et divina sub similitudinibus corporalium.[16] Unde cum trinam dimensionem Deo attribuit sub similitudine quantitatis corporeæ quantitatem virtualem ipsius designat: utpote per profunditatem virtutem ad cognoscendum occulta, per altitudinem excellentiam virtutis super omnia, per longitudinem durationem sui esse, per latitudinem affectum dilectionis ad omnia. Vel ut dicit Dionysius, per profunditatem Dei intelligitur incomprehensibilitas ipsius essentiæ, per longitudinem processus virtutis ejus omnia penetrantis, per latitudinem vero superextensio ejus ad omnia inquantum scilicet sub ejus protectione omnia continentur.[17]

2. Ad secundum dicendum quod homo dicitur esse ad imaginem Dei non secundum corpus sed secundum id quod* homo excellit alia animalia. Unde *Gen* 1. postquam dictum est, *Faciamus hominem ad imaginem et similitudinem nostram,* subditur, *ut præsit piscibus maris, etc.* Excellit autem homo omnia alia animalia quantum ad rationem et intellectum. Unde secundum intellectum et rationem quæ sunt incorporea homo est ad imaginem Dei.

3. Ad tertium dicendum quod partes corporeæ attribuuntur Deo in scripturis ratione suorum actuum secundum quamdam similitudinem. Sicut actus oculi est videre, unde oculus de Deo dictus significat virtutem ejus ad videndum modo intelligibili non sensibili. Et similiter est de aliis partibus.

4. Ad quartum dicendum quod etiam ea quæ ad situm pertinent non attribuuntur Deo nisi secundum quamdam similitudinem. Sicut dicitur sedens propter suam immobilitatem et auctoritatem, et stans propter suam fortitudinem ad debellandum omne quod adversatur.

5. Ad quintum dicendum quod ad Deum non acceditur passibus corporalibus cum ubique sit, sed affectibus mentis, et eodem modo ab eo receditur. Et sic accessus et recessus sub similitudine localis motus designant spiritualem affectum.

---

*Piana, Leonine *quo*, because of that in virtue of which he is superior.
[15]cf 1a. 2, 3   [16]cf 1a. 1, 9

however, there is always potentiality, for the extended as such is potential of division. God, therefore, cannot be a body.

Thirdly, it is evident from what has been said that God is the most excellent of beings,[15] but no body can be the most excellent of beings. For bodies are either living or non-living, and of these living bodies are clearly the more excellent. Now a living body is not alive simply in virtue of being a body (otherwise all bodies would be living); it is alive because of some other principle, in our case, the soul. Such a principle will be more excellent than body as such. God therefore cannot be a body.

Hence: 1. We remarked earlier that the Scriptures make use of bodily metaphors to convey truth about God and about spiritual things.[16] In ascribing, therefore, three dimensions to God, they are using bodily extension to symbolize the extent of God's power: depth, for example, symbolizes his power to know what is hidden; height, the loftiness of his power above all other things; length, the lasting quality of his existence; breadth, the universality of his love. Or there is Dionysius' explanation of depth as the incomprehensibility of God's nature, length as the penetration of all things by God's power, and breadth the boundless reach of God's guardianship enveloping all things.[17]

2. Man is said to be to God's image, not because he has a body, but because of his superiority to other animals; and this is why Genesis, after saying, *Let us make man in our image and likeness*, adds, *that he may have dominion over the fishes of the sea*, and so on. This superiority man owes to reason and intellect. So that man is to God's image because of his intellect and reason, which are not bodily characteristics.

3. Parts of the body are ascribed to God in the Scriptures by a metaphor drawn from their functions. Eyes, for example, see, and so, we call God's power of sight his eye, though it is not a sense-power, but intellect. And so with other parts of the body.

4. The ascribing of posture to God is again simply metaphor. Sitting symbolizes his authority and his steadfastness; standing his might triumphing in the face of all opposition.

5. One comes to God and one departs from him not by bodily movement, since he is everywhere, but by movement of the heart. Approaching and drawing away are metaphors which picture being moved in spirit as being moved in space.

---

[17]*De Divinis Nominibus* 9, 5. PG 3, 913. Denis or Dionysius the Areopagite, now generally called the Pseudo-Denis, probably a fifth-century Syrian monk, was presented as a disciple of St Paul. His writings, Platonist in character, were therefore of great authority in the Middle Ages.

articulus 2. *utrum sit in eo compositio formæ et materiæ*

AD SECUNDUM sic proceditur:[1] 1. Videtur quod in Deo sit compositio formæ et materiæ. Omne enim quod habet animam est compositum ex materia et forma, quia anima est forma corporis. Sed scriptura attribuit animam Deo, introducitur enim *ad Hebr.* ex persona Dei: *justus autem meus ex fide vivit, quod si subtraxerit se, non placebit animæ meæ.*[2] Ergo Deus est compositus ex materia et forma.

2. Præterea, ira, gaudium et hujusmodi sunt passiones conjuncti, ut dicitur I *de Anima.*[3] Sed huiusmodi attribuuntur Deo in Scriptura, dicitur enim in *Psalmo*: *iratus est furore Dominus in populum suum.*[4] Ergo Deus ex materia et forma est compositus.

3. Præterea, materia est principium individuationis. Sed Deus videtur esse individuum, non enim de multis prædicatur. Ergo est compositus ex materia et forma.

SED CONTRA, omne compositum ex materia et forma est corpus, quantitas enim dimensiva est quæ primo inhæret materiæ. Sed Deus non est corpus, ut ostensum est.[5] Ergo Deus non est compositus ex materia et forma.

RESPONSIO: Dicendum quod impossibile est in Deo esse materiam.

Primo quidem quia materia id quod est in potentia est.* Ostensum est autem quod Deus est purus actus non habens aliquid de potentialitate.[6] Unde impossibile est quod Deus sit compositus ex materia et forma.

Secundo quia omne compositum ex materia et forma est perfectum et

---

*Piane, Leonine: *est id quod est in potentia*, matter is that which is potential.

[1]cf Ia. 50, 2. For second objection cf Ia. 19, 11. For third objection cf 3a. 77, 2. See also I *Sent.* 35, 1, 1. *CG* I, 17. *Compendium Theol.* 28

[2]*Hebrews* 10, 38

[3]*De anima* I, 1. 403a3 ff

[4]*Psalms* 105 (106), 40

[5]cf Ia. 3, 1

[6]cf Ia. 3, 1

[a]This is technical vocabulary, but easily mastered. For we often speak of things assuming a variety of forms: water and ice, for example, are different forms of one substance, represented chemically by the formula H_2O. We can expand this way of talking by saying that, when water changes to ice, beneath the change of form there persists a more fundamental *substantial form*, represented by the formula H_2O, which does not change. Further, since material things can change even their under-lying nature, one substance changing into another, there are some changes in which no latent and more fundamental form persists; all that persists is, so to speak, the ability or potentiality of the things to change into one another, the potentiality of assuming new substantial forms. This potentiality St Thomas, following Aristotle,

article 2. *is God composed of 'form' and 'matter'?*

THE SECOND POINT:[1] I. God seems to be composed of 'form' and 'matter'.[a] For since soul is the form of the body, anything with a soul is composed of matter and form. Now the Scriptures ascribe soul to God; thus in *Hebrews* we find quoted as if from the mouth of God: *my righteous one shall live by faith, and if he shrinks back my soul will have no pleasure in him.*[2] God therefore is composed of matter and form.

2. Moreover, according to Aristotle, anger, joy and the like, affect body and soul together.[3] Now the Scriptures ascribe such dispositions to God: *the anger of the Lord*, says the psalm, *was kindled against his people.*[4] God then is composed of matter and form.

3. Moreover, individualness derives from matter. Now God seems to be an individual, and not something common to many individuals. So God must be composed of matter and form.

ON THE OTHER HAND, since dimension is an immediate property of matter, anything composed of matter and form will be a body. Now we have seen that God is not a body.[5] God therefore is not composed of matter and form.

REPLY: God cannot contain matter.

First, because the very existence of matter is a being potential; whilst God, as we have seen, contains no potentiality, but is sheer actuality.[6] God cannot therefore be composed of matter and form.

Secondly, in complexes of form and matter it is the form which gives

---

called *matter*. Matter of itself has no form, and cannot therefore exist except it assume a form; nevertheless, it must be postulated if fundamental changes of nature are to be possible.

In living things 'form' and 'matter' are called by St Thomas 'body' and 'soul'. Here an ambiguity arises. 'Body' in this sense (which is the sense generally throughout article 2) must be distinguished from 'body' in the sense used throughout article 1. In article 1 'body' meant an already dimensioned thing, living or nonliving; in article 2 it refers rather to the capacity or potentiality of living things to decay and assume new substantial forms, and therefore, as a consequence, new dimensions. Since some common properties reappear with every new form, and since dimension is the most fundamental of these, everything with 'body' in the sense of article 2 will be a 'body' in the sense of article 1. A similar ambiguity must be noticed later in article 2 where it is said that 'dimension is an immediate property of matter': this is not implying that matter is an already dimensioned thing; only a complex of form and matter, of body and soul, can be extended or dimensioned, for indeed only a complex of matter and form can exist.

bonum per suam formam, unde oportet quod sit bonum per participationem secundum quod materia participat formam. Primum autem quod est bonum et optimum quod Deus est non est bonum per participationem, quia bonum per essentiam prius est bono per participationem. Unde impossibile est quod Deus sit compositus ex materia et forma.

Tertio quia unumquodque agens agit per suam formam, unde secundum quod aliquid se habet ad formam sic se habet ad hoc quod sit agens. Quod igitur primum est et per se agens oportet quod sit primo et per se forma. Deus autem est primum agens cum sit prima causa efficiens, ut ostensum est.[7] Est igitur per essentiam suam forma et non compositus ex materia et forma.

1. Ad primum ergo dicendum quod anima attribuitur Deo per similitudinem actus. Si enim volumus aliquid nobis ex anima nostra est, unde illud dicitur esse placitum animæ Dei quod est placitum voluntati ejus.

2. Ad secundum dicendum quod ira et hujusmodi attribuuntur Deo secundum similitudinem effectus. Quia enim proprium est irati punire, ira ejus punitio metaphorice vocatur.

3. Ad tertium dicendum quod formæ quæ sunt receptibiles in materia individuantur per materiam, quæ non potest esse in alio cum sit primum subjectum; forma vero quantum est de se nisi aliquid aliud impediat recipi potest a pluribus. Sed illa forma quæ non est receptibilis in materia sed est per se subsistens ex hoc ipso individuatur quod non potest recipi in alio, et hujusmodi forma est Deus. Unde non sequitur quod habeat materiam.

---

[7] cf Ia. 2, 3

[b] The properties of a thing not only contribute to the perfection of that thing, but are also more or less perfect in themselves when compared to the properties of other things. Hence properties can belong to things in three ways, according to Aquinas. The *strict* property perfects the thing it is in, and is itself fully perfect in that thing. When a property perfects, but is itself not fully perfect, the thing is said to *partake* the property. When the property, though itself fully perfect in a thing, leaves that thing not yet perfected, the thing is said to possess the property *eminently*. Thus, if intellectuality reaches its perfection only in God, whilst sense-life is already fully perfect in animals, man can be said to partake intellectuality, to be strictly rational and eminently sensible (cf Ia. 108, 5). That matter merely partakes form will become clear from the next note.

[c] For the sake of clearness the translation transposes the two halves of the first sentence of the text of this answer. We here take a step forward from the notion of

goodness and perfection. Such complexes therefore are but partakers of goodness, for matter merely partakes of form.[b] Now whatever is good of itself is prior to anything merely partaking goodness; so that God, the first and most perfect good, is no mere partaker of goodness, and thus cannot be composed of matter and form.

Thirdly, an agent acts in virtue of its form, and so the way in which it is an agent will depend upon the way in which it has form. A primary and immediate source of activity must therefore be primarily and immediately form. Now God is the primary source of all activity, since, as we saw, he is the first cause.[7] God then is essentially form, and not composed of matter and form.

Hence: 1. Soul is ascribed to God by a metaphor drawn from its activity. For since soul is the seat of volition in men, we call what is pleasing to God's will, pleasing to his soul.

2. Anger and the like are ascribed to God by a metaphor drawn from their effects. For it is characteristic of anger that it stimulates men to requite wrong. Divine retribution is therefore metaphorically termed anger.

3. If form be considered in itself, free of extraneous factors, then any form assumed by one material thing can be assumed by more than one; individualness derives from matter, which, as the primary substrate of form, cannot be assumed by anything else. A form however of the sort that is not assumed by material things, but itself subsists as a thing, cannot be assumed by anything else, and is thus individual of itself. Now God is such a form, and therefore does not require matter.[c]

'form' described in note *a* above. There we were considering material things, things, namely, which persist for a time under one form, but sooner or later as a result of some change assume another form. The ability or potentiality of such things to assume a variety of forms we called 'matter'. Here we go on to ask: may not things exist which are permanently what they are, things that cannot change and therefore cannot assume new forms? Such things would possess no potentiality to assume a variety of forms, and thus, by definition, would not possess matter. The arguments already given for the existence of God must be taken as proving that at least one such sheer form exists; later (1a. 50, 2) St Thomas will take up the question of whether there can be others. In the terminology of the last note we can see that he would consider that material things partook of form, immaterial things were forms strictly, and God was a form eminently.

articulus 3. *utrum sit in eo compositio quidditatis sive essentiæ*
vel naturæ et subjecti

AD TERTIUM sic proceditur:[1] 1. Videtur quod non sit idem Deus quod sua essentia vel natura. Nihil enim est in seipso, sed essentia vel natura Dei quæ est deitas dicitur esse in Deo. Ergo videtur quod Deus non sit idem quod sua essentia vel natura.

2. Præterea, effectus assimilatur suæ causæ, quia omne agens agit sibi simile. Sed in rebus creatis non est idem suppositum quod sua natura, non enim idem est homo quod sua humanitas. Ergo nec Deus est idem quod sua deitas.

CONTRA, de Deo dicitur quod est vita, non solum quod est vivens, ut patet *Ioan*. *Ego sum via, veritas et vita*.[2] Sicut autem se habet vita ad viventem ita deitas ad Deum. Ergo Deus est ipsa deitas.

RESPONSIO: Dicendum quod Deus est idem quod sua essentia vel natura.

Ad cujus intellectum sciendum est quod in rebus compositis ex materia et forma necesse est quod differant natura vel essentia et suppositum. Quia essentia vel natura comprehendit in se illa tantum quæ cadunt in definitione speciei: sicut humanitas comprehendit in se ea quæ cadunt in definitione hominis, his enim homo est homo, et hoc significat humanitas, hoc scilicet quo homo est homo. Sed materia individualis cum accidentibus omnibus individuantibus ipsam non cadunt in definitione speciei; non enim in definitione hominis cadunt hæ carnes et hæc ossa, aut albedo vel nigredo, vel aliquid hujusmodi. Unde hæ carnes et hæc ossa et accidentia designantia hanc materiam non concluduntur in humanitate, et tamen in eo qui est homo includuntur. Unde id quod est homo habet in se aliquid quod non habet humanitas, et propter hoc non est totaliter idem homo et humanitas, sed humanitas significatur ut pars formalis hominis; quia principia definientia habent se formaliter respectu materiæ individuantis.

In his igitur quæ non sunt composita ex materia et forma, in quibus individuatio non est per materiam individualem, idest per hanc materiam, sed ipsæ formæ per se individuantur, oportet quod ipsæ formæ sint supposita subsistentia. Unde in eis non differt suppositum et natura.

Et sic, cum Deus non sit compositus ex materia et forma, ut ostensum est,[3] oportet quod Deus sit sua deitas, sua vita, et quidquid aliud sic de Deo prædicatur.

1. Ad primum ergo dicendum quod de rebus simplicibus loqui non possumus nisi per modum compositorum a quibus cognitionem accepimus.

---

[1]cf Ia. 11, 3; 13, 9; 29, 2 ad 3; 3a. 2, 2. Also I *Sent*. 34, 1, I. *CG* I, 21. *De un. Verb*. I. *De anima* 17 ad 10. *Quodl*. II 2, 2. *De quatuor oppos*. 4

article 3. is God to be identified with his own essence or nature,
with that which makes him what he is?

THE THIRD POINT:[1] 1. It seems that God is not to be identified with his essence or nature. For the essence or nature of God is godhead, and godhead is said to reside in God. Now nothing resides in itself. It seems therefore that God must differ from his essence or nature.

2. Moreover, effects resemble their causes, for what a thing does reflects what it is. Now we do not identify created things with their natures: human nature is not a man. Neither then is godhead God.

ON THE OTHER HAND, God is not only called living, but life: *I am the way, the truth and the life.*[2] Now godhead bears the same relationship to God, as life does to the living. God then is godhead itself.

REPLY: God is to be identified with his own essence or nature.

We shall understand this when we see why things composed of matter and form must not be identified with their natures or essences. Essence or nature includes only what defines the species of a thing: thus human nature includes only what defines man, or what makes man man, for by 'human nature' we mean that which makes man man. Now the species of a thing is not defined by the matter and properties peculiar to it as an individual; thus we do not define man as that which has this flesh and these bones, or is white, or black, or the like. This flesh and these bones and the properties peculiar to them belong indeed to this man, but not to his nature. An individual man then possesses something which his human nature does not, so that a man and his nature are not altogether the same thing. 'Human nature' names, in fact, the formative element in man; for what gives a thing definition is formative with respect to the matter which gives it individuality.

The individuality of things not composed of matter and form cannot however derive from this or that individual matter, and the forms of such things must therefore be intrinsically individual and themselves subsist as things. Such things are thus identical with their own natures.

In the same way, then, God, who, as we have seen, is not composed of matter and form,[3] is identical with his own godhead, with his own life and with whatever else is similarly said of him.

Hence: 1. In talking about simple things we have to use as models the composite things from which our knowledge derives. Thus when God is

---

[2]*John* 14, 6
[3]cf 1a. 3, 2

29

Et ideo de Deo loquentes utimur nominibus concretis ut significemus ejus subsistentiam, quia apud nos non subsistunt nisi composita; et utimur nominibus abstractis ut significemus ejus simplicitatem. Quod ergo dicitur deitas vel vita vel aliquid hujusmodi esse in Deo referendum est ad diversitatem quæ est in acceptione intellectus nostri, et non ad aliquam diversitatem rei.

2. Ad secundum dicendum quod effectus Dei imitantur ipsum non perfecte, sed secundum quod possunt. Et hoc ad defectum imitationis pertinet quod id quod est simplex et unum non possunt repræsentare nisi per multa, et sic accidit in eis compositio ex qua provenit quod in eis non est idem suppositum quod natura.

articulus 4. utrum sit in eo compositio quæ est ex essentia et esse

AD QUARTUM sic proceditur:[1] 1. Videtur quod in Deo non sit idem essentia et esse. Si enim hoc sit tunc ad esse divinum nihil additur. Sed esse cui nulla fit additio est esse commune quod de omnibus prædicatur; sequitur ergo quod Deus sit ens commune prædicabile de omnibus. Hoc autem est falsum secundum illud *Sap. incommunicabile nomen lignis et lapidibus imposuerunt.*[2] Ergo esse Dei non est ejus essentia.

2. Præterea, de Deo scire possumus an sit, non autem possumus scire quid sit, ut supra dictum est.[3] Ergo non est idem esse Dei et quod quid est ejus sive quidditas vel natura.

SED CONTRA est quod Hilarius dicit: *esse non est accidens in Deo sed subsistens veritas.*[4] Id ergo quod subsistit in Deo est suum esse.

RESPONSIO: Dicendum quod Deus non solum est sua essentia, ut ostensum est,[5] sed est suum esse, quod quidem multipliciter ostendi potest.

---

[1]Ia. 13, 11; 44, 1; 50, 2 ad 3; 75, 5 ad 4. Also I *Sent.* 8, 4, 1; 5, 2; 34, 1, 1; II, 1, 1, 1. *CG* I, 22; II, 52. *De potentia* VII, 2. *De spirit. creat.* 1. *Compend. Theol.* II. *De quatuor oppos.* 4. *De ente et essentia* 5. *Quodl.* II, 2, 1.

[2]*The Wisdom of Solomon* 14, 21   [3]cf Ia. 2, 2

[4]*De Trinitate* VII. PL 10, 208. St Hilary, Bishop of Poitiers, died A.D. 368, an early Latin father much influenced by Greek theology, and a strong opponent of the Arian heresy   [5]cf Ia. 3, 3

[a]The words translated as 'existence' and 'essence' both derive from the Latin verb *to be*, and it would have been possible to translate them both by the English word 'being'. This would naturally have led to confusion, particularly as the word 'being' is usually chosen to translate yet a third derivative of the Latin verb *to be*. A discussion of the three Latin terms (*esse, essentia, ens*) will be found in Appendices 8(3) and 12(7); what follows is merely a summary of that discussion. St Thomas conceives the being of a thing on the model of an action which that thing exerts, and this universal action of the thing being itself is thought of as the inner significance

being referred to as a subsistent thing, we use concrete nouns (since the subsistent things with which we are familiar are composite); but to express God's simpleness we use abstract nouns. So that when we talk of godhead or life or something of that sort residing in God, the diversity this implies is not to be attributed to God himself, but to the way in which we conceive him.

2. God's effects resemble God as far as they can, but not perfectly. One of the defects in resemblance is that they can reproduce only manifoldly what in itself is one and simple. As a result they are composite, and so cannot be identified with their natures.

article 4. can one distinguish in God nature and existence?

THE FOURTH POINT:[1] 1. It is not, it seems, the nature of God simply to exist. If it were, there would be nothing to specify that existence; and since unspecified existence is existence in general and belongs to everything, the word 'God' would mean an existent in general, and would name anything. Now this is false, as the book of *Wisdom* shows: *they invested stocks and stones with the incommunicable name.*[2] So it is not God's nature simply to exist.

2. Moreover, as we remarked earlier, we can know clearly that there is a God, and yet cannot know clearly what he is.[3] So the existence of God is not to be identified with what God is, with God's 'whatness' or nature.

ON THE OTHER HAND, Hilary writes: *Existence does not add anything to God; it is his very substance.*[4] The substance of God is therefore his existence.

REPLY: That God is his own essence, we have seen;[5] that he is also his own existence can be shown in a number of ways.[a]

─────────────────────────────

of all the particular actions in which the thing engages. One might perhaps call it the action of being be-ing being, where the word 'being' is at once subject, verb and complement. 'Being' as verb (*esse*) denotes the quasi-action of be-ing (*actus essendi*), which might be compared to talking of the act of living. *Esse* I have usually translated 'existence' though the translation has some disadvantages. 'Being' as subject (*ens*) denotes anything which exerts this action of be-ing, anything which exists: one may compare this use to the use of the word 'living' in the phrase 'the living and the dead'. I have translated *entia* by a motley of terms: 'existents', 'existent things', 'existing things', 'things which exist', 'beings', etc., etc. Finally, we have 'being' as complement. Now just as when seeking to specify any deed done we ask 'What is the thing doing?', so we can seek to specify the be-ing of the thing itself by asking 'What is it?'. When being is thus seen as specifying the act of existing St Thomas uses a third derivative of the verb *to be* (*essentia*), and this I have generally translated as 'nature', and sometimes as 'essence' or 'whatness'.

Primo quidem quia quidquid est in aliquo quod est præter essentiam ejus oportet esse causatum, vel a principiis essentiæ, sicut propria consequentia speciem (ut risibile quidem consequitur hominem et causatur ex principiis essentialibus speciei), vel ab aliquo exteriori (sicut calor in aqua causatur ab igne). Si igitur ipsum esse rei sit aliud ab ejus essentia, necesse est quod esse illius rei vel sit causatum ab aliquo exteriori vel a principiis essentialibus ejusdem rei. Impossibile est autem quod esse sit causatum tantum a principiis essentialibus rei, quia nulla res sufficit quod sit sibi causa essendi (si habeat esse causatum). Oportet ergo quod illud cujus esse est aliud a sua essentia habeat esse causatum ab alio. Hoc autem non potest dici de Deo, quia Deum dicimus esse primam causam efficientem.[6] Impossibile est ergo quod in Deo sit aliud esse et aliud ejus essentia.

Secundo quia esse est actualitas omnis formæ vel naturæ: non enim bonitas vel humanitas significatur in actu nisi prout significamus eam esse. Oportet igitur quod ipsum esse comparetur ad essentiam quæ est aliud ab ipso sicut actus ad potentiam. Cum igitur in Deo nihil sit potentiale, ut ostensum est supra,[7] sequitur quod non sit aliud in eo essentia quam suum esse. Sua igitur essentia est suum esse.

Tertio quia sicut illud quod habet ignem et non est ignis est ignitum per participationem, ita illud quod habet esse et non est esse est ens per participationem. Deus autem est,* ut supra ostensum est.[8] Si igitur non sit suum esse, erit ens per participationem et non per essentiam. Non ergo erit primum ens.† Est igitur Deus suum esse et non solum sua essentia.

1. Ad primum ergo dicendum quod aliquid cui non fit additio potest intelligi dupliciter. Uno modo ut de ratione ejus sit quod non fiat ei additio, sicut de ratione animalis irrationalis est quod sit sine ratione. Alio modo intelligitur aliquid cui non fit additio quia non est de ratione ejus quod sibi fiat additio, sicut animal commune est sine ratione, quia non est de ratione animalis communis ut habeat rationem, sed nec de ratione ejus est ut careat ratione. Primo igitur modo esse sine additione est esse divinum, secundo modo esse sine additione est esse commune.

2. Ad secundum dicendum quod esse dupliciter dicitur: uno modo significat actum essendi, alio modo significat compositionem propositionis quam anima adinvenit conjungens prædicatum subjecto. Primo igitur modo accipiendo esse non possumus scire esse Dei sicut nec ejus essentiam, sed

---

*Piana, Leonine add *sua essentia*, God and his nature, as we saw, are identical; and change note 8 accordingly to read: cf 1a. 3, 3.
†Piana, Leonine add *quod absurdum est dicere*, not, the primary existent: an absurd conclusion.

[6]cf 1a. 2, 3   [7]cf 1a. 3, 1   [8]cf 1a. 2, 3
[b]These properties peculiar to a species are referred to further in note *a* to article 6 as accidents of a thing that do not belong to it 'by accident'.

First, properties that belong to a thing over and above its own nature must derive from somewhere, either from that nature itself, as do properties peculiar to a particular species (for example, the sense of humour peculiar to man derives from his specific nature),[b] or from an external cause (as heat in water derives from some fire).[c] If therefore the existence of a thing is to be other than its nature, that existence must either derive from the nature or have an external cause. Now it cannot derive merely from the nature, for nothing with derived existence suffices to bring itself into being. It follows then that, if a thing's existence differs from its nature, that existence must be externally caused. But we cannot say this about God, whom we have seen to be the first cause.[6] Neither then can we say that God's existence is other than his nature.

Secondly, forms and natures are realized by existing: thus, we express actual realization of goodness or human nature by saying that goodness or human nature exists. When a nature is not itself existence, then, it must be potential of existence. Now, as we have seen, God does not contain potentialities,[7] so in him nature must not differ from existence. It is therefore God's very nature to exist.

Thirdly, anything on fire either is itself fire or has caught fire.[d] Similarly, anything that exists either is itself existence or partakes of it. Now, God, as we have seen, exists.[8] If then he is not himself existence, and thus not by nature existent, he will only be a partaker of existence. And so he will not be the primary existent. God therefore is not only his own essence, but also his own existence.

Hence: 1. 'Unspecified' is an ambiguous word. For it may imply on the one hand that further specification is excluded by definition, as reason is excluded by definition from irrational animals. Or it may imply that further specification is not included in the definition, as reason is not included in the definition of animals in general, though neither is it excluded. Understood in the first way, unspecified existence is divine existence; understood in the second way, unspecified existence is existence in general.

2. The verb 'to be' is used in two ways: to signify the act of existing, and to signify the mental uniting of predicate to subject which constitutes a proposition. Now we cannot clearly know the being of God in the first sense any more than we can clearly know his essence. But in the second

---

[c] cf note *b* to 2, 3 above. According to the theory of the four elements water was by nature cold and moist, whilst fire was hot and dry (cf Aristotle, *On Generation and Corruption* II 3, 330a30–b5).

[d] For the notion of 'participation' used in this argument cf note *b* to article 2 above and Appendix 3.

solum secundo modo. Scimus enim quod hæc propositio quam formamus de Deo cum dicimus Deus est vera est. Et hoc scimus ex ejus effectibus, ut supra dictum est.[9]

articulus 5. utrum sit in eo compositio generis et differentiæ

AD QUINTUM sic proceditur:[1] 1. Videtur quod Deus sit in genere aliquo. Substantia enim est ens per se subsistens. Hoc autem maxime convenit Deo. Ergo Deus est in genere substantiæ.

2. Præterea, unumquodque mensuratur per aliquid sui generis, sicut longitudines per longitudinem, et numeri per numerum. Sed Deus est mensura omnium substantiarum, ut patet per Commentatorem.[2] Ergo Deus est in genere substantiæ.

SED CONTRA, genus est prius secundum intellectum eo quod in genere continetur. Sed nihil est prius Deo nec secundum rem nec secundum intellectum. Ergo Deus non est in aliquo genere.

RESPONSIO: Dicendum quod aliquid est in genere dupliciter: uno modo simpliciter et proprie, sicut species et quæ sub eis* continentur; alio modo per reductionem, sicut punctum et unitas reducuntur ad genus quantitatis sicut principia, cæcitas autem et omnis privatio reducitur ad genus sui habitus. Neutro autem modo Deus est in genere.

Quod enim non possit esse species alicujus generis tripliciter ostendi potest.

Primo quidem quia species constituitur ex genere et differentia. Semper autem id a quo sumitur differentia constituens speciem se habet ad illud unde sumitur genus sicut actus ad potentiam. Animal enim sumitur a natura sensitiva per modum concretionis (hoc enim dicitur animal quod naturam sensitivam habet), rationale vero sumitur a natura intellectiva (quia rationale est quod naturam intellectivam habet); intellectivum autem

---

*Leonine, *quæ sub genere*, as do the species of a genus.

[9]cf 1a. 2, 2, especially the reply to argument 2

[1]cf 1a. 4, 3 ad 2; 6, 2 ad 3; 88, 2 ad 4. 1 *Sent.* 8, 4, 2; 19, 4, 2. *CG* 1, 25. *De potentia* VIII, C. *Compend. Theol.* 12. *De ente et essentia* 6

[2]Ibn Roschd, the greatest of the medieval Arab philosophers, died 1198. Quotation from *Commentary on Aristotle's Metaphysics* x, 7 (Venice edition of Aristotle's works, 1574, vol viii 257a)

[e]It is clearly nonsensical to say that the proposition 'God is' makes a true assertion, but an assertion quite unrelated to the divine act of existing. And St Thomas does not here say anything of the kind. What he says is that we clearly know (*scimus*) the proposition 'God exists' to be true, even though we cannot have clear knowledge of the divine act of existing referred to. And this is because clear knowledge of that act of existing would demand clear knowledge of God's essential nature; whilst

sense we can, for when we say that God is we frame a proposition about God which we clearly know to be true. And this, as we have seen, we know from his effects.[9] [e]

article 5. can one distinguish in God genus and difference?

THE FIFTH POINT:[1] 1. God seems to belong to a genus. For the definition of a substance—something self-subsistent—is most fully applicable to God. God therefore belongs to the genus of substance.

2. Moreover, any measure must belong to the same genus as the things it measures: lengths are measured by length, and numbers by number. Now it appears from Averroes that God is the measure of all substances.[2] God must therefore belong to the genus of substance.

ON THE OTHER HAND, a generic idea is logically prior to the things which exemplify it. Now nothing is prior to God in either the real or logical order.[a] Hence God does not belong to a genus.

REPLY: There are two ways of belonging to a genus: immediately and strictly, as do species and members of species; and mediately, as unity and the point belong to the genus of quantity because they generate number and extension, or as a defect like blindness belongs mediately to the genus of the corresponding perfection. In neither of these ways does God belong to a genus.

That he cannot be a species within a genus can be shown in three ways.

First, because species are defined by differentiating some generic notion.[b] Such differentiation is always based on some actualization of the potentiality which gave rise to the generic notion. Thus sense-life, envisaged in the concrete, gives rise to the notion of animal (an animal being that which lives by sense-perception); whilst mental life gives rise to the notion of a reasoning creature (that is a creature which lives by its mind);

---

clear knowledge of the truth that God exists results from a 'demonstration that', based not on knowledge of God's nature but on knowledge of his effects. For further discussion see appendix 5.

[a]That nothing is logically prior to God is not strictly true. For the necessary distinctions and cautions see 1a. 13, 6.

[b]That is to say, one arrives at a determinate notion of what a thing is (defines its species), by determining (differentiating) some relatively indeterminate notion of what it is (some generic notion). Thus, St Thomas would define man as a rational animal, where all three words 'man', 'rational', and 'animal' express the whole of what man is; but 'animal' does this in a relatively indeterminate way, 'rational' in a determining way, and 'man' in a fully determinate way. This example must be kept in mind during the next few lines of text.

comparatur ad sensitivum sicut actus ad potentiam. Et similiter manifestum est in aliis. Unde, cum in Deo non adjungatur potentia actui, impossibile est quod sit in genere tanquam species.

Secundo quia cum esse Dei sit ejus essentia, ut ostensum est,[3] si Deus esset in aliquo genere oporteret quod genus ejus esset ens, nam genus significat essentiam rei cum prædicetur in eo quod quid est. Ostendit autem Philosophus[4] quod ens non potest esse genus alicujus: omne enim genus habet differentias quæ non participant essentiam generis, nulla autem differentia posset inveniri quæ esset extra ens (quia non ens non potest esse differentia). Unde relinquitur quod Deus non sit in genere.

Tertio quia omnia quæ sunt in genere uno communicant in quidditate vel essentia generis quod prædicatur de eis in eo quod quid. Differunt autem secundum esse, non enim idem est esse hominis et equi, nec hujus hominis et illius hominis. Et sic oportet quod quæcumque sunt in genere differant in eis esse et quod quid est, idest essentia. In Deo autem non differant, ut ostensum est.[5] Unde manifestum est quod Deus non est in genere sicut species.

Et ex hoc patet quod non habet genus neque differentias, neque est definitio ipsius neque demonstratio nisi per effectum, quia definitio est ex genere et differentia, demonstrationis autem medium est definitio.

Quod autem Deus non sit in genere per reductionem ut principium manifestum est ex eo quod principium quod reducitur in aliquod genus non se extendit ultra genus illud, sicut punctum non est principium nisi quantitatis continuæ et unitas quantitatis discretæ. Deus autem est principium totius esse, ut infra ostendetur.[6] Unde non continetur in aliquo genere sicut principium.

1. Ad primum ergo dicendum quod substantiæ nomen non significat hoc solum quod est per se esse, quia hoc quod est esse non potest* esse genus, ut ostensum est. Sed significat essentiam cui competit sic esse, idest per se esse, quod tamen esse non sit ipsa ejus essentia. Et sic patet quod Deus non est in genere substantiæ.

2. Ad secundum dicendum quod objectio illa procedit de mensura proportionata, hanc enim oportet esse homogeneam mensurato. Deus autem non est mensura proportionata alicui. Dicitur tamen mensura omnium ex eo quod unumquodque tantum habet de esse quantum ei appropinquat.

---

*Piana, Leonine add *per se,* cannot as such determine.

[3]cf 1a. 3, 4

[4]*Metaphysics* III, 3. 998b22

[5]cf 1a. 3, 4

[6]cf 1a. 44, 1

cIn the translation of the last few lines I have used 'to live by' as a shorthand for 'to have a nature such that one lives by'; and I have used 'sense-life' and 'mind-life'

the mind-life of man, however, realizes potentialities of his sense-life.[c] And we see the like in other cases. So, since realization of potentialities does not occur in God, he cannot be a species within a genus.

Secondly, since the genus of a thing states what the thing is, a genus must express a thing's nature. Now God's nature, as we have seen,[3] is to exist; so that the only genus to which God could belong would be the genus of existent. Aristotle,[4] however, has shown that there is no such genus: for genera are differentiated by factors not already contained within those genera, and no differentiating factor could be found which was not already existent (it could not differentiate if it did not exist). So we are left with no genus to which God could belong.

Thirdly, all members of a genus share one essence or nature, that of the genus stating what they are. As existents, however, they differ, for a horse's existence is not a man's, and this man's existence is not that man's. So that when something belongs to a genus, its nature, or what it is, must differ from its existence. In God, however, we saw that there is not this difference.[5] Clearly then God cannot be a species within a genus.

And this shows why one cannot assign either genus or difference to God, nor define him, nor demonstrate anything of him except by means of his effects; for definitions are composed of genus and difference, and demonstration depends upon definition.

That God does not belong mediately to a genus by initiating or generating it, is also clear. For anything which so initiates a genus that it mediately belongs to that genus, is ineffective outside the genus: the point generates only extension and unity only number. Now God initiates everything that is, as we shall see later.[6] He does not therefore so initiate any particular genus that he belongs to it.

Hence: 1. The word 'substance' does not mean baldly that which exists of itself, for existence, as we have seen, cannot determine a genus. Rather 'substance' means that which is possessed of a nature such that it will exist of itself. But this nature is not itself the thing's existence. So it is plain that God does not belong to the genus of substance.

2. This argument holds of measurement by commensuration in the strict sense, for then measure and measured must be of the same genus. Now nothing is commensurate with God; though he is called the measure of all things, inasmuch as the nearer things come to God, the more fully they exist.

---

as shorthand for 'a nature such that the life of the thing possessing the nature is a sense-life' or 'is a mental life'. The shorthand is harmless in itself, but the note is made in view of the answer which follows later to the first argument.

articulus 6. utrum sit in eo compositio subjecti et accidentis

AD SEXTUM sic proceditur:[1] 1. Videtur quod in Deo sint aliqua accidentia. Substantia enim *nulli est accidens*, ut dicitur in 1 *Phys.*[2] Quod ergo in uno est accidens non potest in alio esse substantia, sicut probatur quod calor non sit forma substantialis ignis quia in aliis est accidens. Sed sapientia, virtus et hujusmodi quæ in nobis sunt accidentia, Deo attribuuntur. Ergo et in Deo sunt accidentia.

2. Præterea, in quolibet genere est unum primum. Multa autem sunt genera accidentium. Si igitur prima illorum generum non sunt in Deo erunt multa prima extra Deum, quod est inconveniens.

SED CONTRA, omne accidens in subjecto est. Deus autem non potest esse subiectum, quia *forma simplex non potest esse subiectum*, ut dicit Boëtius *lib. de Trin.*[3] Ergo in Deo non potest esse accidens.

RESPONSIO: Dicendum secundum præmissa quod manifeste apparet quod in Deo accidens esse non potest.

Primo quidem quia subjectum comparatur ad accidens sicut potentia ad actum, subjectum enim secundum accidens est aliquo modo in actu. Esse autem in potentia omnino removetur a Deo, ut ex prædictis patet.[4]

Secundo quia Deus est suum esse, et* ut Boëtius dicit, *licet id quod est, aliquid aliud possit habere adjunctum, tamen ipsum esse nihil aliud adjunctum habere potest*[5] (sicut quod est calidum potest habere aliud extraneum quam calidum, ut albedinem, sed ipse calor nihil habet præter calorem).

---

*manuscripts, *et* omitted.
[1]cf Ia. 14, 4; 28, 2; 54, 3 ad 2. 1 *Sent.* 8, 4, 3. *CG* I, 23. *De potentia* VII, 4. *Compendium Theologiæ* 23   [2]*Physics* I, 3. 186b1–4
[3]*De Trinitate* 2, PL 64, 1250   [4]cf Ia. 3, 1   [5]*De Hebdomadibus.* PL 64, 1311
[a]In note *c* to 2, 2 it was remarked that a definition does not merely state the sense of a word, i.e. how the word is used, but also the significance of a thing, i.e. how the word *must* be used if it is to mean this thing. Defining a thing implicitly legislates for all that may or may not be significantly said about that thing. For a definition can be regarded as a concise statement of what it is possible to assert or deny significantly concerning the thing (whether truly or falsely), and which affirmations and denials would not make significant sense. Once one has defined a typewriter one knows that it does not make sense even to consider whether a typewriter yawns or not. This is why a definition is said to declare what a thing is, or to express a thing's *essence*.

An *accident* is a property which can be asserted of a thing without that assertion defining the thing. Indeed, the assertion of an accident assumes previous definition of the thing, for only when we know from a thing's definition whether the accident can be significantly asserted of it, can we turn to the question of whether it is truly or falsely asserted.

Sometimes, however, a thing's definition determines not only whether a particular

article 6. is God composed of substance and accidents?

THE SIXTH POINT:[1] 1. It seems that there must be accidents[a] in God. For Aristotle says that *substance is never accidental to anything;*[2] so that one cannot have something that is accidental in one thing being the substance of another. The fact that heat, for example, is an accidental form of some things proves that it cannot be the substantial form of fire. Now wisdom, power and the like which are ascribed to God are accidental in us. They must therefore be accidental in God as well.

2. Moreover, each genus has its prototype.[b] So, unless the prototypes of the many genera of accidents are to be found in God, there will be many other prototypes besides God; and this does not seem right.

ON THE OTHER HAND, every accident is an accident of some subject. Now God cannot be a subject, since, as Boëthius says, *no simple form can be a subject.*[3] So there cannot be accidents in God.

REPLY. What we have already said makes it clear that accidents cannot exist in God.

First, because accidents realize some potentialities of their subject, an accident being a mode in which the subject achieves actuality. But we have seen already that potentiality is to be altogether ruled out from God.[4]

Secondly, because God is his own existence, and as Boëthius says, *you may add to an existent, but you cannot add to existence itself*[5] (just as a hot thing can be other things than hot—white, for example—but heat itself is nothing else but heat).

---

accident can be significantly asserted of the thing, but also whether it is truly or falsely asserted. For certain accidents do not belong 'by accident' to a thing, but necessarily belong (or necessarily do not belong) to it 'by nature'. Thus, man does not have a sense of humour 'by accident', if we take sense of humour to mean the basic human capacity to appreciate absurdity. Nevertheless, having a sense of humour does not define man. It is possible to understand what a thing is without knowledge of such properties, though it is not possible to assert that the thing exists without such properties.

Accidents are real differences in mode of being, and not merely aspects under which a thing is considered. They are therefore said to exist, although only in the sense of existing in some thing called their subject; or better, only in the sense that they are modes in which some subject exists. For a thing can both exist in the unqualified sense of that word (and thus have definition and essence), and also exist in qualified senses (and thus have accidents). Under the aspect of having accidents, but of not itself being an accident, a thing is said to be a *substance*.

b'Prototype': literally 'a principal member'. The doctrine has already occurred in the 'third way' (1a. 2, 3) where St Thomas said that 'when many things possess some property in common the one most fully possessing it causes it in the others'. Comment on the doctrine will be found in Appendix 9.

Tertio quia omne quod est per se, prius est eo quod est per accidens. Unde cum Deus sit simpliciter primum ens, nihil in eo potest esse per accidens. Sed nec accidentia per se in eo esse possunt, sicut risibile est per se accidens hominis, quia hujusmodi accidentia causantur ex principiis subjecti, in Deo autem nihil potest esse causatum cum sit causa prima. Unde relinquitur quod in Deo nullum sit accidens.

1. Ad primum ergo dicendum quod virtus et sapientia non univoce dicuntur de Deo et de nobis, ut infra patebit.[6] Unde non sequitur quod accidentia sint in Deo sicut in nobis.

2. Ad secundum dicendum quod cum substantia sit prior accidentibus principia accidentium reducuntur in principia substantiæ sicut in priora, quamvis Deus non sit primum contentum in genere substantiæ sed primum extra omne genus respectu totius esse.

articulus 7. utrum sit quocumque modo compositus, vel totaliter simplex

AD SEPTIMUM sic proceditur:[1] 1. Videtur quod Deus non sit omnino simplex. Ea enim quæ sunt a Deo imitantur ipsum, unde a primo ente sunt omnia entia et a primo bono sunt omnia bona. Sed in rebus quæ sunt a Deo nihil est omnino simplex. Ergo Deus non est omnino simplex.

2. Præterea, omne quod est melius Deo attribuendum est. Sed apud nos composita sunt meliora simplicibus, sicut corpora mixta elementis et elementa suis partibus. Ergo non est dicendum quod Deus sit omnino simplex.

SED CONTRA est quod Augustinus dicit quod Deus vere et summe simplex est.[2]

RESPONSIO: Dicendum quod Deum omnino esse simplicem multipliciter potest esse manifestum.

Primo quidem per supradicta. Cum enim in Deo non sit compositio neque quantitativarum partium, quia corpus non est, neque compositio formæ et materiæ, neque in eo sit aliud natura et suppositum, neque aliud natura et esse, neque in eo sit compositio generis et differentiæ, neque subjecti et accidentis, manifestum est quod Deus nullo modo compositus est sed est omnino simplex.

---

[6]cf Ia. 13, 5
[1]cf Ia. 4, 2; 13, 12. Also I *Sent.* 8, 4, 1. *CG* I, 16, 18. *De pententia* VII, 1. *Compend. Theol.* 9. *De quatuor oppos.* 4. *In De causis,* 21. For homogeneous and heterogeneous composites cf Ia. 11, 2 ad 2
[2]*De Trinitate* VI, 4–8. PL 42, 927–9
[c]See note *a* above.

Thirdly, because what exists by nature is prior to what exists by accident, so that if God is to be the absolutely prime existent, nothing can exist in him by accident. Nor can there be accidents existing in him by nature,[c] as a sense of humour exists in man by nature; for such accidents are derivative from the essential nature of the subject. In God however there is nothing derivative, but all derivation starts from him. We are left to conclude that God contains no accidents.

Hence: 1. Power and wisdom are not ascribed to God and to us in the same sense, as we shall see later.[6] For this reason it does not follow that, because they are accidental in us, they will be accidental in God also.

2. Substance is prior to accidents, so that prototypal accidents are themselves subordinate to prior substantial prototypes. Although God is not even a prototype within the genus of substance, but the prototype of all being, transcending all genera.

article 7. is there any way in which God is composite, or is he altogether simple?

THE SEVENTH POINT:[1] 1. God, it seems, is not altogether simple. For the things which derive from God resemble him: thus everything deriving from the first being exists, and everything deriving from the first good is good. Now nothing deriving from him is altogether simple. Neither then is God altogether simple.

2. Moreover, whatever attributes display the more perfection must be ascribed to God. Now, in the world with which we are familiar, composite things are more perfect than simple ones: compounds than elements, for example, and elements than their constituent parts.[a] So we ought not to assert that God is altogether simple.

ON THE OTHER HAND, Augustine says that God is the most truly simple thing there is.[2]

REPLY: There are many ways of showing that God is altogether simple.

First, relying on what we have already said. For God, we said, is not composed of extended parts, since he is not a body; nor of form and matter; nor does he differ from his own nature; nor his nature from his existence; nor can one distinguish in him genus and difference; nor substance and accidents. It is clear then that there is no way in which God is composite, and he must be altogether simple.

---

[a]The elements referred to are the elements of medieval physical theory: earth, air, fire and water. By constituent parts of such elements St Thomas must mean either the extended parts into which a certain bulk of the element might be divided, or, more probably, the form and matter of which even elements must be composed.

Secundo quia omne compositum est posterius suis componentibus et dependens ex eis. Deus autem est primum ens, ut supra ostensum est.[3] Tertio quia omne compositum causam habet; quæ enim secundum se diversa sunt non conveniunt in unum nisi per aliquam causam adunantem ipsa. Deus autem non habet causam, ut supra ostensum est, cum sit prima causa efficiens.[4] Quarto quia in omni composito oportet esse potentiam et actum, quod in Deo non est: quia vel una partium est actus alterius, vel saltem omnes partes sunt sicut in potentia respectu totius. Quinto quia omne compositum est aliquid quod non convenit alicui suarum partium. Et quidem in totis dissimilium partium manifestum est, nulla enim partium hominis est homo neque aliqua partium pedis est pes. In totis vero similium partium, licet aliquid quod dicitur de toto dicatur de parte (sicut pars aëris est aër et aquæ aqua), aliquid tamen dicitur de toto quod non convenit alicui partium (non enim si tota aqua est bicubita et pars ejus). Sic igitur in omni composito est aliquid quod non est ipsum. Hoc autem etsi possit dici de habente formam, quod scilicet habeat aliquid quod non est ipsum (puta in albo est aliquid quod non pertinet ad rationem albi), tamen in ipsa forma nihil est alienum. Unde, cum Deus sit ipsa forma vel potius ipsum esse, nullo modo compositus esse potest. Et hanc rationem tangit Hilarius dicens: *Deus qui virtus est ex infirmis non continetur, neque qui lux est ex obscuris coaptatur.*[5]

1. Ad primum ergo dicendum quod ea quæ sunt a Deo imitantur Deum sicut causata primam causam. Est autem hoc de ratione causati quod sit aliquo modo compositum, quia ad minus esse ejus est aliud quam quod* est, ut infra patebit.[6]

2. Ad secundum dicendum quod apud nos composita sunt meliora simplicibus quia perfectio bonitatis creaturæ non invenitur in uno sed in multis. Sed perfectio divinæ bonitatis invenitur in uno simplici, ut infra ostendetur.[7]

articulus 8. utrum veniat in compositionem cum aliis

AD OCTAVUM sic proceditur:[1] 1. Videtur quod Deus in compositionem aliorum veniat. Dicit enim Dionysius, *esse omnium est quæ super esse est deitas.*[2] Sed esse omnium intrat compositionem uniuscujusque. Ergo Deus in compositionem aliorum venit.

---

*Leonine adds *quid*, it is not of an effect's nature simply to exist.
[3] cf Ia. 2, 3   [4] cf Ia. 2, 3
[5] *De Trinitate* VII. PL 10, 223
[6] cf Ia. 50, 2 ad 3.

Secondly, everything composite is subsequent to its components and dependent upon them; whilst God, as we have seen, is the first of all beings.[3]

Thirdly, everything composite is caused; for essentially diverse elements will not combine unless made to do so by a cause. God however is not caused, as we have seen,[4] but is himself the first cause.

Fourthly, in any composite there is a realizing of potentialities, such as cannot occur in God: for either the potentialities of one component are realized by another, or at any rate all the components together are potentially the whole.

Fifthly, nothing composite can be predicated of its own component parts. In heterogeneous composites this is obvious, for no part of a man is a man, and no part of the foot a foot. And, although in homogeneous composites certain ways of describing the whole apply also to the parts (every bit of air, for example, is air, and every drop of water water), yet there are other ways which do not (thus if all the water occupies two cubic feet, no part of it will do so). So that in all composites there is some element not sharing a common predicate with the whole. Now even though one grants that a thing possessed of a form may contain such elements (thus, a white thing contains elements not covered by the predicate 'white'), nevertheless in the form itself there can be nothing foreign. Now God is form itself, indeed existence itself; so he can in no way be composite. And this was what Hilary was pointing out when he said: *God, being power, is not compounded of weakness; and, being light, is not pieced together from darkness.*[5]

Hence: 1. Things deriving from God resemble him as effects resemble a primary cause. Now it is in the nature of an effect to be composite in some way, because even at its simplest it is not its own existence. This we shall see later.[6]

2. In the world with which we are familiar composite things excel simple ones, because created perfection needs building up from many elements, and not just from one. Divine perfection is, however, simple and single, as we shall show shortly.[7]

article 8. does God enter into composition with other things?

THE EIGHTH POINT:[1] 1. God seems to enter into composition with other things. For Dionysius declares that *the being of everything is the godhead beyond being.*[2] Now the being of everything enters into the composition of each. God therefore enters into composition with other things.

---

[7]cf 1a. 4, 2 ad 1   [1]cf 1a. 90, 1; 3a. 2, 1; 5, 1 ad 2; 50, 2 ad 3. Also
1 *Sent.* 8, 1, 2. *CG* 1, 17, 26, 27; III, 51. *De potentia* VI, 6. *De veritate* XXI, 4.
[2]*De Cælesti Hierarchia*, 4, 1. PG 3, 177

2. Præterea, Deus est forma: dicit enim Augustinus quod *Verbum Dei* quod est Deus *est forma quædam non formata*.[3] Sed forma est pars compositi. Ergo Deus est pars alicujus compositi.

3. Præterea, quæcumque sunt et nullo modo differunt sunt idem. Sed Deus et materia prima sunt et nullo modo differunt. Ergo penitus sunt idem. Sed materia prima intrat compositionem rerum. Ergo et Deus.— Probatio mediæ: quæcumque differunt aliquibus differentiis differunt, et ita oportet ea esse composita; sed Deus et materia prima sunt omnino simplicia, ergo nullo modo differunt.

SED CONTRA est quod dicit Dionysius quod *neque tactus est ejus* (scilicet Dei) *neque alia quædam ad partes commiscendi communio*.[*4]

RESPONSIO: Dicendum quod circa hoc fuerunt tres errores. Quidam enim posuerunt quod Deus esset anima mundi, ut patet per Augustinum,[5] et ad hoc reducitur quod quidam etiam dixerunt Deum esse animam primi cæli. Alii dixerunt Deum esse principium formale omnium rerum, et hæc dicitur fuisse opinio Almarianorum. Tertius error fuit David de Dinando qui stultissime posuit Deum esse materiam primam. Omnia enim hæc manifestam continent falsitatem, neque est possibile Deum aliquo modo in compositionem alicujus venire nec sicut principium formale nec sicut principium materiale.

Primo quidem quia supra diximus Deum esse primam causam efficientem.[6] Causa autem efficiens cum forma rei perfectæ non incidit in idem numero sed solum in idem specie, homo enim generat hominem. Materia vero cum causa efficiente non incidit in idem numero nec in idem specie, quia hoc est in potentia, illud in actu.

Secundo, quia cum Deus sit† causa efficiens, ejus est primo et per se agere. Quod autem venit in compositionem alicujus non est primo et per se agens, sed magis compositum, non enim manus agit sed homo per manum, et ignis calefacit per calorem. Unde Deus non potest esse pars alicujus compositi.

Tertio quia nulla pars compositi potest esse simpliciter prima in entibus, neque etiam materia et forma quæ sunt primæ partes compositorum. Nam

---

*Leonine adds *Præterea, dicitur in libro de Causis quod causa prima regit omnes res, præterquam commisceatur eis.* Moreover, the Book of Causes (prop. 20 ed. Bardenhewer 181, 7) says that the first cause governs all things but does not mingle with them.

†Leonine adds *prima,* God is the first cause.

³*Sermon to the People* no. 117, ch 2. PL 38, 662. Referred to by St Thomas in the text by an alternative title, 'On the Lord's words'.

2. Moreover, God is a form, for Augustine says that *the Word of God* (which is God) *is unformed form.*[3] Now form is a component of things. God then must be a component in something.

3. Moreover, things which exist without differing are identical. Now God and the ultimate matter of things exist without differing. They are therefore completely identical. And since ultimate matter enters into the composition of things, God must do so too.—To prove the middle step in this argument: things that differ do so by certain differentiating factors, and must therefore be composite. God and ultimate matter are however altogether simple, and so cannot differ.

ON THE OTHER HAND, Dionysius says that *nothing can come into contact with God or partially intermingle with him in any way.*[4]

REPLY: On this point three mistakes have been made. Some people have held that God is the soul of the world, as we learn from Augustine;[5] and with these people we can include those who said that God was the soul of the outermost heaven. Others have said that God is the form of all things: the view, it is said, of Amaury of Bène and his followers. The third mistake was the really stupid thesis of David of Dinant that God was the ultimate unformed matter of things.[a] All these opinions are clearly wrong: God cannot enter into composition with anything in any way, be it as form or as matter.

First, because we have said above that God is the first cause of things.[6] Now the form of an effect, though similar in species to its cause (man begets man), is not to be identified with the cause. And matter is neither identifiable with the cause nor similar to it in species, since matter is only able to be what the cause is already.

Secondly, since God is a cause, he is a primary and immediate source of activity. A component, however, is not itself a primary and immediate source of activity; this belongs rather to the composite thing. Thus a hand does not act, but man by means of his hand; and it is the fire which warms by virtue of its heat. God then cannot be a component of anything.

Thirdly, no component, not even those primary components of composite things, matter and form, can be called, without qualification, a

---

[4]*On the Divine Names* 2, 5. PG 3, 643
[5]*De Civitate Dei* VII, 6. PL 41, 199. The reference is to Varro
[6]cf 1a. 2, 3
[a]Amaury of Bène and David of Dinant were two French professors of the late twelfth and early thirteenth century. Their views were condemned in 1210 by a provincial council at Paris. See E. Gilson, *Christian Philosophy in the Middle Ages* (London, New York, 1955), pp. 240–4.

materia est in potentia, potentia autem est posterior actu simpliciter, ut ex dictis patet.[7] Forma autem quæ est pars compositi est forma participata; sicut autem participans est posterius eo quod est per essentiam, ita et ipsum participatum, sicut ignis in ignitis est posterior eo quod est per essentiam. Ostensum est autem quod Deus est primum ens simpliciter.[8]

1. Ad primum ergo dicendum quod deitas dicitur esse omnium effective et exemplariter, non autem per essentiam.

2. Ad secundum dicendum quod Verbum est forma exemplaris, non autem forma quæ est pars compositi.

3. Ad tertium dicendum quod simplicia non differunt aliquibus aliis differentiis, hoc enim compositorum est. Homo enim et equus differunt rationali et irrationali differentiis, quæ quidem differentiæ non differunt amplius ab invicem aliis differentiis. Unde si fiat vis in verbo non proprie dicuntur differre sed diversa esse, nam secundum Philosophum diversum absolute dicitur sed omne differens aliquo differt.[9] Unde si fiat vis in verbo materia prima et Deus non differunt sed sunt diversa seipsis. Unde non sequitur quod sint idem.

---

[7] cf Ia. 3, 1
[8] cf Ia. 2, 3
[9] *Metaphysics* x, 3. 1054b24

primary being. For matter is potential, and it is only in a qualified sense, as we have shown, that the potential precedes the actual.[7] Again, form, when a component, is something of which a composite partakes.[b] Now, just as that which is essentially *x* takes precedence over that which partakes *x*, so also over *x* as partaken: that which is by nature fire takes precedence over the being on fire of other things. We have however already shown that God is the primary being, without qualification.[8]

Hence: 1. Dionysius means that godhead is archetypally and causatively the being of all things, but not substantially their being.

2. The Word is not a component form, but a form upon which things are patterned.

3. Simple things do not differ from one another by added differentiating factors as composites do. Thus, although the factors 'rational' and 'irrational' differentiate men and horses, these factors themselves do not then require further factors to differentiate them one from another. Indeed, if we may point the words we are using, these factors are not *differentiated*, but *diverse*. According to Aristotle diversity is absolute, but difference is difference in some respect.[9] So, emphasizing our words, God and ultimate matter are not *differentiated*, but are of themselves *diverse*. One cannot conclude therefore to their identity.

---

[b]For the notion of 'participation' cf note *b* to article 2 above and Appendix 2.

POST CONSIDERATIONEM divinæ simplicitatis de perfectione ipsius Dei agendum est. Et quia unumquodque secundum quod perfectum est sic dicitur bonum,

> primo agendum est de perfectione divina,
> secundo de ejus bonitate.

Quæstio 4. de Dei perfectione

Circa primum quæruntur tria;
1. utrum Deus sit perfectus,
2. utrum sit universaliter perfectus, quasi omnium in se perfectiones habens,
3. utrum creaturæ possint dici Deo similes.

articulus I. utrum Deus sit perfectus

AD PRIMUM sic proceditur:[1] 1. Videtur quod esse perfectum non conveniat Deo. Perfectum enim dicitur quasi totaliter factum. Sed Deo non convenit esse factum. Ergo nec esse perfectum.

2. Præterea, Deus est primum rerum principium. Sed principia rerum videntur esse imperfecta, semen enim est principium animalium et plantarum. Ergo Deus est imperfectus.

3. Præterea, ostensum est supra quod natura Dei est ipsum esse.[2] Sed ipsum esse videtur esse imperfectissimum, cum sit communissimum et recipiens omnium additiones. Ergo Deus non est perfectus.

SED CONTRA est quod dicitur *Matt. estote perfecti sicut et Pater vester cælestis perfectus est.*[3]

RESPONSIO: Dicendum quod sicut Philosophus narrat quidam antiqui philosophi, scilicet Pythagorici et Speusippus,* non attribuerunt optimum et perfectissimum primo principio.[4] Cujus ratio est quia philosophi antiqui consideraverunt principium materiale tantum, primum autem principium materiale imperfectissimum est. Cum enim materia inquantum hujusmodi sit in potentia, oportet quod primum principium materiale sit maxime in potentia, et ita maxime imperfectum.

---

*manuscripts: *Leucippus.*
[1]cf Ia. 6; 13; 25, 1. Also *CG* I, 28. *De veritate* II, 3 ad 13. *Compend. Theol.* 20. *In De div. nom.* 13, *lect.* 1
[2]cf Ia. 3, 4   [3]*Matthew* 5, 48   [4]*Metaphysics* XII, 7. 1072b30

DISCUSSION OF God's simpleness must be followed by a study of his perfection. And since things perfect are called 'good', we shall discuss

> first, God's perfection,
> secondly, his goodness.

Question 4. God's perfection

About the first of these questions there are three points of inquiry:[a]

1. is God perfect?
2. is his perfection all-embracing, containing, so to say, the perfection of everything else?
3. can creatures be said to resemble God?

article 1. is God perfect?

THE FIRST POINT:[1] 1. 'Perfect' does not seem a suitable term to apply to God, for etymologically it means 'thoroughly made'. Now since we would not say that God is made, we should not say that he is perfect.

2. Moreover, God is the first origin of things. But things have imperfect origins: plants and animals, for example, begin from seed. God therefore is imperfect.

3. Moreover, as we have shown, the nature of God is simply to exist.[2] Now simply to exist is seemingly most imperfect: the lowest common denominator of all things. God then is not perfect.

ON THE OTHER HAND, we read in *Matthew*: *be ye perfect, as your heavenly Father is perfect*.[3]

REPLY. Aristotle[4] tells us that certain ancient philosophers—the Pythagoreans and Speusippus—did not regard the first origin of things as the acme of goodness and perfection; the reason being that they only paid attention to the matter out of which things originated, and primordial matter is the most imperfect of all things. For matter as such is only potential, and primordial matter is therefore sheer potentiality and entirely imperfect.[b]

---

[a]See Appendix 13.

[b]So imperfect in fact that it is a contradiction in terms for primordial or 'sheer' matter to exist (cf 1a. 7, 2 ad 3). Matter cannot exist except it assume some form, except in some material thing. But then it exists really: that is to say, material things are not 'sheer' forms (cf again note *a* to 3, 2).

Deus autem ponitur primum principium non materiale sed in genere causæ efficientis, et hoc oportet esse perfectissimum. Sicut enim materia inquantum hujusmodi est in potentia, ita agens inquantum huiusmodi est in actu. Unde primum principium activum oportet maxime esse in actu, et per consequens maxime perfectum. Secundum hoc enim dicitur aliquid esse perfectum quod est actu, nam perfectum dicitur cui nihil deest secundum modum suæ perfectionis.

1. Ad primum ergo dicendum quod sicut dicit Gregorius *balbutiendo ut possumus excelsa Dei resonamus,*[5] quod enim factum non est perfectum proprie dici non potest. Sed quia in his quæ fiunt tunc dicitur aliquid esse perfectum cum de potentia educitur in actum, transumitur hoc nomen perfectum ad significandum omne illud cui non deest esse in actu sive hoc habeat per modum factionis sive non.

2. Ad secundum dicendum quod principium materiale quod apud nos imperfectum invenitur non potest esse simpliciter primum sed præceditur ab aliquo perfecto. Nam semen licet sit principium animalis generati ex semine, tamen habet ante se animal vel plantam unde decidit. Oportet enim ante id quod est in potentia esse aliquid actu, cum ens in potentia non reducatur in actum nisi per aliquod ens in actu.

3. Ad tertium dicendum quod ipsum esse est perfectissimum omnium, comparatur enim ad omnia ut actus. Nihil enim habet actualitatem nisi inquantum est, unde ipsum esse est actualitas omnium rerum et etiam ipsarum formarum. Unde non comparatur ad alia sicut recipiens ad receptum, sed magis sicut receptum ad recipiens. Cum enim dico esse hominis vel equi vel cujuscumque alterius, ipsum esse consideratur ut formale et receptum, non autem* illud cui competit esse.

---

articulus 2. utrum Deus sit universaliter perfectus, omnium in se perfectiones habens

AD SECUNDUM sic proceditur:[1] 1. Videtur quod in Deo non sint perfectiones omnium rerum. Deus enim simplex est, ut ostensum est.[2] Sed perfectiones rerum sunt multæ et diversæ. Ergo in Deo non sunt omnes perfectiones rerum.

2. Præterea, opposita non possunt esse in eodem. Sed perfectiones rerum sunt oppositæ, unaquæque enim species perficitur per suam differentiam specificam, differentiæ autem quibus dividitur genus et constituuntur

---

*Leonine adds *ut,* not as the thing to which existence belongs.
[5]*Magna Moralia,* 5, 36. PL 75, 715. St Gregory the Great, Pope, died A.D. 604

We however hold God to be not primordial matter but the primary operative cause of things, and thus the most perfect of things. For just as matter as such is potential, so an acting thing as such is actual. Thus the first origin of all activity will be the most actual, and therefore the most perfect, of all things. For things are called perfect when they have achieved actuality, the perfect thing being that in which nothing required by the thing's particular mode of perfection fails to exist.

Hence: 1. What is not made cannot properly be called perfect, but, as Gregory says, *stammering, we echo the heights of God as best we can.*[5] And so, because things that are made are called perfect when the potentiality of them has been actualized, we extend the word to refer to anything that is not lacking in actuality, whether made or not.

2. The imperfect matter from which the things around us originate, is not their ultimate origin, but is itself preceded by something perfect. For even when an animal is generated from seed, the original seed itself derives from some previous animal or plant. Anything potential must be preceded by something actual, since only the already actual can actualize a thing which exists potentially.

3. The most perfect thing of all is to exist, for everything else is potential compared to existence. Nothing achieves actuality except it exist, and the act of existing is therefore the ultimate actuality of everything, and even of every form. So it is that things acquire existence, and not existence things. For in the very phrases 'the existence of man' or 'of a horse' or 'of some other thing', it is existence that is regarded as an acquisition like a form, not the thing to which existence belongs.

article 2. is God's perfection all-embracing, containing, so to say, the perfection of everything?

THE SECOND POINT:[1] 1. God, it seems, does not contain the perfections of everything. For God, as we have seen, is simple,[2] and the perfections of things are many and diverse. So God does not contain every perfection of things.

2. Moreover, opposites cannot exist together. Now the perfections of things are opposed to one another; for each species is perfected by that which differentiates it from other species in the same genus, and such constitutive differences are opposed to one another. So it seems that, because

---

[1]cf Ia. 14, 6; 47, 1; 91, 1; Ia2æ. 2, 5 ad 2. Also *In* I *Sent.* 2, 1, 2–3. *CG* I, 28, 31. *De veritate* II. 1. *Compend. Theol.* 21, 22. *In De div. nom.* 5, lect. 1, 2
[2]cf Ia. 3, 7

species sunt oppositæ. Cum ergo opposita non possint simul esse in eodem videtur quod non omnes rerum perfectiones sint in Deo.

3. Præterea, vivens est perfectius quam ens et sapiens quam vivens, ergo et vivere est perfectius quam esse et sapere quam vivere. Sed essentia Dei est ipsum esse. Ergo non habet in se perfectionem vitæ et sapientiæ et alias hujusmodi perfectiones.

SED CONTRA est quod dicit Dionysius quod Deus *in uno existentia omnia præhabet.*[3]

RESPONSIO: Dicendum quod in Deo sunt perfectiones omnium rerum, unde et dicitur universaliter perfectus, quia non deest ei aliqua nobilitas quæ inveniatur in aliquo genere, ut dicit Commentator.[4] Et hoc quidem ex duobus considerari potest.

Primo quidem ex hoc quod quidquid perfectionis est in effectu oportet inveniri in causa effectiva, vel secundum eamdem rationem si sit agens univocum (ut homo generat hominem), vel eminentiori modo si sit agens æquivocum (sicut in sole est similitudo eorum quæ generantur per virtutem solis). Manifestum est enim quod effectus præexistit virtute in causa agente. Præexistere autem in virtute causæ agentis non est præexistere imperfectiori modo sed perfectiori, licet præexistere in potentia causæ materialis sit præexistere imperfectiori modo, eo quod materia inquantum hujusmodi est imperfecta, agens vero inquantum hujusmodi est perfectum. Cum ergo Deus sit prima causa effectiva rerum oportet omnium rerum perfectiones præexistere in Deo secundum eminentiorem modum. Et hanc rationem tangit Dionysius dicens de Deo quod *non hoc quidem est hoc autem non est, sed omnia est ut omnium causa.*[5]

Secundo vero ex hoc quod supra ostensum est quod Deus est ipsum esse per se subsistens,[6] ex quo oportet quod totam perfectionem essendi in se contineat. Manifestum est enim quod si aliquod calidum non habeat totam perfectionem caloris* hoc ideo est quia calor non participatur secundum perfectam rationem, sed si calor esset per se subsistens non posset ei aliquid deesse de virtute caloris. Unde cum Deus sit ipsum esse subsistens nihil de perfectione essendi potest ei deesse. Omnium autem perfectiones pertinent ad perfectionem essendi, secundum hoc enim aliqualiter perfecta sunt quod aliquo modo esse habent. Unde sequitur quod nullius rei perfectio Deo desit. Et hanc rationem tangit Dionysius dicens quod *Deus non*

---

*Leonine *calidi*, the full perfection of a hot thing.
[3]*On the Divine Names* 5, 9. PG 3, 825
[4]Ibn Roschd, *Commentary on Aristotle's Metaphysics* V, 21 (Venice edition of Aristotle's works, 1574, vol viii, 131c)
[5]*On the Divine Names* 5, 8. PG 3, 824   [6]cf Ia. 3, 4

opposites cannot exist together in the same thing, God does not contain all the perfections of things.

3. Moreover, a living thing is more perfect than a merely existent thing, and one that is wise more perfect than one that is merely alive; so that to live is more perfect than to be, and to be wise more perfect than to live. Now it is the nature of God simply to be. Perfections like life and wisdom therefore are not to be found in him.

ON THE OTHER HAND, we have Dionysius saying that *all existent things are contained in a primordial unity in God*.[3]

REPLY: The perfections of everything exist in God. For this reason we call his perfection 'all-embracing', for, as Averroes says, he lacks no excellence of any sort.[4] There are two ways of showing this.

Firstly, because any perfection found in an effect must be found also in the cause of that effect; and this either without modification when cause and effect are of the same sort (thus man begets man), or in a more perfect manner when cause and effect are not of the same sort (thus the sun's power produces things having a certain likeness to the sun).[a] This is because effects obviously pre-exist potentially in their causes. Now to pre-exist potentially in a cause is to pre-exist in a more perfect, not in a less perfect, manner, even if to pre-exist potentially in matter is to pre-exist less perfectly; for although matter as such is imperfect, agents as such are perfect. Since God then is the primary operative cause of all things, the perfections of everything must pre-exist in him in a higher manner. And Dionysius is touching upon this argument when he refuses any description of God as *this and not that*, saying *God is everything, inasmuch as he is everything's cause*.[5]

Secondly, because as we have seen God is self-subsistent being itself,[6] and therefore necessarily contains within himself the full perfection of being. For clearly a hot thing falls short of the full perfection of heat only because it does not fully partake of the nature of heat; to a self-subsistent heat nothing of the virtue of heat could be lacking. Nothing therefore of the perfection of existing can be lacking to God, who is subsistent existence itself. Now every perfection is a perfection of existing, for it is the manner in which a thing exists that determines the manner of its perfection. No perfection can therefore be lacking to God. And Dionysius is touching upon this argument when he says that *God does not exist in any qualified*

---

[a]The word 'likeness' is here being stretched to cover any correspondence at all between the form of the cause and the form of its effect. There must always be some aptness of this cause to produce this effect, and to this extent a 'likeness' of effect to cause. cf next article.

quodammodo est existens sed simpliciter et incircumscripte totum in seipso★ esse præaccipit, et postea subdit quod *ipse est esse subsistentibus.*[7]

1. Ad primum ergo dicendum quod sicut sol ut dicit Dionysius *sensibilium substantias et qualitates multas et differentes, ipse unus existens et uniformiter lucendo, in seipso uniformiter præaccipit, multo magis in causa omnium necesse est præexistere omnia secundum naturalem unitionem.*[8] Et sic quæ sunt diversa et opposita in seipsis in Deo præexistunt ut unum absque detrimento simplicitatis ipsius.

2. Et per hoc etiam patet solutio ad secundum.

3. Ad tertium dicendum quod, sicut in eodem capite idem dicit,[9] licet ipsum esse sit perfectius quam ipsa vita et ipsa vita quam ipsa sapientia si considerentur secundum quod distinguuntur ratione, tamen vivens est nobilius quam ens tantum, quia vivens etiam est ens, et sapiens est ens et vivens. Licet igitur ens non includat in se vivens et sapiens, quia non oportet quod illud quod participat esse participet ipsum secundum omnem modum essendi, tamen ipsum esse† includit in se vitam et sapientiam, quia nulla de perfectionibus essendi potest deesse ei quod est ipsum esse subsistens.

articulus 3. *utrum creaturæ similes Deo dici possunt*

AD TERTIUM sic proceditur:[1] 1. Videtur quod nulla creatura possit esse similis Deo. Dicitur enim in psalmo, *non est similis tui in diis, Domine.*[2] Sed inter excellentiores creaturas, sunt quæ dicuntur dii participatione. Multo ergo minus aliæ creaturæ possunt dici Deo similes.

★Leonine adds *uniformiter*, without diversity.
†Leonine adds *Dei*, God's existence.
[7]*On the Divine Names* 5, 4. PG 3, 817
[8]*On the Divine Names* 5, 8. PG 3, 824
[9]*On the Divine Names* 5, 3. PG 3, 817
[1]cf Ia. 13, 5; 25, 2 ad 2, 3; 44, 3 ad 1; 57, 2 ad 2; 1a2æ. 60, 1. Also I *Sent.* 48, 1, 1; II, 16, 1, 1 ad 3. *CG* I, 29. *De veritate* II, 11; III, 1 ad 9; XXIII, 7 ad 9 sqq. *De potentia* VII, 7. *In De div. nom.* 9, *lect.* 3
[2]*Psalms* 85 (86), 8
[b]The sun, by its light, not only gives colour to things, but also causes their life and growth. This involves a relation of 'exemplarity' and imitation as explained in note *a*.
[c]The pseudo-Denis and St Thomas are here uncovering a very important ambiguity of the words 'wise', 'living' and 'existent'. We could regard the word 'wise' as a shorthand for 'wise and living and existent', and we could perhaps say that, in comparison, 'living' meant 'non-wise and living and existent', and 'existent' meant 'non-wise and non-living and existent'. It is on these interpretations of the words that a 'wise' person can be said to be more perfect than a 'living' one, and the 'living' thing more perfect than the 'existent' one. But, St Thomas points out, the

way, but possesses primordially in himself all being, without qualification and without circumscription. And later he adds that *God is the being of all that subsists.*[7]

Hence: 1. If the sun, as Dionysius says, *possesses in itself, primordially and without diversity, the divers qualities and substances of the things we can sense,*[b] *while yet maintaining the unity of its own being and the homogeneity of its light, how much more must everything pre-exist in unity of nature in the cause of all?*[8] Perfections therefore which are diverse and opposed in themselves, pre-exist as one in God, without detriment to his simpleness.

2. The above answer solves this argument also.

3. In the same chapter Dionysius[9] tells us that, when considered as notionally separate, existence as such is more perfect than life as such, and life as such more perfect than wisdom as such. Nevertheless, living things, which both live and exist, are more perfect than things which merely exist; and one who is wise also exists and also lives.[c] So, although being an existent thing does not involve being living or wise (for nothing partaking of existence need partake every mode of existence), nevertheless, existence itself[d] does involve life and wisdom (for subsistent existence itself cannot lack any perfection of existence).

article 3. can creatures be said to resemble God?

THE THIRD POINT:[1] 1. No creature, it seems, can resemble God. For the psalm says *there is none like thee among the gods, O Lord.*[2] Now the creatures to which we extend the word 'god' are among the more excellent ones.[a] So one has even less grounds for saying that other creatures resemble God.

---

use of the words 'wise' and 'living' and 'existent' *within* the above definitions of the words is very different. *Within* the definitions we must define 'wise' as 'wise abstracting from life and abstracting from existence'; 'living' will similarly abstract from wisdom and existence, and so on. Now, it is remarked, in *these* senses of the words, existence is more perfect than life, and life than wisdom. For by such abstraction wisdom is cut off, so to speak, from what gives it desirability, significance, actuality. Wisdom is desirable, significant, actual only as a mode of life; life is desirable, significant, actual only as a mode of existence; only existence is in itself desirable, significant and actual.

[d]'Existence itself' must be taken here to mean 'unspecified existence' in the first sense given to that phrase at 1a. 3, 4 ad 1: namely, divine existence. This is why certain editions (including the Leonine) have added the word 'Dei' to the text at this point (see textual note).

[a]Although the name 'God' belongs strictly only to one being, the name is used of other things like idols because of a (mistaken) belief, and can be extended to certain other things, in so far as these things partake of a likeness to God. cf note *b* to 3, 2; and also 1a. 13, 9 and 10.

2. Præterea, similitudo est comparatio quædam. Non est autem comparatio eorum quæ sunt diversorum generum ergo nec similitudo, non enim dicimus quod dulcedo est similis albedini. Sed nulla creatura est ejusdem generis cum Deo, cum Deus non sit in genere, ut supra ostensum est.[3] Ergo nulla creatura est similis Deo.

3. Præterea, similia dicuntur quæ conveniunt in forma. Sed nihil convenit cum Deo in forma, nullius enim rei essentia est ipsum esse nisi solius Dei. Ergo nulla creatura potest esse similis Deo.

4. Præterea, in similibus est mutua similitudo, nam simile est simili simile. Si igitur aliqua creatura est similis Deo et Deus esset similis alicui creaturæ, quod est contra id quod dicitur Isaiæ: *cui similem fecistis Deum?*[4]

SED CONTRA est quod dicitur *Gen. Faciamus hominem ad imaginem et similitudinem nostram,*[5] et I *Ioan. cum apparuerit similes ei erimus.*[6]

RESPONSIO: Dicendum quod cum similitudo attendatur secundum convenientiam in forma multiplex est similitudo secundum multos modos communicandi in forma.

Quædam enim dicuntur similia quia communicant in eadem forma secundum eamdem rationem et secundum eumdem modum (et hæc non solum dicuntur similia sed æqualia in similitudine), sicut duo æqualiter alba dicuntur similia in albedine. Et hæc est perfectissima similitudo.

Alio modo dicuntur similia quæ communicant in forma secundum eamdem rationem sed non secundum eundem modum sed secundum magis et minus, ut minus album dicitur simile magis albo. Et hæc est similitudo imperfecta.

Tertio modo dicitur aliquid simile alteri quia communicant in forma sed non secundum eamdem rationem, ut patet in agentibus non univocis. Cum enim omne agens agat sibi simile inquantum est agens, agit autem unumquodque secundum suam formam, necesse est quod in effectu sit similitudo formæ agentis. Si ergo agens sit contentum in eadem specie erit similitudo inter faciens et factum in forma secundum eamdem rationem speciei, sicut homo generat hominem. Si autem agens non sit contentum in specie erit similitudo sed non secundum eamdem rationem speciei, sicut ea quæ generantur ex virtute solis accedunt quidem ad aliquam similitudinem solis, non tamen ut recipiant formam solis secundum similitudinem speciei.* Si igitur sit aliquod agens quod non in genere contineatur, effectus ejus adhuc magis accedent remote ad similitudinem agentis, non tamen ita quod participent similitudinem formæ agentis secundum eamdem rationem speciei

---

*Leonine adds *sed secundum similitudinem generis,* but a form generically like.
[3]cf Ia. 3, 5   [4]*Isaiah* 40, 18

2. Moreover, resemblance is a sort of comparison; so that things of diverse genera, which cannot be compared, cannot be alike. Thus no one talks of a resemblance between sweetness and whiteness. Now no creature can be of one genus with God, for God, as we say, does not belong to a genus.[3] No creature then can resemble God.

3. Moreover, things are said to be alike when they agree in form. Now nothing agrees with God in form, for nothing but God alone has as its nature simply to exist. No creature then can be like God.

4. Moreover, resemblance is mutual, for like is like to like. If then some creature were like God, God would be like a creature, which Isaiah denies: *to whom will you liken God?*[4]

ON THE OTHER HAND, we read in *Genesis*: *Let us make man after our image and likeness*,[5] and in John's first epistle: *when he appears we shall be like him.*[6]

REPLY: Resemblance results from sharing a common form, and there are as many sorts of resemblance as there are ways of sharing a form.

Some things are called alike because they share a form of the same type to the same degree (and such we call not merely alike, but exactly alike). Thus, two equally white things are said to resemble one another in whiteness. And this is the best likeness.

Other things are called alike because they share a form of the same type, though to different degrees. Thus, something less white is said to resemble something more white. And this is a less perfect likeness.

Thirdly, things are called alike because they share a form, though not of one type. An example would be an agent and its effect, when not in the same genus. For what a thing does reflects what its active self is; and, since a thing is active in virtue of its form, its effect must bear a likeness to that form. If then agent and effect are of one species their like forms will be of the same specific type, as when man begets man. If, however, the agent is outside the species, the forms will be alike, but not of the same specific type: thus a certain likeness exists between the sun and the things the sun produces, even though such things do not receive a form of like species to the sun's.[b] If now there be an agent outside even genus, its effects will bear an even remoter resemblance to the agent. The likeness borne will not now be of the same specific or generic type as the form of the agent,

---

[5]*Genesis* 1, 26
[6]I *John* 3, 2
[b]cf note *a* to article 2 above.

aut generis sed secundum aliqualem analogiam sicut ipsum esse est commune omnibus. Et hoc modo illa quæ sunt a Deo assimilantur ei inquantum sunt entia, ut primo et universali principio totius esse.

1. Ad primum ergo dicendum quod sicut dicit Dionysius quod sacra scriptura dicit aliquid non esse simile Deo *non est contrarium assimilationi ad ipsum. Eadem enim sunt similia Deo et dissimilia: similia quidem secundum quod imitantur ipsum, prout contingit imitari eum qui non perfecte imitabilis est; dissimilia vero secundum quod deficiunt a sua causa*,[7] non solum secundum intensionem et remissionem (sicut minus album deficit a magis albo), sed quia non est communicantia nec secundum speciem nec secundum genus.

2. Ad secundum dicendum quod Deus non se habet ad creaturas sicut res diversorum generum, sed sicut id quod est extra omne genus et principium omnium generum.

3. Ad tertium dicendum quod non dicitur esse similitudo creaturæ ad Deum propter communicantiam in forma secundum eamdem rationem generis et speciei, sed secundum analogiam tantum, prout scilicet Deus est ens per essentiam et alia per participationem.

4. Ad quartum dicendum quod licet aliquo modo concedatur quod creatura est similis Deo nullo tamen modo concedendum est quod Deus sit similis creaturæ; quia ut dicit Dionysius *in his quæ unius ordinis sunt recipitur mutua similitudo, non autem in causa et causato*:[8] dicimus enim quod imago sit similis homini sed non e converso. Et similiter dici potest aliquo modo quod creatura sit similis Deo, non tamen quod Deus sit similis creaturæ.

but will present the sort of analogy that holds between all things because they have existence in common. And this is how things receiving existence from God resemble him; for precisely as things possessing existence they resemble the primary and universal sources of all existence.

Hence: 1. As Dionysius says, when the scriptures state that nothing is like to God, *they are not denying all likeness to him. For the same things are like and unlike God: like in so far as they imitate as best they can him whom it is not possible to imitate perfectly; unlike in so far as they fall short of their cause,*[7] not only in degree (as less white falls short of more white), but also because they do not share a common species or genus.

2. Creatures are not related to God as to a thing of a different genus, but as to something outside of and prior to all genera.

3. Creatures are said to resemble God, not by sharing a form of the same specific or generic type, but only analogically, inasmuch as God exists by nature, and other things partake existence.

4. Although we may admit in a way that creatures resemble God, we may in no way admit that God resembles creatures; for, as Dionysius points out, *mutual likeness obtains between things of the same order, but not between cause and effect:*[8] thus we would call a portrait a likeness of a man, but not vice-versa. Similarly, we can say in a way that creatures resemble God, but not that God resembles creatures.

---

[7] *On the Divine Names* 9, 7. PG 3, 916
[8] *On the Divine Names* 9, 6. PG 3, 913

DEINDE QUÆRITUR de bono, et

> primo de bono in communi,
> secundo de bonitate Dei.

Quæstio 5. de bono in communi

Circa primum quæruntur sex:

> 1. utrum bonum et ens sint idem secundum rem,
> 2. supposito quod differant ratione tantum, quid sit prius secundum rationem, utrum bonum vel ens,
> 3. supposito quod ens sit prius, utrum omne ens sit bonum,
> 4. ad quam causam ratio boni reducatur,
> 5. utrum ratio boni consistat in modo, specie et ordine,
> 6. de divisione boni in honestum, utile et delectabile.

articulus I. *utrum bonum et ens sint idem secundum rem*

AD PRIMUM sic proceditur:[1] I. Videtur quod bonum differat secundum rem ab ente. Dicit enim Boëtius in libro *de Hebd.*: *intueor in rebus aliud esse quod sunt bona et aliud esse quod sunt.*[2] Ergo bonum et ens differunt secundum rem.

2. Præterea, nihil informatur seipso. Sed bonum dicitur per informationem entis, ut habetur in commento *libri de Causis.*[3] Ergo bonum differt secundum rem ab ente.

3. Præterea, bonum suscipit magis et minus. Esse autem non suscipit magis et minus. Ergo bonum differt secundum rem ab ente.

SED CONTRA est quod Augustinus dicit in libro *de Doct. Christ.* quod *inquantum sumus boni sumus.*[4]

RESPONSIO: Dicendum quod bonum et ens sunt idem secundum rem, sed

---

[1]cf Ia. 16, 3 & 4; Ia2æ. 18, I; 2a2æ. 109, 2 ad I. Also I *Sent.* I, exp; 8, I, 3; 19, 5, I ad 3. *De veritate* I, I; XXI, I–3. *De potentia* IX, 7 ad 6. *CG* II, 41; III, 20. *In De hebdomadibus, lect.* 3   [2]*De Hebdomadibus.* PL 64, 1312 [3]cf the Book of Causes (prop. 19, ed. Bardenhewer 181) Fribourg, 1882. Largely excerpts from the *Elementatio Theologica* of Proclus, translated into Latin by an unknown author either from the Greek or Arabic in the twelfth century. [4]*De Doctrina Christiana* I, 32. PL 34, 32

WE ASK next about good.

> first, the general notion of good,
> secondly, the goodness of God.

Question 5. the general notion of good

The first question has six points of inquiry:

1. is being good really the same thing as existing?
2. if one assumes that being good and existing differ merely as ideas, which idea is the more fundamental?
3. if one assumes that existing is more fundamental, is everything that exists good?
4. what kind of causality is implicit in the notion of goodness?
5. is goodness a matter of being in condition, form and order?
6. the division of good into the worthy, the useful and the delightful.

article 1. is being good really the same thing as existing?

THE FIRST POINT:[1] 1. There is a real difference, it seems, between being good and existing.[a] For Boëthius says: *I observe that it is one thing for things to be good, another for them to exist.*[2] So there is a real difference between being good and existing.

2. Moreover, nothing can be a mode of itself. The commentary on the *Book of Causes* remarks, however, that being good is a mode of existing.[3] So existing and being good really differ.

3. Moreover, there are degrees of goodness but not of existence. So being good and existing must really differ.

ON THE OTHER HAND Augustine says that *inasmuch as we exist, we are good.*[4]

REPLY: To be good is really the same thing as to exist, but the words have

---

[a] The reader will notice that articles 1 and 3 raise practically the same question and give it practically the same answer. But whereas article 3 is asking whether any particular things qualified as beings escape being qualified as goods, article 1 is rather asking whether these are different qualifications at all. One might say that article 3 treats the words *ens* and *bonum* as nouns, article 1 as adjectives. It is to mark this difference that I have translated *ens* as 'existing' and *bonum* as 'being good' quite often in the following pages.

differunt secundum rationem tantum. Quod sic patet. Ratio enim boni in hoc consistit quod aliquid sit appetibile, unde Philosophus in 1 *Ethic.* dicit quod *bonum est quod omnia appetunt.*[5] Manifestum est autem quod unumquodque est appetibile secundum quod est perfectum, nam omnia appetunt suam perfectionem. Intantum est autem perfectum unumquodque inquantum est actu. Unde manifestum est quod intantum est aliquid bonum inquantum est ens, esse enim est actualitas omnis rei, ut ex superioribus patet.[6] Unde manifestum est quod bonum et ens sunt idem secundum rem, sed bonum dicit rationem appetibilitatis quam non dicit ens.

1. Ad primum ergo dicendum quod licet bonum et ens sint idem secundum rem quia tamen differunt secundum rationem non eodem modo dicitur aliquid ens simpliciter et bonum simpliciter. Nam cum ens dicat proprie esse in actu, actus autem proprie ordinem habeat ad potentiam, secundum hoc simpliciter aliquid dicitur ens secundum quod primo discernitur ab eo quod est in potentia tantum. Hoc autem est esse substantiale rei uniuscujusque, unde per suum esse substantiale dicitur unumquodque ens simpliciter. Per actus autem superadditos dicitur aliquid esse secundum quid, sicut esse album significat esse secundum quid; non enim esse album aufert esse in potentia simpliciter cum adveniat rei iam præexistenti in actu. Sed bonum dicit rationem perfecti quod est appetibile, et per consequens dicit rationem ultimi. Unde id quod est ultimo perfectum dicitur bonum simpliciter; quod autem non habet ultimam perfectionem quam debet habere, quamvis habeat aliquam perfectionem inquantum est actu, non tamen dicitur perfectum simpliciter nec bonum simpliciter sed secundum quid.

Sic ergo secundum primum esse quod est substantiale dicitur aliquid ens simpliciter et bonum secundum quid (idest inquantum est ens), secundum vero ultimum actum dicitur aliquid ens secundum quid et bonum simpliciter. Sic ergo quod dicit Boëtius, quod *in rebus aliud est quod sunt bona et aliud quod sunt,* referendum est ad esse bonum et ad esse simpliciter, quia secundum primum actum est aliquid ens simpliciter et secundum ultimum bonum simpliciter. Et tamen secundum primum actum est quodammodo bonum, et secundum ultimum actum est quodammodo ens.

2. Ad secundum dicendum quod bonum dicitur per informationem prout accipitur bonum simpliciter secundum ultimum actum.

---

[5]*Ethics* I, 1. 1094a3
[6]cf Ia. 3, 4; 4, 1 ad 3
[b]St Thomas extends the notion of 'desire' to cover not only the appetites of beings endowed with sense-perception or with reason, but also the tendencies exhibited by beings altogether without knowledge, yet he is well aware that in the proper sense of the term most things do not 'desire' the good, but rather tend by nature to some determinate goal which their creator desires for them (cf for example the 5th way

different meanings. This is made clear as follows. The goodness of a thing consists in its being desirable; hence Aristotle's dictum that *good is what all things desire*.[5] [b] Now clearly desirability is consequent upon perfection, for things always desire their perfection. And the perfection of a thing depends on how far it has achieved actuality. It is clear then that a thing is good inasmuch as it exists, for as we saw above it is by existing that everything achieves actuality.[6] Obviously then being good does not really differ from existing, though the word 'good' expresses a notion of desirability not expressed by the word 'existent'.

Hence: 1. Although being good is really the same thing as existing, one cannot use the words 'good' and 'existent' interchangeably without qualification, due to a difference in meaning. For 'existent' properly means actual, and actuality properly involves reference to potentiality, so that, used without qualification, 'existent' names a thing in its initial distinctness from sheer potentiality. Now it is being a substance that thus distinguishes a thing, and things are therefore said to exist, without qualification, when they exist as substances. As possessed of some further actuality they are said to exist only in a certain respect; to be white, for example, is to exist only in a certain respect; it is not being white which removes a thing from sheer potentiality, for to be white a thing must already actually exist. 'Good', on the other hand, expresses the idea of desirable perfection and thus the notion of something complete. So things are called 'good', without qualification, when they are completely perfect; when their perfection is not so complete as it should be, then, even though having some perfection inasmuch as they actually exist, they will nonetheless not be called perfect or good without qualification but only in a certain respect.

It follows therefore that when we consider the initial existence of something as substance we talk of it existing without qualification and being good in a certain respect (namely, inasmuch as it exists); but when we consider the actualization which completes a thing we talk of that thing existing in a certain respect and being good without qualification. Hence Boëthius' remark that *it is one thing for things to be good and another for them to exist* refers to existing and being good understood without qualification; for to exist without qualification is to achieve an initial actuality, and to be good without qualification is to achieve complete actuality. However, a thing's initial actuality is a sort of goodness, and the actuality completing it a sort of existence.

2. 'Being good' describes a mode of existence when used without qualification to mean achieving complete actuality.

---

in 1a. 2, 3; and also 1a. 6, 1 ad 2: 1a2æ. 1, 2). Aristotle's tag says therefore that to call a thing good means that it is the determinate object of some tendency or other.

3. Et similiter dicendum ad tertium quod bonum dicitur secundum magis et minus secundum actum supervenientem, puta secundum scientiam vel virtutem.

articulus 2. quid sit prius secundum rationem, utrum bonum vel ens

AD SECUNDUM sic proceditur:[1] 1. Videtur quod bonum secundum rationem sit prius quam ens. Ordo enim nominum est secundum ordinem rerum significatarum per nomen. Sed Dionysius inter alia nomina Dei prius ponit bonum quam ens, ut patet in iii cap. *de Div. Nom.*[2] Ergo bonum secundum rationem est prius quam ens.

2. Præterea, illud est prius secundum rationem quod ad plura se extendit. Sed bonum ad plura se extendit quam ens, quia ut dicit Dionysius v cap. de Div. Nom. *bonum se extendit ad existentia et non existentia, ens vero se extendit ad existentia tantum.*[3] Ergo bonum est prius secundum rationem quam ens.

3. Præterea, quod est universalius est prius secundum rationem. Sed bonum videtur universalius esse quam ens, quia bonum habet rationem appetibilis, quoddam autem appetibile est ipsum non esse (dicitur enim Matth. xxvi de Iuda: *bonum erat ei si natus, etc.*).[4] Ergo bonum est prius secundum rationem quam ens.

4. Præterea, non solum esse est appetibile, sed etiam vita et sapientia et multa hujusmodi. Et sic videtur quod esse sit quoddam particulare appetibile et bonum.* Bonum ergo simpliciter est prius secundum rationem quam ens.

SED CONTRA est quod dicitur in *libro de Causis,* quod *prima rerum creatarum est esse.*[5]

RESPONSIO: Dicendum quod ens secundum rationem est prius quam bonum. Ratio enim significata per nomen est id quod concipit intellectus de re et significat illud per vocem. Illud ergo est prius secundum rationem quod prius cadit in conceptione intellectus. Primo autem in conceptione intellectus cadit ens, quia secundum hoc unumquodque cognoscibile est quod est actu, ut dicitur in IX *Meta.*[6] Unde ens est proprium objectum

---

*Leonine adds *universale,* many desirable things, and good the desirable in general.
[1]cf references quoted for first article   [2]*On the Divine Names* 3, 1. PG 3, 680
[3]*On the Divine Names* 5, 1. PG 3, 816   [4]*Matthew* 26, 24
[5]*De Causis* 4. ed. Bardenhewer 166. 19   [6]*Metaphysics* IX, 9. 1051a31
[a]There seems to be no essential difference between arguing from wider application of an idea as in argument 2, and from universality of an idea as in argument 3.

3. In the same way, degrees of goodness result from actuality over and above existence, such as knowledge or virtue.

article 2. which idea is the more fundamental, being good or existing?

THE SECOND POINT:[1] 1. Being good seems to be a more fundamental idea than existing. For one lists epithets in the order of the ideas they express. Now in Dionysius' list of divine epithets 'good' precedes 'existent'.[2] The idea of the good is therefore prior to the idea of the existent.

2. Moreover, the more fundamental idea is the one with wider application. Now good is of wider application than existent, for as Dionysius says *good comprehends things that exist and things that do not exist, but existent only things that exist.*[3] Hence good is a more fundamental idea than existent.

3. Moreover, the more universal an idea the more fundamental it is.[a] Now good seems more universal than existent, for it conveys the notion of desirability, and even non-existence is desirable (thus we read of Judas that *it would have been good for him never to have been born*).[4] The good is therefore a more fundamental idea than the existent.

4. Moreover, not only existence is desirable, but also life, wisdom and many similar things. Existence seems then to be only one of many desirable goods. So the good is without qualification a more fundamental idea than the existent.

ON THE OTHER HAND the *Book of Causes* says that *existence is the first thing created.*[5]

REPLY: Existing is a more fundamental idea than being good. For the idea expressed in a word is something the intellect conceives from things and expresses in speech.[b] A more fundamental idea then is one met with earlier in this process of intellectual conception. Now the first idea met with in intellectual conception is that of an existent, for as Aristotle says in order to be known a thing must actually be.[6] This is why existent being is the primary and distinctive object of intellect, just as sound is the primary

---

The reason for there being two arguments emerges only in the solutions: argument 2 understands by non-existence potential existence, argument 3 understands the term strictly.

[b]Understanding is, for St Thomas, an action. To think of it simply as a passive reflection of things is to think of it abstractly; in the concrete it is an action of reproduction, of conception which cannot be separated from the expression of what is conceived in images or in words. See 1a. 27, 1; 84, 7; 85, 2 ad 3.

intellectus, et sic est primum intelligibile, sicut sonus est primum audibile. Ita ergo secundum rationem prius est ens quam bonum.

1. Ad primum ergo dicendum quod Dionysius determinat de divinis nominibus secundum quod important circa Deum habitudinem causæ, nominamus enim Deum ut ipse dicit ex creaturis sicut causam ex effectibus.[7] Bonum autem cum habeat rationem appetibilis importat habitudinem causæ finalis, cujus causalitas prima est; quia agens non agit nisi propter finem et ab agente materia movetur ad formam, (unde dicitur quod finis est causa causarum). Et sic in causando bonum est prius quam ens sicut finis quam forma, et hac ratione inter nomina designantia causalitatem divinam prius ponitur bonum quam ens.

Et iterum quia secundum Platonicos, qui materiam a privatione non distinguentes dicebant materiam esse non ens, ad plura se extendit participatio boni quam participatio entis. Nam materia prima participat bonum cum appetat ipsum (nihil autem appetit nisi sibi simile), non autem participat ens cum ponatur non ens. Et ideo dicit Dionysius quod *bonum extenditur ad non existentia.*[8]

2. Unde patet solutio ad secundum. Vel dicendum quod *bonum extenditur ad existentia et non existentia* non secundum prædicationem sed secundum causalitatem, ut per non existentia intelligamus non ea simpliciter quæ penitus non sunt sed ea quæ sunt in potentia et non in actu. Quia bonum habet rationem finis, in quo non solum quiescunt quæ sunt in actu sed ad ipsum moventur quæ in actu non sunt sed in potentia tantum. Ens autem non importat habitudinem causæ nisi formalis tantum, vel inhærentis vel exemplaris, cujus causalitas non se extendit nisi ad ea quæ sunt in actu.

3. Ad tertium dicendum quod non esse secundum se non est appetibile sed per accidens, inquantum scilicet ablatio alicujus mali est appetibilis quod malum quidem aufertur per non esse. Ablatio vero mali non est appetibilis nisi inquantum per malum privatur quoddam esse. Illud igitur quod per se est appetibile est esse, non esse vero per accidens tantum inquantum quoddam esse appetitur quo homo non sustinet privari. Et sic etiam per accidens non esse dicitur bonum.

4. Ad quartum dicendum quod vita et scientia et alia hujusmodi sic

---

[7]*On the Divine Names* 1, 7. PG 3, 596
[8]*On the Divine Names* 5, 1. PG 3, 816
[c]On causality, and the primacy of the end in causality, see Appendix 2.
[d]Arguments 1 and 2 have been answered with the same two alternative solutions: on the one hand, that good is prior to existent as a cause but not as a predicate; and on the other, that given a view of matter as non-existent and yet desirous of good, good is prior to existent because of its wider application. This latter view

object of hearing. Existing therefore is a more fundamental idea than being good.

Hence: 1. Dionysius is concerned with divine epithets implying causality in God, for as he himself says God's names are drawn from creatures like those of other causes from their effects.[7] Now being good, conveying as it does the notion of desirability, implies being an end or goal, and this is where causality starts, for no agent acts except for some end, and except some agent acts no matter acquires form (hence we call the end the cause of causes).[c] In causation then the good precedes the existent as end precedes form; and for this reason in any list of epithets signifying divine causality 'good' will precede 'existent'.

A further reason is that the Platonists, not differentiating between potential being and lack of being, said that matter was non-existent, and consequently held that goodness is partaken of more widely than existence. For since unformed matter desires good, it partakes it (what a thing desires reflects what it is); it does not however partake existence since supposed to be non-existent. And this is why Dionysius says that *good comprehends things that do not exist*.[8]

2. Clearly this answers the second argument also. Or one could say instead that it is not to good as predicate but to good as cause that both existent and non-existent things are subject; understanding by non-existence not total and absolute non-existence but potential existence not yet actualized. For the good is a goal, in which not only things that have achieved actuality come to rest, but towards which things not actualized but only potential are in movement. Existing, on the other hand, involves no causal relation at all, unless it be that of form—either intrinsic form or extrinsic pattern—, and only actually existent things are subject to the casuality of form.[d]

3. Non-existence is desirable not in itself, but for the incidental reason that it removes an evil which it is desirable to remove. Now removing evil is desirable only because evil is lack of some sort of existence. So that the desirable thing itself is existence, and non-existence is desirable only incidentally, inasmuch as a man can no longer abide the lack of an existence such as he desires. And it is for such incidental reasons that non-existence is called good.

4. Life, wisdom and so on are desired as modes of actual existence; so

---

St Thomas calls Platonist, but it ought more accurately perhaps to be called neo-Platonist. In any case, the two alternative solutions seem to be merely two aspects of one Platonic position. For Plato's 'idea' is really an 'ideal', and he sees no difference between the notions of form and end as St Thomas uses them here: to desire the good is the highest form of actuality for Plato.

appetuntur ut insint actu, unde in omnibus appetitur quoddam esse. Et sic nihil est appetibile nisi ens, et per consequens nihil est bonum nisi ens.

articulus 3. *utrum omne ens sit bonum*

AD TERTIUM sic proceditur:[1] 1. Videtur quod non omne ens sit bonum. Bonum enim addit supra ens, ut ex dictis patet.[2] Ea vero quæ addunt supra ens contrahunt ipsum, sicut substantia, quantitas, qualitas et alia hujusmodi. Ergo bonum contrahit ens. Non igitur omne ens est bonum.

2. Præterea, nullum malum est bonum: Isaiæ v, *Væ qui dicunt malum bonum.*[3] Sed aliquod ens dicitur malum. Ergo non omne ens est bonum.

3. Præterea, bonum habet rationem appetibilis. Sed materia prima non habet rationem appetibilis sed appetentis tantum. Ergo materia prima non habet rationem boni. Non igitur omne ens est bonum.

4. Præterea, Philosophus dicit in III *Meta.* quod in mathematicis non est bonum.[4] Sed mathematica sunt quædam entia, alioquin de eis non esset scientia. Ergo non omne ens est bonum.

SED CONTRA, omne ens quod non est Deus est Dei creaturæ. Sed *omnis creatura Dei est bona* ut dicitur I *ad Tim.* iv.[5] Deus vero est maxime bonus. Ergo omne ens est bonum.

RESPONSIO: Dicendum quod omne ens inquantum est ens est bonum. Omne enim ens inquantum est ens est in actu et quodammodo perfectum, quia omnis actus perfectio quædam est. Perfectum vero habet rationem appetibilis et boni, ut ex dictis patet.[6] Unde sequitur omne ens inquantum hujusmodi bonum esse.

1. Ad primum ergo dicendum quod substantia, quantitas et qualitas et ea quæ sub eis continentur contrahunt ens applicando ens ad aliquam quidditatem seu naturam. Sic autem non addit aliquid bonum super esse, sed rationem tantum appetibilitatis et perfectionis quod convenit ipsi esse in quacumque natura sit. Unde bonum non contrahit ens.

2. Ad secundum dicendum quod nullum ens dicitur malum inquantum est ens sed inquantum caret quodam esse, sicut homo dicitur malus inquantum caret esse virtutis, et oculus dicitur malus inquantum caret actione visus.

---

[1]cf references quoted for article 1
[2]cf Ia. 5, 1   [3]*Isaiah* 5, 20
[4]*Metaphysics* III, 2. 996a29
[5]I *Timothy* 4, 4   [6]cf Ia. 5, 1

that what is desired from them is existence of a certain sort. Nothing therefore is desirable except it exist, and in consequence nothing is good except it exist.

article 3. *is everything that exists good?*

THE THIRD POINT:[1] 1. Not everything that exists is good, it seems. For previous discussion has shown that being good adds something to existing.[2] Now adding something to the idea of existing will produce a narrower idea: being a substance, for example, or being of such a size or such a sort. Being good is therefore a narrower idea than existing. And so not everything that exists is good.

2. Moreover, nothing bad is good: witness Isaiah, crying *woe to those who call evil good*.[3] Now some things that exist are called bad. So not everything that exists is good.

3. Moreover, the good is, by definition, desirable. Now the ultimate matter of things is not desirable but only desires.[a] Matter then is not good. And so not everything that exists is good.

4. Moreover, Aristotle says that mathematics does not concern itself with the good.[4] Nevertheless the objects of mathematics must somehow exist for there to be science of them. So not everything that exists is good.

ON THE OTHER HAND, anything that exists is either God or created by God. Now *every creature of God is good*, says St Paul.[5] And God himself is supremely good. So everything that exists is good.

REPLY: Inasmuch as they exist, all things are good. For everything, inasmuch as it exists, is actual and therefore in some way perfect, all actuality being a sort of perfection. Now we have shown above that anything perfect is desirable and good.[6] It follows then that, inasmuch as they exist, all things are good.

Hence: 1. Being a substance, or being of such a size or sort, as also any idea less general than these, narrows the idea of existing by mentioning what kind of thing is existing. Being good does not add to existing in this way, but adds merely the notion of a desirability and perfection associated with the very existence of things, whatever kind of things they be. Being good then is no narrower than existing.

2. Nothing that exists is called bad because it exists, but rather because it fails to exist in some way; thus a man is called bad when he fails to be virtuous, and an eye bad when its vision fails.

---

[a]On the use of the word 'desires', see note *b* to article 1.

3. Ad tertium dicendum quod materia prima sicut non est ens nisi in potentia ita nec bonum nisi in potentia. Licet secundum Platonicos dici possit quod materia prima est non ens propter privationem adjunctam, sed tamen participat aliquid de bono scilicet ipsum ordinem vel aptitudinem ad bonum. Et ideo non competit sibi quod sit appetibile sed quod appetat.

4. Ad quartum dicendum quod mathematica non subsistunt separata secundum esse, quia si subsisterent esset in eis bonum, scilicet ipsum esse ipsorum. Sunt autem mathematica separata secundum rationem tantum prout abstrahuntur a motu et a materia, et sic abstrahuntur a ratione finis quod habet rationem moventis. Non est autem inconveniens quod in aliquo ente secundum rationem non sit ratio boni, cum ratio entis sit prior quam ratio boni, sicut supra dictum est.[7]

articulus 4. ad quam causam ratio boni reducatur

AD QUARTUM sic proceditur:[1] 1. Videtur quod bonum non habeat rationem causæ finalis sed magis aliarum. Ut enim dicit Dionysius iv cap de Div. Nom. *bonum laudatur ut pulchrum.*[2] Sed pulchrum importat rationem causæ formalis. Ergo bonum habet rationem causæ formalis.

2. Item, bonum est diffusivum sui esse, ut ex verbis Dionysii accipitur quibus dicitur quod *bonum est ex quo omnia subsistunt et sunt.*[3] Sed esse effusivum importat rationem causæ efficientis. Ergo bonum habet rationem causæ efficientis.

3. Præterea, dicit Augustinus in I *de Doct. Christ.* quod *quia Deus bonus est sumus.*[4] Sed ex Deo sumus sicut ex causa efficiente. Ergo bonum importat rationem causæ efficientis.

SED CONTRA est quod Philosophus dicit in II *Phys.* quod *illud cujus causa est est sicut finis et bonum aliorum.*[5] Bonum ergo habet rationem causæ finalis.

RESPONSIO: Dicendum quod bonum cum sit quod omnia appetunt, hoc autem habet rationem finis, manifestum est quod bonum rationem finis importat. Sed tamen ratio boni præsupponit rationem causæ efficientis et rationem causæ formalis.

---

[7]cf Ia. 5, 2
[1]cf Ia2æ. I, 2; I, 4; 25, 2. I *Sent.* 34, 2, ad I, 4. *De veritate* XXI, I, 2. *CG* I, 40. *In De div. nom.* I, *lect.* 3. *In Physic.* II, *lect* 5. Also especially about good and beauty Ia2æ. 27, I ad 3
[2]*On the Divine Names* 4, 7. PG 3, 701
[3]cf *On the Divine Names* 4, 4. PG 3, 700. Dionysius uses the vocabulary of 'pouring forth' at several points in chapter 4 of this work: e.g. 4, 20. PG 3, 717–20
[4]*De Doctrina Christiana* I, 32. PL 34, 32

3. Just as matter only potentially exists, so it is only potentially good. Although one might say if one were a Platonist that matter is non-existent, being accompanied by lack of existence, and yet partakes something of goodness, being a predisposition towards good.[b] This is why matter, though not desirable, nevertheless desires.

4. Mathematical objects have no separate existence; if they did, that existence itself would be good. We separate them only conceptually, by prescinding from matter and change, and thus from the idea of an end or goal motivating change. Now conceiving something to exist without conceiving it to be good is admissible, for as we have already seen existing is a more fundamental concept than being good.[7]

article 4. what kind of causality is implicit in the notion of goodness?

THE FOURTH POINT:[1] 1. Being good seems to imply not so much being an end or goal as being one of the other kinds of cause.[a] For Dionysius says that *the good is esteemed beautiful.*[2] Now beauty involves the notion of form. Goodness therefore conveys the idea of form.

2. Or another approach: good things pour forth their own being, as Dionysius gives us to understand, saying that *from the good comes all subsistence and existence.*[3] Now pouring out involves the idea of an operative cause. Being good therefore conveys the idea of being an operative cause.

3. Moreover, Augustine says *we exist because God is good.*[4] Now existence comes from God as an operative cause. So being good implies being an operative cause.

ON THE OTHER HAND we have the words of Aristotle: *that for the sake of which things exist is their good and their goal.*[5] Being good therefore involves being an end or goal.

REPLY: Since good is what all things desire, and this involves the idea of a goal, clearly being good involves being a goal. Nevertheless, presupposed to the idea of good are the notions of operative cause and form.

---

[5]*Physics* II, 3. 195a23-4
[b]For the notion of participation cf note *b* on 1a. 3, 2. Also cf here the answers to the first two objections in 1a. 5, 2.
[a]The Aristotelian and Thomist division of causes will be found in Appendix 2.

Videmus enim quod primum est in causando ultimum esse in causato, ignis enim primo calefacit quam formam ignis inducat, cum tamen calor in igne consequatur formam substantialem. In causando autem primum invenitur bonum et finis qui movet efficientem, secundo actio efficientis movens ad formam, tertio advenit forma. Unde e converso oportet esse in causato, quod primum sit ipsa forma per quam est ens, secundo consideretur in eo virtus effectiva secundum quod est perfectum in esse (quia unumquodque tunc perfectum est quando potest sibi simile facere, ut dicit Philosophus in IV *Meteor.*);[6] tertio consequitur ratio boni per quam in ente perfectio fundatur.

1. Ad primum ergo dicendum quod pulchrum et bonum in subjecto quidem sunt idem quia super eamdem rem fundantur, scilicet super formam, et propter hoc *bonum laudatur ut pulchrum.* Sed ratione differunt. Nam bonum proprie respicit appetitum (est enim bonum *quod omnia appetunt*), et ideo habet rationem finis (nam appetitus est quasi quidam motus ad rem). Pulchrum autem respicit vim cognitivam, pulchra enim dicuntur quæ visa placent. Unde pulchrum in debita proportione consistit, quia sensus delectatur in rebus debite proportionatis sicut in sibi similibus, nam et sensus ratio quædam est et omnis virtus cognoscitiva. Et quia cognitio fit per assimilationem, similitudo autem respicit formam, pulchrum proprie pertinet ad rationem causæ formalis.

2. Ad secundum dicendum quod bonum dicitur diffusivum sui ipsius esse eo modo quo finis dicitur movere.

3. Ad tertium dicendum quod quilibet habens voluntatem dicitur bonus inquantum habet bonam voluntatem, quia per voluntatem utimur omnibus quæ in nobis sunt. Unde non dicitur bonus homo qui habet bonum intellectum, sed qui habet bonam voluntatem. Voluntas autem respicit finem ut objectum proprium, et sic quod dicitur *quia Deus est bonus sumus* refertur ad causam finalem.

---

[6]*Meteorology* IV, 3. 380a 12 ff
[b]St Thomas is concerned with goodness, activity and existence. In causing, he says, goodness precedes existence, for the goodness of the end arouses the activity of the agent which causes the existence of the effect. But within the caused thing, existence precedes goodness, for a thing must exist before it can act, and must be active and therefore perfect before it can be desired as a good. St Thomas equates 'being desired as a good' to 'pouring forth perfection within being', an equation

For we observe that an act of causation begins from what will be caused last; thus fire begins by heating other things and then elicits the form of fire in them, and yet the heat of a fire is consequent upon its substantial form. Now in the act of causation we begin with the good end which influences the agent to act, then follows the action of the agent eliciting the form, and finally there arises the form. Necessarily then the opposite order is found within the caused thing: first, there occurs the form itself which gives the thing existence; second for consideration occurs the thing's operative power through which it achieves perfect existence (for a thing is perfect Aristotle says when it can reproduce itself);[6] and finally the thing realizes the idea of good and so can pour forth perfection within being.[b]

Hence: 1. A good thing is also in fact a beautiful thing, for both epithets have the same basis in reality, namely, the possession of form; and this is why *the good is esteemed beautiful*. Good and beautiful are not however synonymous. For good (being *what all things desire*) has to do properly with desire and so involves the idea of end (since desire is a kind of movement towards something). Beauty, on the other hand, has to do with knowledge, and we call a thing beautiful when it pleases the eye of the beholder. This is why beauty is a matter of right proportion, for the senses delight in rightly proportioned things as similar to themselves, the sense-faculty being a sort of proportion itself like all other knowing faculties.[c] Now since knowing proceeds by imaging, and images have to do with form, beauty properly involves the notion of form.

2. Good things are said to pour forth their being in the same way that ends are said to move one.

3. Beings with wills are called good when those wills are good, since will determines the use to which everything else in us is put. A good man therefore is not one who has a good intellect, but one who has a good will. Now the special function of the will is the pursuit of ends. So saying that *we exist because God is good* does have reference to the causality of an end.

---

which he further refers to in the answer to the second objection. For fuller explanation see Appendix 7, where the translation of this passage is also commented upon.
[c]That the sense-faculty is a sort of proportion is a phrase derived from Aristotle, *De Anima* III, 2. 426b4. Any great intensity in an object of sense—a very loud sound for example, or a very bright light—upsets this proportion, and as a result destroys the faculty.

articulus 5. utrum ratio boni consistat in modo, specie et ordine

AD QUINTUM sic proceditur:[1] 1. Videtur quod ratio boni non consistat in modo, specie et ordine. Bonum enim et ens ratione differunt ut supra dictum est.[2] Sed modus, species et ordo pertinere ad rationem entis videntur. Quia, sicut dicitur *Sap.* xi, *omnia in numero, pondere et mensura constituisti*;[3] ad quæ tria reducuntur species, modus et ordo, quia ut dicit Augustinus IV *super Gen. ad litt. mensura omni rei modum præfigit, et numerus omni rei speciem præbet, et pondus omnem rem ad quietem et stabilitatem trahit.*[4] Ergo ratio boni non consistit in modo, specie et ordine.

2. Præterea, ipse modus, species et ordo bona quædam sunt. Si ergo ratio boni consistit in modo, specie et ordine oportet etiam quod modus habeat modum, speciem et ordinem, et similiter species et ordo. Ergo procederetur in infinitum.

3. Præterea, malum est privatio modi et speciei et ordinis. Sed malum non tollit totaliter bonum. Ergo ratio boni non consistit in modo, specie et ordine.

4. Præterea, illud in quo consistit ratio boni non potest dici malum. Sed dicitur malus modus, mala species, malus ordo. Ergo ratio boni non consistit in modo, specie et ordine.

5. Præterea, modus, species et ordo ex pondere, numero et mensura causantur, ut ex auctoritate Augustini inducta patet. Non autem omnia bona habent pondus, numerum et mensuram, dicit enim Ambrosius in Hexæm. quod *lucis natura est ut non in numero, non in pondere, non in mensura creata sit.*[5] Non ergo ratio boni consistit in modo, specie et ordine.

SED CONTRA est quod dicit Augustinus in libro *de Natura Boni: Hæc tria— modus, species et ordo—tanquam generalia bona sunt in rebus a Deo factis, et ita hæc tria ubi magna sunt magna bona sunt, ubi parva parva bona sunt, ubi nulla nullum bonum est.*[6] Quod non esset nisi ratio boni in eis consisteret. Ergo ratio boni consistit in modo, specie et ordine.

RESPONSIO: Dicendum quod unumquodque dicitur bonum inquantum est perfectum, sic enim est appetibile ut supra dictum est.[7] Perfectum autem dicitur cui nihil deest secundum modum suæ perfectionis. Cum autem unumquodque sit id quod est per suam formam, forma autem præsupponit quædam et quædam ad ipsam ex necessitate consequuntur, ad hoc quod aliquid sit perfectum et bonum necesse est quod formam habeat et ea quæ forma præexigit et ea quæ consequuntur ad ipsam.

---

[1]cf Ia2æ. 85, 4. And Ia. 6, 1 ad 1. Also *De veritate* XXI, 6
[2]cf Ia. 5, 1   [3]*Wisdom* 11, 21
[4]*Super Genesim ad litteram* (a literal commentary on Genesis) IV, 3. PL 34, 299

article 5. is goodness a matter of being in condition, form and order?

THE FIFTH POINT:[1] 1. Goodness does not seem a matter of being in condition, form and order. For we have already seen that being good does not mean the same as existing.[2] Condition, form and order, however, seem part of what existence means. For the book of *Wisdom* declares: *thou hast created all things by number and weight and measure,*[3] a threefoldness Augustine shows to be the basis of form, condition and order, when he says: *measure determines the condition of everything, number supplies everything with form, and weight attracts everything toward steadiness and rest.*[4] Goodness therefore does not consist in condition, form and order.

2. Moreover, condition, form and order are themselves goods of a certain sort. If then being good is to consist in being in condition, form and order, each of these must be in a condition, form and order of its own. And so on for ever.

3. Moreover, to be bad is to be out of condition, form and order. Now a bad thing never lacks goodness altogether. So that goodness does not consist in condition, form and order.

4. Moreover, that in which goodness consists cannot be called bad. But we talk of things being in bad condition, bad form and bad order. Goodness does not therefore consist in condition, form and order.

5. Moreover, condition, form and order are caused by weight, number and measure, as the above quotation from Augustine shows. But some good things do not possess weight, number and measure, for Ambrose declares that *it is the nature of light not to be created in number, weight and measure.*[5] Goodness therefore does not consist in condition, form and order.

ON THE OTHER HAND Augustine says that *these three—condition, form and order—are goods always found in everything God makes; where these three bulk large things are very good, where they are of small account things are of little good, where they do not exist at all things are no good.*[6] Now none of this would be so unless goodness consisted in these three things. Goodness therefore consists in condition, form and order.

REPLY: To be called 'good' things must be perfect, for only then as we have said are they desirable.[7] Being perfect means lacking nothing requisite to one's own mode of perfection. Now what a thing is its form determines, and form presupposes certain things and has certain necessary consequences. So, to be perfect and good, a thing must possess form and the prerequisites and consequences of form.

---

[5]*In Hexæm.* (on the six days of creation) I, 9. PL 14, 143
[6]*De Natura Boni* 3. PL 42, 553   [7]cf 1a. 5, 1

Præexigitur autem ad formam determinatio sive commensuratio principiorum seu materialium seu efficientium ad* ipsam, et hoc significatur per modum, unde dicitur quod *mensura modum præfigit.*[8] Ipsa autem forma significatur per speciem quia per formam unumquodque in specie constituitur. Et propter hoc dicitur quod *numerus speciem præbet,*† quia definitiones significantes speciem sunt sicut numeri secundum Philosophum in VIII *Meta*; sicut enim in numeris unitas addita vel subtracta variat speciem numeri, ita in definitionibus differentia apposita vel subtracta.[9] Ad formam autem consequitur inclinatio ad finem aut ad actionem aut ad aliquid hujusmodi, quia unumquodque inquantum est actu agit, et tendit in id quod sibi convenit secundum suam formam. Et hoc pertinet ad pondus et ordinem. Unde ratio boni secundum quod consistit in perfectione, consistit etiam in modo, specie et ordine.

1. Ad primum ergo dicendum quod ista tria non consequuntur ens nisi inquantum est perfectum, et secundum hoc est bonum.

2. Ad secundum dicendum quod modus, species et ordo eo modo dicuntur bona sicut et entia, non quia ipsa sint quasi subsistentia sed quia eis aliqua sunt et entia et bona. Tamen non oportet quod ipsa habeant aliqua alia quibus sint bona. Non enim sic dicuntur bona quasi formaliter aliis ipsa sint bona, sed quia ipsis formaliter aliqua sunt bona, sicut albedo non dicitur ens quia ipsa aliquo sit, sed quia ipsa aliquid est secundum quid (scilicet, album).

3. Ad tertium dicendum quod quodlibet esse est secundum formam aliquam, unde secundum quodlibet esse rei consequitur ipsam modus, species et ordo. Sicut homo habet speciem, modum et ordinem inquantum est homo, et similiter inquantum est album habet aliter‡ modum, speciem et ordinem, et inquantum est virtuosus, et inquantum est sciens, et secundum omnia quæ de ipso dicuntur. Malum autem privat quoddam esse, sicut cæcitas privat esse visus, unde non tollit omnem modum, speciem et ordinem, sed solum modum, speciem et ordinem quæ consequuntur esse visus.

4. Ad quartum dicendum quod sicut dicit Augustinus, *omnis modus inquantum modus bonus est* (et similiter potest dici de specie et ordine), *sed malus modus vel mala species vel malus ordo aut ideo dicuntur quia minora sunt quam esse debuerunt, aut quia non his rebus accommodantur quibus accommodanda sunt, ut ideo dicantur mala quia sunt aliena et incongrua.*[10]

---

*Leonine omits *ad* to that form.
†ms: *imprimit vel præbet*, to imprint or supply.
‡Leonine *similiter*, and a like condition, form and order again.
[8]*Super Genesim ad litteram* IV, 3. PL 34, 299
[9]*Metaphysics* VIII, 3. 1043b34   [10]*De Natura Boni* 22 and 23. PL 42, 558
[a]In the phrase 'condition, form and order' the English word 'form' is translating

Now form presupposes that a thing's material elements and operative causes are somehow appropriate or commensurate to that form, and this is expressed in the word 'condition'. This is why *measure* is said to *determine condition.*[8] To express form itself Augustine used the word *species* since form determines the species of things.[a] And this is why *number* is said to *supply form*; for according to Aristotle definitions of species are like numbers, and just as adding or subtracting one changes the species of numbers, so also does adding or subtracting a differentiating factor in definitions.[9] Finally, form issues in a proneness to some end or action or the like, for activity is consequent upon actuality, and things gravitate toward what is natural to them. And this is expressed by 'weight' and 'order'. So because being good consists in being perfect, it also consists in being in condition, form and order.

Hence: 1. An existent thing possesses these three qualities only when it is perfect, and then it is good.

2. We talk of condition, form and order as good in the same way that we talk of them existing, not as subjects of existence themselves, but as constituting other things in existence and goodness. Nevertheless they themselves are good without being so constituted in goodness. For they are not called good as being formally constituted good, but because other things are formally constituted good by them, in the same way that whiteness is said to exist inasmuch as it constitutes things in a mode of existence (namely, existing as white) and not because it is constituted in any mode of existence itself.

3. Every mode of existence is determined by some form, and so condition, form and order accompany every mode in which a thing exists. Thus man has one condition, form and order as a man, and another condition, form and order again as white, or as virtuous, or as knowledgeable, or as anything else he is. Now something gone bad, like a blind eye, lacks some particular mode of existence, in this case being able to see; and so loses, not all condition, form and order, but only that condition, form and order associated with being able to see.

4. Augustine says that *condition as such is always good* (and the same could be said of form and order) *but condition, form and order are called bad either because they fall short of what they should be, or because they are unfitted for the things for which they are meant, and thus bad in the sense of foreign and incongruous.*[10]

---

the Latin word *species*. But otherwise in the body of this article *form* is used to translate the Latin word *forma*. It has been necessary therefore to translate the sentence which St Thomas wrote here (namely, 'to express form we use the word *species*') as 'to express form Augustine used the word *species*'.

5. Ad quintum dicendum quod natura lucis dicitur esse sine numero et pondere et mensura non simpliciter sed per comparationem ad corporalia, quia virtus lucis ad omnia corporalia se extendit inquantum est qualitas activa primi corporis alterantis, scilicet cæli.

articulus 6. de divisione boni in honestum, utile et delectabile

AD SEXTUM sic proceditur:[1] 1. Videtur quod non convenienter dividatur bonum per honestum, utile et delectabile. Bonum enim sicut dicit Philosophus in I Ethic. dividitur per decem prædicamenta;[2] honestum autem, utile et delectabile inveniri possunt in uno prædicamento. Ergo non convenienter per hæc dividitur bonum.

2. Præterea, omnis divisio fit per opposita. Sed hæc tria non videntur esse opposita, nam honesta etiam sunt delectabilia, nullumque inhonestum est utile, ut etiam dicit Tullius in libro *de Officiis.*[3] Ergo prædicta divisio non est conveniens.

3. Præterea, ubi unum propter alterum ibi unum tantum. Sed utile non est bonum nisi propter delectabile vel honestum. Ergo non debet utile dividi contra delectabile et honestum.

SED CONTRA est quod Ambrosius in libro *de Officiis* utitur ista divisione boni.[4]

RESPONSIO: Dicendum quod hæc divisio proprie videtur esse boni humani. Si tamen altius et communius rationem boni consideremus invenitur hæc divisio proprie competere bono secundum quod bonum est. Nam bonum est aliquid inquantum est appetibile et terminus motus appetitus. Cujus quidem motus terminatio considerari potest ex consideratione motus corporis naturalis. Terminatur autem motus corporis naturalis simpliciter quidem ad ultimum, secundum quid autem etiam medium per quod itur ad ultimum terminat motum et dicitur aliquis terminus motus inquantum aliquam partem motus terminat. Id autem quod est ultimus terminus motus potest accipi dupliciter: vel ipsa res in quam tenditur (utpote locus vel forma), vel quies in re illa. Sic ergo in motu appetitus id quod est appetibile terminans motum appetitus secundum quid ut medium per quod tenditur in aliud vocatur 'utile'. Id autem quod appetitur ut ultimum terminans

---

[1]cf Ia2æ. 16, 3; 34, 2 ad 1; 2a2æ. 145, 3. Also II *Sent.* 21, 1, 3. *In Ethic.* I, *lect.* 5
[2]*Ethics* I, 6. 1096a23
[3]*De Officiis* II, 3. Roman orator and writer, 106–43 B.C.
[4]*De Officiis* I, 9. PL 16, 31

5. No one says it is the nature of light to lack number, weight and measure altogether, but only as compared to bodies; for light is all-pervasive in its influence on bodies, being the form of energy proper to the ultimate physical source of change, namely, the heavens.[b]

article 6. the division of good into the worthy, the useful and the delightful

THE SIXTH POINT:[1] 1. It seems wrong to divide good into the worthy, the useful and the delightful. For as Aristotle says goods are divided into ten categories,[2] in each of which we can find worthy, useful and delightful things. Such a division is therefore inappropriate.

2. Moreover, all division results from dissociation. Now these three classes of goods do not seem dissociate, for worthy things are also delight-ful, and nothing unworthy is useful, as even Cicero remarks.[3] So the suggested division is inappropriate.

3. Moreover, things related as means to end must be treated as one. Now the useful is good only as a means to either the delightful or the worthy. We should not then divide the useful from the delightful and the worthy.

ON THE OTHER HAND Ambrose divided the good in this way.[4]

REPLY: This division seems properly to apply to what is good for man. Nevertheless, a deeper and more general consideration of the concept of good reveals that the division properly applies to good as such. For a thing is good because desirable, and because movements of desire terminate in it. Now the termination of such movements can be discussed on analogy with the movements of physical bodies. Physical movement terminates, simply speaking, at its final point; but also, in a certain sense, at points part of the way there, which since they end some part of the movement can be called stops in the movement. Moreover, one can consider that which finally stops the movement to be either the actual thing aimed at (a place, say, or a form), or rest in that thing. By analogy then in movements of desire things desirable as putting a partial stop to the movement, being partway toward some other thing, we call 'useful'. That which is desirable

---

[b]According to the Aristotelian theory all changes on the earth below are eventually traceable to the influence of the changes in the heavens. This is evidently true to a very great extent where seasonal and biological changes are concerned. For further information cf Aristotle's works *De Cælo et Mundo* and *De Generatione et Corruptione*.

totaliter motum appetitus sicut quædam res in quam per se appetitus tendit vocatur 'honestum', quia honestum dicitur quod per se desideratur. Id autem quod terminat motum appetitus ut quies in re desiderata est 'delectatio'.

1. Ad primum ergo dicendum quod bonum inquantum est idem subjecto cum ente dividitur per decem prædicamenta, sed secundum propriam rationem competit sibi ista divisio.

2. Ad secundum dicendum quod ista divisio non est per oppositas res sed per oppositas rationes. Dicuntur tamen illa proprie delectabilia quæ nullam habent aliam rationem appetibilitatis nisi delectationem, cum aliquando sint et noxia et inhonesta. Utilia vero dicuntur quæ non habent in se unde desiderentur, sed desiderantur solum ut sunt ducentia in alterum (sicut sumptio medicinæ amaræ). Honesta vero dicuntur quæ in seipsis habent unde desiderentur.

3. Ad tertium dicendum quod bonum non dividitur in ista tria sicut univocum æqualiter de eis prædicatum, sed sicut analogum quod prædicatur secundum prius et posterius. Per prius enim prædicatur de honesto, secundario de delectabili, et tertio de utili.

as putting a full stop to the movement of desire because it is the actually desired thing itself we call 'worthy', for worthy means desirable in itself. That which puts a stop to the movement of desire because it is rest in the desired thing is 'delight'.

Hence: 1. As existent things goods divide into ten categories; the suggested division however is proper to goods precisely as good.

2. The division is based not on dissociation of things, but on dissociation of ideas. Although those things are properly called delightful which are desirable solely because they give delight and can at times be harmful and unworthy. And those things are said to be useful which are desirable not in themselves but solely as means to other things (for example, the drinking of bitter medicine). Those things are called worthy which are desirable in themselves.

3. The word 'good' is not used in exactly the same sense within these three divisions, but in a graded sequence of analogical senses. The primary sense of 'good' is worthy, the second delightful, and the third useful.

DEINDE QUÆRITUR de bonitate Dei

Quæstio 6. de bonitate Dei

Et circa hoc quæruntur quatuor:

1. utrum esse bonum conveniat Deo,
2. utrum Deus sit summe bonus,
3. utrum ipse solus sit bonus per suam essentiam,
4. utrum omnia sint bona bonitate divina.

articulus 1. utrum esse bonum conveniat Deo

AD PRIMUM sic proceditur:[1] 1. Videtur quod esse bonum non conveniat Deo. Ratio enim boni consistit in modo, specie et ordine; hæc autem non videntur Deo convenire, cum Deus immensus sit et ad aliquid non ordinetur. Ergo esse bonum non convenit Deo.

2. Præterea, *bonum est quod omnia appetunt*.[2] Sed Deum non omnia appetunt quia non omnia cognoscunt ipsum, nihil autem appetitur nisi notum. Ergo esse bonum non convenit Deo.

SED CONTRA est quod dicitur *Thren.* iii. *Bonus est Dominus sperantibus in eum, animæ quærenti illum.*[3]

RESPONSIO: Dicendum quod bonum præcipue Deo convenit. Bonum enim aliquid est secundum quod est appetibile. Unumquodque autem appetit suam perfectionem; perfectio autem et forma effectus est quædam similitudo agentis, cum omne agens agat sibi simile. Unde ipsum agens est appetibile et habet rationem boni, hoc enim est quod de ipso appetitur ut ejus similitudo participetur. Cum ergo Deus sit prima causa effectiva omnium, manifestum est quod sibi competit ratio boni et appetibilis. Unde Dionysius in libro de Div. Nom. attribuit bonum Deo sicut primæ causæ efficienti dicens quod bonus dicitur Deus *sicut ex quo omnia subsistunt.*[4]

1. Ad primum ergo dicendum quod habere modum, speciem et ordinem pertinet ad rationem boni creati.* Sed bonum in Deo est sicut in causa,

---

*Leonine *causati*, caused goodness.
[1]cf 1a. 5, 2 ad 1; 13, 11 ad 2; 44, 4; 105, 2 ad 2. Also *CG* 1, 37. *In Meta.* xii, lect. 7
[2]cf Aristotle, *Ethics* I, 1. 1094a3

WE ASK next about the goodness of God

Question 6. the goodness of God

This question is composed of four points of inquiry:

    1. can one associate goodness with God?
    2. is God supremely good?
    3. is God alone good by nature?
    4. does God's goodness make everything good?

article 1. can one associate goodness with God?

THE FIRST POINT:[1] 1. One must not it seems associate goodness with God. For goodness consists in condition, form and order, which seem out of place in a God who is immeasurable and not subordinate to anything.[a] So goodness must not be associated with God.

    2. Moreover, *the good is what everything desires.*[2] But not everything desires God, because not everything knows him and one can only desire what one knows. Goodness therefore must not be associated with God.

ON THE OTHER HAND we read in *Lamentations: The Lord is good to those who wait for him, to the soul that seeks him.*[3]

REPLY: Goodness should be associated above all with God. For goodness is consequent upon desirability. Now things desire their perfection; and an effect's perfection and form consists in resembling its cause, since what a thing does reflects what it is. So the cause itself is desirable and can be called 'good', what is desired from it being a share in resembling it. Clearly then, since God is the primary operative cause of everything, goodness and desirability fittingly belong to him. And so Dionysius ascribes goodness to God as to the primary operative cause, saying that God is called good *as the source of all subsistence.*[4]

    Hence: 1. Goodness consisting in condition, form and order is created goodness. Goodness belongs to God as to a cause, however, so he it is

---

[3]*Lamentations* 3, 25
[4]*On the Divine Names* 4, 4. PG 3, 700
[a]The non-subordination of God is contrasted with the notion of 'order'; the immeasurableness of God is contrasted with 'condition'. cf 1a. 5, 5.

unde ad eum pertinet imponere aliis modum, speciem et ordinem. Unde ista tria sunt in Deo sicut in causa.

2. Ad secundum dicendum quod omnia appetendo proprias perfectiones appetunt ipsum Deum, inquantum perfectiones omnium rerum sunt quædam similitudines divini esse ut ex dictis patet.[5] Et sic eorum quæ Deum appetunt quædam cognoscunt ipsum secundum seipsum, quod est proprium creaturæ rationalis, quædam vero cognoscunt aliquas participationes suæ bonitatis, quod etiam extenditur usque ad cognitionem sensibilem, quædam vero appetitum naturalem habent absque cognitione, utpote inclinata ad suos fines ab aliquo superiori cognoscente.

articulus 2. utrum Deus sit summe bonus

AD SECUNDUM sic proceditur:[1] 1. Videtur quod Deus non sit summum bonum. Summum enim bonum addit aliquid supra bonum, alioquin omni bono conveniret. Sed omne quod se habet ex additione ad aliquid est compositum. Ergo summum bonum est compositum. Sed Deus est simplex, ut supra ostensum est;[2] ergo Deus non est summum bonum.

2. Præterea, *bonum est quod omnia appetunt* ut dicit Philosophus.[3] Sed nihil aliud est quod omnia appetunt nisi solus Deus qui est finis omnium. Ergo nihil aliud est bonum nisi Deus. Quod etiam videtur per aliud quod dicitur *Matth.* xix: *nemo bonus nisi solus Deus.*[4] Sed summum dicitur in comparatione aliorum, sicut summum calidum in comparatione respectu ad omnia calida. Ergo Deus non potest dici summum bonum.

3. Præterea, summum comparationem importat. Sed quæ non sunt unius generis non sunt comparabilia, sicut dulcedo inconvenienter dicitur major vel minor quam linea. Cum igitur Deus non sit in eodem genere cum aliis bonis ut ex superioribus patet,[5] videtur quod non possit dici summum bonum respectu eorum.

SED CONTRA est quod dicit Augustinus I *de Trin.* quod Trinitas divinarum personarum *est summum bonum quod purgatissimis mentibus cernitur.*[6]

RESPONSIO: Dicendum quod Deus est summum bonum simpliciter et non solum in aliquo genere vel ordine rerum. Sic enim bonum Deo attribuitur ut dictum est inquantum omnes perfectiones desideratæ effluunt ab eo sicut a causa.[7] Non autem effluunt ab eo sicut ab agente univoco ut ex

---

[5]cf Ia. 4, 3
[1]cf Ia. 4, 3; 103, 2; Ia2æ. 2, 8; 9, 6. Also II *Sent.* 1, 2, 2 ad 4. *CG* I, 41
[2]cf Ia. 3
[3]*Ethics* I, I. 1094a3

that imposes condition, form and order on others. The three qualities do belong to God, therefore, but as to a cause.

2. In desiring its own perfection everything is desiring God himself, for the perfections of all things, as we saw, somehow resemble divine existence.[5] And so, of the things that desire God, some know him in himself and this is the privilege of reasoning creatures, others know his goodness as participated somewhere or other and this is possible even to sense-knowledge, whilst yet other things, having no knowledge, desire by nature, directed to their goal by some higher being with knowledge.

article 2. is God supremely good?

THE SECOND POINT:[1] 1. It seems that God is not supremely good. For supreme goodness is something over and above goodness, otherwise every good would be supremely good. Now adding one thing to another produces something composite. The supreme good is therefore composite. God, then, who has been shown to be simple,[2] is not the supreme good.

2. Moreover, Aristotle says that *good is what everything desires*.[3] Now the only thing which everything desires is the goal of all things, namely, God. So that nothing except God is good. This is also apparent from something *Matthew* says: *No one is good but God alone*.[4] Now calling a thing 'supreme' involves comparing it with other things: the supremely hot, for example, with all hot things. So one cannot call God supremely good.

3. Moreover, 'supreme' involves a comparison. Now one can only compare things of the same genus: it is odd to say that sweetness is bigger or smaller than a line. Since then we already know that God and other good things are not in the same genus,[5] it seems that he cannot be called supremely good by comparison with them.

ON THE OTHER HAND Augustine tells us that the three divine persons *are the supreme good seen by the supremely clean of heart*.[6]

REPLY: God is not just supremely good within a particular genus or order of reality; he is the absolutely supreme good. For we saw that God was called good as being the first source of every perfection things desire.[7] And these perfections, as we have shown, flow out from God not as from an

---

[4]Actually quoted from *Luke* 18, 19. In the parallel place in *Matthew* 19, 17 we read 'One there is who is good'
[5]cf 1a. 3, 5; 4, 3 ad 3
[6]*De Trinitate* I, 2. PL 42, 822   [7]cf 1a. 6, 1

superioribus patet sed sicut ab agente quod non convenit cum suis effectibus neque in ratione speciei nec in ratione generis.[8] Similitudo autem
effectus in causa quidem univoca invenitur uniformiter, in causa autem
æquivoca invenitur excellentius sicut calor excellentiori modo est in sole
quam in igne. Sic ergo oportet quod cum bonum sit in Deo sicut in prima
causa omnium non univoca quod sit in eo excellentissimo modo. Et
propter hoc dicitur summum bonum.

1. Ad primum ergo dicendum quod summum bonum addit supra bonum
non rem aliquam absolutam sed relationem tantum. Relatio autem qua
aliquid de Deo dicitur relative ad creaturas non est realiter in Deo sed in
creaturis, in Deo vero secundum rationem, sicut scibile relative dicitur ad
scientiam non quia ipsum referatur sed quia scientia refertur ad ipsum.
Et sic non oportet quod in summo bono sit aliqua compositio sed quod
alia deficiant ab ipso.

2. Ad secundum dicendum quod cum dicitur quod *bonum est quod omnia
appetunt* non sic intelligitur quod unumquodque bonum ab omnibus appe-
tatur, sed quia quidquid appetitur rationem boni habet. Quod autem dicitur *nemo bonus nisi solus Deus* intelligitur de bono per essentiam ut post
dicetur.[9]

3. Ad tertium dicendum quod ea quae non sunt in eodem genere si
quidem sint in diversis generibus contenta nullo modo comparabilia sunt.
De Deo autem negatur esse in eodem genere cum aliis bonis non quod ipse
sit in quodam alio genere, sed quia ipse est extra genus et principium
omnis generis. Et sic comparatur ad alia per excessum; et hujusmodi
comparationem importat summum bonum.

articulus 3. utrum ipse solus sit bonus per suam essentiam

AD TERTIUM sic proceditur:[1] 1. Videtur quod esse bonum per essentiam
non sit proprium Dei. Sicut enim unum convertitur cum ente, ita et
bonum, ut supra habitum est.[2] Sed omne ens est unum per suam essentiam
ut patet per Philosophum in IV *Meta*.[3] Ergo omne ens est bonum per
suam essentiam.

2. Præterea, si bonum est quod omnia appetunt, cum ipsum esse sit
desideratum ab omnibus, ipsum esse cujuslibet rei est ejus bonum. Sed
quælibet res est ens per suam essentiam. Ergo quælibet res est bona per
suam essentiam.

3. Præterea, omnis res per suam bonitatem est bona. Si igitur aliqua

---

[8]cf Ia. 4, 3   [9]cf Ia. 6, 3
[1]cf Ia. 3, 2; 103, 2; 2a2æ. 27, 3. Also *CG* I, 38; III, 20. *De veritate* XXI, 1 ad 1;
XXI, 5. *In De hebd., lect.* 3, 4. *In De div. nom.* 4, *lect.* 1; 13, *lect.* 1. *Compendium Theol.*

agent in the same genus, but as from an agent agreeing neither in species nor in genus with its effects.[8] Now an agent in the same genus mirrors its effects with unchanged form, but an agent not in the same genus mirrors them more perfectly, the heat of the sun, for example, excelling that of fire.[a] So, since it is as first source of everything not himself in a genus that God is good, he must be good in the most perfect manner possible. And for this reason we call him supremely good.

Hence: 1. What supreme goodness adds to goodness is something not absolute but merely relative. Now the relations that God is said to bear to creatures, though represented mentally as existing in God, really exist not in God but in the creatures, just as things are called objects of knowledge not because they are related to knowledge, but because knowledge is related to them.[b] So the supreme good does not have to be composite, but other good things must fall short of him.

2. The assertion that *good is what everything desires* does not mean that every good is desired by everything, but that whatever is desired is good. And the assertion that *no one is good but God alone*, means 'good by nature' as we shall see.[9]

3. There is no way of comparing things not in the same genus, when they are actually in different genera. But we say God is not in the same genus as other goods, not because he belongs to another genus but because he exists outside all genera and initiates them all. And so he is related to other things by surpassing them; and this is the comparison implied by supreme goodness.

article 3. is God alone good by nature?

THE THIRD POINT:[1] 1. Not only God it seems is good by nature. For as we saw above everything that exists is good, just as it is one.[2] Now Aristotle shows that every existing thing is one by nature.[3] Every existing thing therefore is good by nature.

2. Moreover, if *good is what everything desires* the very existence of a thing must be its good, for everything desires to exist. Now things exist by nature. Everything then is good by nature.

3. Moreover, there is a goodness in things which makes them good. If

109. On unity and perfection (cf objection 1) see also 1a. 103, 3; 1a2æ. 36, 3
[2]cf 1a. 5, 1–3
[3]*Metaphysics* IV, 2. 1003b32
[a]cf note *a* to 1a. 4, 2.
[b]cf 1a. 13, 7.

res est quæ non sit bona per suam essentiam oportebit quod ejus bonitas non sit sua essentia. Illa ergo bonitas cum sit ens quoddam oportet quod sit bona; et si quidem alia bonitate iterum de illa bonitate quæretur. Aut ergo erit procedere in infinitum, aut devenire ad aliquam bonitatem quæ non est bona per aliam bonitatem. Eadem ergo ratione standum est in primo. Res igitur quælibet est bona per suam essentiam.

SED CONTRA est quod dicit Boëtius in libro *de Hebd.* quod omnia alia a Deo sunt bona per participationem.[4] Non igitur per essentiam.

RESPONSIO: Dicendum quod solus Deus est bonus per suam essentiam.

Unumquodque enim dicitur bonum inquantum est perfectum. Perfectio autem alicujus rei triplex est: prima quidem secundum quod in suo esse constituitur; secunda vero prout ei aliqua accidentia superadduntur ad suam perfectam operationem necessaria; tertia vero perfectio alicujus est per hoc quod aliquid aliud attingit sicut finem. Utpote prima perfectio ignis consistit in esse quod habet secundum suam formam substantialem; secunda vero ejus perfectio consistit in caliditate, levitate et siccitate et hujusmodi; tertia vero perfectio ejus est secundum quod in loco suo quiescit.

Hæc autem triplex perfectio nulli causato* competit secundum suam essentiam sed soli Deo; cujus solius essentia est suum esse, et cui non adveniunt aliqua accidentia (sed quæ de aliis dicuntur accidentaliter sibi conveniunt essentialiter, ut esse potentem, sapientem et alia hujusmodi, sicut ex dictis patet).[5] Ipse etiam ad nihil aliud ordinatur sicut ad finem sed ipse est ultimus finis omnium rerum. Unde manifestum est quod solus Deus habet omnimodam perfectionem secundum suam essentiam. Et ideo ipse solus est bonus per suam essentiam.

1. Ad primum ergo dicendum quod unum non importat rationem perfectionis sed indivisionis tantum quæ unicuique rei competit secundum suam essentiam. Simplicium autem essentiæ sunt indivisæ et actu et potentia, compositorum autem essentiæ sunt indivisæ secundum actum tantum. Et ideo oportet quod quælibet res sit una per suam essentiam, non autem bona ut ostensum est.

2. Ad secundum dicendum quod licet unumquodque sit bonum inquantum habet esse, tamen essentia rei creatæ non est ipsum esse, et ideo non sequitur quod res creata sit bona per suam essentiam.

3. Ad tertium dicendum quod bonitas rei creatæ non est ipsa ejus essentia sed aliquid superadditum: vel ipsum esse ejus, vel aliqua perfectio

---

*Leonine *creato*, no created thing.
[4]*De Hebdomadibus.* PL 64, 1313   [5]cf 1a. 3, 6

then there exists a thing not by nature good, the goodness of such a thing will not be its nature. Yet because it exists in some way, that goodness must itself be good, and if again by some goodness different from itself, we must go on and ask about this other goodness. The only way of stopping the process is by arriving at some goodness not good by another goodness. But then we might as well have begun with this. All things then are good by nature.

ON THE OTHER HAND Boëthius says that everything else besides God participates goodness.[4] Nothing else therefore is by nature good.

REPLY: God alone is good by nature.

For to be called 'good' a thing must be perfect. Now there is a threefold perfection in things: firstly, they are established in existence; secondly, they possess in addition certain accidents necessary to perfect their activity; and a third perfection comes when they attain some extrinsic goal. Thus the primary perfection of fire lies in existing according to its own substantial form, a secondary perfection consists in heat, lightness, dryness, and so on; and a third perfection is being at rest in its appropriate place.[a]

Now this threefold perfection belongs by nature to no caused thing, but only to God; for he alone exists by nature, and in him there are no added accidents (power, wisdom and the like which are accidental to other things belonging to him by nature, as already noted).[5] Moreover, he is not disposed towards some extrinsic goal, but is himself the ultimate goal of all other things. So it is clear that only God possesses every kind of perfection by nature. He alone therefore is by nature good.

Hence: 1. Being one does not involve being perfect, but only being undivided, and this belongs to everything by nature. For the natures of simple things are both undivided and indivisible, and the natures of composite things are at least undivided. So things whilst necessarily one by nature, are not, as we have shown, necessarily good by nature.

2. Although things are good inasmuch as they exist, nevertheless existence is not the nature of any created thing, and so it does not follow that created things are good by nature.

3. The goodness of a created thing is not its nature, but something additional: either its existence, or some added perfection, or some relatedness

---

[a]It was the Aristotelian theory of the elements that each had its proper place in the universe, and would tend naturally to move there and rest there. Earth's place was in the centre of the universe, and its natural movement was inwards to that centre: such was the explanation of gravity. Fire's place, on the other hand, was in the upper regions beyond the air, and its natural movement was therefore upward. For the validity of such examples in modern times refer again to note *b* on 1a. 2, 3.

superaddita, vel ordo ad finem. Ipsa autem bonitas superaddita sic dicitur bona sicut et ens. Hac autem ratione dicitur ens quia ea est aliquid, non quia ipsa aliquo alio sit. Unde hac ratione dicitur bona quia est aliquid ea bonum, non quia ipsa habeat aliquam aliam bonitatem qua sit bona.

articulus 4. utrum omnia sint bona bonitate divina

AD QUARTUM sic proceditur:[1] 1. Videtur quod omnia sint bona bonitate divina. Dicit enim Augustinus VIII *de Trin.*: *Bonum hoc et bonum illud, tolle hoc et tolle illud, et vide ipsum bonum si potes; ita Deum videbis non alio bono bonum sed bonum omnis rei.*[*2] Ergo unumquodque est bonum ipso bono quod est Deus.

2. Præterea, sicut dicit Boëtius in libro *de Hebd.* omnia dicuntur bona inquantum ordinantur ad Deum,[3] et hoc ratione bonitatis divinæ. Ergo omnia sunt bona bonitate divina.

SED CONTRA est quod omnia sunt bona inquantum sunt. Sed non dicuntur omnia entia per esse divinum sed per esse proprium. Ergo non omnia sunt bona bonitate divina sed bonitate propria.

RESPONSIO: Dicendum quod nihil prohibet in his quæ relationem important aliquid ab extrinseco denominari, sicut aliquid denominatur 'locatum' a loco et 'mensuratum' a mensura. Circa vero ea quæ absolute dicuntur diversa fuit opinio. Plato enim posuit omnium rerum species esse separatas, et quod ab eis individua nominantur quasi species separatas participando; ut puta quod Socrates dicitur homo secundum Ideam hominis separatam. Et sicut ponebat Ideam hominis et equi separatam quam vocabat Per Se Hominem et Per Se Equum, ita ponebat Ideam entis et Ideam unius separatam quam dicebat Per Se Ens et Per Se Unum, et ejus participatione unumquodque dicitur ens vel unum. Hoc autem quod est Per Se Bonum† et Per Se Unum ponebat esse summum Deum,‡ a quo omnia dicuntur bona per modum participationis. Et quamvis hæc opinio irrationabilis videatur quantum ad hoc quod ponebat species rerum naturalium separatas per se subsistentes, ut Aristoteles multipliciter probat, tamen hoc absolute verum est quod est aliquid primum per essentiam suam§ bonum

---

*Leonine adds *Sed unumquodque est bonum suo bono*, now the good of a thing is what makes it good.
†Leonine *Ens*, the Existent Being itself.
‡Leonine *bonum. Et quia bonum convertitur cum ente, sicut et unum, ipsum Per Se Bonum dicebat esse Deum*, the supreme good. And because everything that exists is good and is one, he called this Good Itself God.
§Leonine adds *ens et*, existent and good by nature.

to a goal. This additional goodness however is said to be good in the same way that it is said to exist. Now it is said to exist as a mode in which something exists, not as something having its own mode of existence. And so it is said to be good because things that possess it are good, not because it itself possesses some other goodness making it good.

article 4. does God's goodness make everything good?

THE FOURTH POINT:[1] 1. It seems that God's goodness makes all things good. For Augustine writes: *Consider this good and that good; abstract from the this and the that and gaze simply at good, if you can; so shall you see God, the good of all things, himself not good by any other good.*[2] So everything is good by the good we call God.

2. Moreover, Boëthius says that everything is called good because it has God for its goal,[3] and this is because of the goodness of God. So it is the goodness of God that makes all things good.

ON THE OTHER HAND things are good inasmuch as they exist. Now things are said to exist, not by divine existence, but by their own. So things are good, not by God's goodness, but by their own.

REPLY: There is nothing to stop things being named by reference to others, if the name is a relative term, as when things are said to be 'in place' by reference to place, or 'measured' by reference to measure. But concerning non-relative terms opinions have differed. Plato believed that the forms of things exist separately, and that individual things are named after these separate forms which they participate in some way: Socrates, for example, is called a 'man' by reference to some separate Idea of man. And just as he believed in separate Ideas of man and horse, calling them Man Himself and Horse Itself, so also Plato believed in separate Ideas of being and unity, called Being Itself and Unity Itself, by participating which everything was said to be or to be one. The existent Good Itself and Unity Itself he believed to be the supreme God, by reference to whom all things were said to be good by participation. And although, as Aristotle repeatedly proves, the part of this opinion which postulates separate, self-subsistent Ideas of natural things appears to be absurd, nonetheless that there exists

---

[1]cf 1a. 16, 6; 2a2æ. 23, 2 ad 1. Also 1 *Sent.* 19, 5, 2 ad 3. *De veritate* XXI, 4 *CG* I, 40
[2]*De Trinitate* VIII, 3. PL 42, 949
[3]*De Hebdomadibus.* PL 64, 1312

quod dicimus Deum, ut ex superioribus patet.[4] Huic etiam sententiæ concordat Aristoteles.

A primo igitur per essentiam ente et bono unumquodque potest dici bonum et ens inquantum participat ipsum per modum cujusdam assimilationis, licet remote et deficienter ut ex superioribus patet.[5] Sic ergo unumquodque dicitur bonum bonitate divina sicut primo principio exemplari, effectivo et finali totius bonitatis. Nihilominus tamen unumquodque dicitur bonum similitudine divinæ bonitatis sibi inhærente quæ est formaliter sua bonitas denominans ipsum. Et sic est bonitas una omnium et multæ bonitates.

Et per hoc patet responsio ad objecta.

---

[4]cf Ia. 6, 3. (Also Ia. 3, 4 if the reading 'existent and good by nature' is adopted)
[5]cf Ia. 4, 3
[a]The view of Plato here put forward derives partly from Aristotle and partly from the neo-Platonists of six or so centuries later. Most of the original works of Plato

some first thing called God, good by nature, is absolutely true, as we have shown.[4] And with this opinion Aristotle also is in agreement.[a]

One may therefore call things good and existent by reference to this first thing, existent and good by nature, inasmuch as they somehow participate and resemble it, even if distantly and deficiently, as was pointed out earlier.[5] And in this sense all things are said to be good by divine goodness, which is the pattern, source and goal of all goodness. Nevertheless the resemblance to divine goodness which leads us to call the thing good is inherent in the thing itself, belonging to it as a form and therefore naming it. And so there is one goodness in all things, and yet many.

And this clears up the difficulties.

---

were not available to St Thomas. A typical passage on Plato by Aristotle will be found in the *Metaphysics* I, 9. 990a33. That Aristotle accepts some first thing good by nature St Thomas deduces from *Metaphysics* II, 1. 993b24.

POST CONSIDERATIONEM divinæ perfectionis considerandum est de ejus infinitate et de existentia ejus in rebus. Attribuitur enim Deo quod sit ubique et in omnibus rebus inquantum est incircumscriptibilis et infinitus.

Quæstio 7. de infinitate Dei

Circa primum quæruntur quatuor:

1. utrum Deus sit infinitus,
2. utrum aliquid præter ipsum sit infinitum secundum essentiam,
3. utrum aliquid possit esse infinitum secundum magnitudinem,
4. utrum possit esse infinitum in rebus secundum multitudinem.

articulus 1. utrum Deus sit infinitus

AD PRIMUM sic proceditur:[1] 1. Videtur quod Deus non sit infinitus. Omne enim infinitum est imperfectum, quia habet rationem partis et materiae ut dicitur in III *Phys.*[2] Sed Deus est perfectissimus. Ergo non est infinitus.

2. Præterea, secundum Philosophum in I *Phys.* finitum et infinitum conveniunt quantitati.[3] Sed in Deo non est quantitas cum non sit corpus, ut supra ostensum est.[4] Ergo non competit sibi esse infinitum.

3. Præterea, quod ita est hic quod non alibi est finitum secundum locum, ergo quod ita est hoc quod non est aliud est finitum secundum substantiam. Sed Deus est hoc et non aliud, non enim est lapis nec lignum. Ergo Deus non est infinitus secundum substantiam.

SED CONTRA est quod dicit Damascenus quod Deus est *infinitus et æternus et incircumscriptibilis.*[5]

RESPONSIO: Dicendum quod omnes antiqui philosophi attribuunt infinitum primo principio ut dicitur in III *Phys.*,[6] et hoc rationabiliter considerantes res effluere a primo principio in infinitum. Sed quia* erraverunt circa naturam primi principii consequens fuit ut errarent circa infinitatem ipsius. Quia enim ponebant primum principium materiam consequenter

---

*Leonine adds *quidam,* some of them made a mistake.

[1]cf Ia. 12, 1 ad 2; 42, 1 ad 1; 86, 2 ad 1; 3a. 10, 3. Also I *Sent.* 43, 1, 1. *De veritate* II, 2 ad 5; XXIX, 3. *CG* I, 43. *De potentia* I, 2. *Quodlibet* III, 2, 1. *Compendium Theol.* 18; 20

[2]*Physics* III, 6. 207a27   [3]*Physics* I, 2. 185b2

NEXT FOR CONSIDERATION after God's perfection we have his limitlessness and then his presence in things. For it is because he is boundless and unlimited that God is said to exist everywhere in everything.

Question 7. God's limitlessness

The first of these questions contains four points of inquiry:[a]

1. is God unlimited?
2. is anything other than God unlimited in being?
3. can anything be unlimited in size?
4. can there exist an unlimited number of things?

article 1. is God unlimited?

THE FIRST POINT:[1] 1. God, it seems, is not unlimited. For to be unlimited is to be incomplete and unrealized, as Aristotle says, and therefore imperfect.[2] [b] Now God is the very summit of perfection. He is not therefore limitless.

2. Moreover, Aristotle says that to be limited or unlimited a thing must first be extended.[3] Now God is not extended, since he is not a body, as we have shown.[4] Unlimited is therefore not an apt description of God.

3. Moreover, so to be in one place that one is not in another is to be spatially limited; so to be one thing, then, that one is not another is to be limited in being. Now God is one thing and no other: not a stone, for example, nor a piece of wood. He is therefore not limitless in being.

ON THE OTHER HAND Damascene calls God *limitless, eternal and unbounded.*[5]

REPLY: Aristotle tells us that in ancient times all philosophers considered the first principle to be unlimited,[6] and reasonably so since they saw no limit to the things deriving from the first principle. But because they made a mistake about the nature of the first principle they made a corresponding

---

[4]cf 1a. 3, 1   [5]*De Fide Orthodoxa* I, 4. PG 94, 800   [6]*Physics* III, 4. 203b4
[a]See Appendix 14.
[b]Aristotle 'defines' the infinite as that which always has something further to offer, which you can therefore never 'define' or complete. It is in this sense that he says it resembles a part (lacking wholeness) or matter (lacking form). I have translated 'incomplete and unrealized'.

attribuerunt primo principio infinitatem materialem, dicentes aliquod corpus infinitum esse primum principium rerum.

Considerandum est igitur quod infinitum dicitur aliquid ex eo quod non est finitum. Finitur autem quodammodo et materia per formam et forma per materiam. Materia quidem per formam inquantum materia antequam recipiat formam est in potentia ad multas formas, sed cum recipit unam terminatur per illam. Forma vero finitur per materiam inquantum forma in se considerata communis est ad multa, sed per hoc quod recipitur in materia fit forma determinate hujus rei. Materia autem perficitur per formam per quam finitur, et ideo infinitum secundum quod attribuitur materiæ habet rationem imperfecti, est enim quasi materia non habens formam. Forma autem non perficitur per materiam sed magis per eam eius amplitudo contrahitur, unde infinitum secundum quod se tenet ex parte formæ non determinatæ per materiam habet rationem perfecti.

Illud autem quod est maxime formale omnium est ipsum esse, ut ex superioribus patet.[7] Cum igitur esse divinum non sit esse receptum in aliquo, sed ipse est suum esse subsistens, ut supra ostensum est,[8] manifestum est quod ipse Deus sit infinitus et perfectus.

1. Et per hoc patet responsio ad primum.

2. Ad secundum dicendum quod terminus quantitatis est sicut forma ipsius, cujus signum est quod figura quæ consistit in terminatione quantitatis est quædam forma circa quantitatem. Unde infinitum quod competit quantitati est infinitum quod se tenet ex parte materiæ, et tale infinitum non attribuitur Deo ut dictum est.

3. Ad tertium dicendum quod ex hoc ipso quod esse Dei est per se subsistens non receptum in aliquo, prout dicitur infinitum, distinguitur ab omnibus aliis et alia removentur ab eo; sicut, si esset albedo subsistens, ex hoc ipso quod non esset in alio discerneretur ab omni albedine existente in subjecto.

articulus 2. utrum aliquid præter ipsum sit infinitum secundum essentiam

AD SECUNDUM sic proceditur:[1] 1. Videtur quod aliquid aliud quam Deus possit esse infinitum per essentiam. Virtus enim rei proportionatur essentiæ ejus. Si igitur essentia Dei est infinita oportet quod ejus virtus sit infinita. Ergo potest producere effectum infinitum cum quantitas virtutis per effectum cognoscatur.

2. Præterea, quidquid habet virtutem infinitam habet essentiam infinitam. Sed intellectus creatus habet virtutem infinitam, apprehendit enim

---

[7]cf Ia. 3, 4; 4, 3 ad 1   [8]cf Ia. 3, 4
[1]cf Ia. 10, 5 ad 4; 45, 5 ad 3; 50, 2 ad 4; 86, 2; Ia2æ. 30, 4 ad 2. Also I *Sent.* 43, 1, 2. *De veritate* XX, 4 ad 1; XXIX, 3. *Quodlibet* IX, 1, 1; X, 2, 1 ad 2; XII, 2, 1 ad 2

mistake about its limitlessness. They thought of the first principle as matter, and hence assigned to it a material limitlessness, saying that the first principle of things was some limitless body.

We must therefore remember that anything not limited can be called limitless. Now there is both a sense in which matter is limited by form, and a sense in which form is limited by matter. Form limits matter because before assuming form matter is potential of many forms, but afterwards is determined by the one assumed. Matter limits form because a form as such may be shared by many things, but when acquired by matter becomes determinately the form of this thing. Now a form in limiting matter perfects it, so that material limitlessness is imperfect in character: a sort of matter without form. Matter however does not perfect a form but rather restricts its full scope, so that the limitlessness of a form undetermined by matter is perfect in character.

Now the notion of form is most fully realized in existence itself, as we showed above.[7] And in God existence is not acquired by anything, but, as we saw earlier, God is existence itself subsistent.[8] It is clear then that God himself is both limitless and perfect.

Hence: 1. The answer to the first difficulty is now plain.

2. The boundary of an extended thing is, so to speak, the form of its extension; the fact that setting bounds to extension produces shape, a sort of dimensional form, indicates this. So limitlessness of extension is the kind of limitlessness associated with matter, and such limitlessness, as we have said, is not to be ascribed to God.

3. The very fact that God's existence itself subsists without being acquired by anything, and as such is limitless, distinguishes it from everything else, and sets other things aside from it. Just so, if whiteness subsisted of itself, the very fact that it was not the whitenesss of something would distinguish it from all whiteness ingredient in things.

article 2. is anything other than God unlimited in being?

THE SECOND POINT:[1] 1. Other things, it seems, can be unlimited in being besides God.[a] For a thing's power is commensurate with its being; so that if God is unlimited in being he must also be unlimited in power. This means that he can produce an unlimited effect, for power is measured by the effects it can produce.

2. Moreover, unlimited power is a mark of unlimited being. Now the powers of a created intellect are unlimited, for it perceives universal ideas

---

[a]'Being' is here translating the Latin word *essentia*. cf note *a* on 1a. 3, 4.

universale quod se potest extendere ad infinita singularia. Ergo omnis substantia intellectualis creata est infinita.

3. Præterea, materia prima aliud est a Deo, ut supra ostensum est.[2] Sed materia prima est infinita. Ergo aliquid aliud præter Deum potest esse infinitum.

SED CONTRA est quod infinitum non potest esse ex principio alio ut dicitur in III *Phys*.[3] Omne autem quod est præter Deum est ex Deo sicut ex primo principio. Ergo nihil quod est præter Deum est infinitum.

RESPONSIO: Dicendum quod aliquid præter Deum potest esse infinitum secundum quid sed non simpliciter. Si enim loquamur de infinito secundum quod competit materiæ manifestum est quod omne existens in actu habet aliquam formam et sic materia ejus est terminata per formam. Sed quia materia secundum quod est sub una forma substantiali remanet in potentia ad multas formas accidentales, quod est finitum simpliciter potest dici infinitum secundum quid, utpote lignum est finitum secundum suam formam sed tamen est infinitum secundum quid, inquantum est in potentia ad figuras infinitas.

Si autem loquamur de infinito secundum quod convenit formæ sic manifestum est quod illa quorum formæ sunt in materia sunt simpliciter finita et nullo modo infinita. Si autem sint aliquæ formæ creatæ non receptæ in materia sed per se subsistentes, ut quidam de angelis opinantur, erunt quidem infinitæ secundum quid inquantum formæ non terminantur neque contrahuntur per aliquam materiam. Sed quia forma creata sic subsistens habet esse et non est suum esse, necesse est quod ipsum esse ejus sit receptum et contractum ad determinatam naturam. Unde non potest esse infinitum simpliciter.

1. Ad primum ergo dicendum quod hoc est contra rationem facti quod essentia rei sit ipsum esse ejus, quia esse subsistens non est esse creatum, unde contra rationem facti est quod sit simpliciter infinitum. Sicut ergo Deus licet habeat potentiam infinitam non tamen potest facere aliquid non factum (hoc enim esset contradictoria esse simul), ita non potest facere aliquid infinitum simpliciter.

2. Ad secundum dicendum quod hoc ipsum quod virtus intellectus extendit se quodammodo ad infinitum procedit ex hoc quod intellectus est forma non in materia, sed vel totaliter separata sicut sunt substantiæ

---

[2]cf Ia. 3, 8
[3]*Physics* III, 4. 203b7
[b]A note on substantial and accidental forms will be found at Ia. 3, 6, note *a*.
[c]St Thomas includes himself in this reference to 'some people'. cf later Ia. 50, 2.

capable of applying to an unlimited number of individuals. So every created being endowed with intellect is unlimited.

3. Moreover, the ultimate matter of things, though not God as we have shown,[2] is nonetheless unlimited. So something other than God can be unlimited.

ON THE OTHER HAND Aristotle says that what is unlimited cannot be derived from anything else.[3] Now everything other than God derives primarily from him. Nothing other than God then is unlimited.

REPLY: Things other than God can be unlimited in some, but not in all, respects. For if we talk of the limitlessness associated with matter, then clearly everything that actually exists possesses form, and its matter therefore is determined by that form. But because matter determined by a substantial form is still potential of many accidental forms, that which simply speaking is limited may yet in some respect be called unlimited.[b] Wood, for example, limited by its form, is yet in a certain respect unlimited, inasmuch as it is capable of an unlimited number of shapes.

If however we talk of the limitlessness associated with form, then clearly things composed of form and matter are limited in all respects and unlimited in none. But if there exist created forms not assumed by matter but subsisting themselves, as some people say is the case with angels,[c] then such forms will be in a certain respect unlimited, inasmuch as they are not contained or restricted by matter. Since such subsistent created forms however acquire their existence, and are not identical with it, that existence itself is of necessity contained and restricted by some specifying nature. Such a form then cannot be in all respects unlimited.

Hence: 1. To make something the nature of which is simply to exist, is a contradiction in terms, for subsistent existence is noncreated existence; and so it is a contradiction in terms to make something in all respects unlimited. Hence, although God's power is unlimited, he still cannot make an absolutely unlimited thing, no more than he can make an unmade thing (for this involves contradictories being true together).[d]

2. That the extent of an intellect's powers is in some sense unlimited follows from the fact that the intellect is a form not contained by matter. For either it is completely separate, as angelic beings are, or, in the case

---

[d]Later, in 1a. 25, 3, St Thomas will explain what he means by saying that God's power is unlimited power, just as his being is unlimited being. That God cannot create an uncreated thing is only an apparent restriction, like that he cannot *be* a created thing. It is really the words 'power', 'making' and 'being' that are restricted, not the God of whom they are predicated.

angelorum, vel ad minus potentia intellectiva* non est actus alicujus organi in anima intellectiva corpori conjuncta.

3. Ad tertium dicendum quod materia prima non existit in rerum natura per seipsam cum non sit ens in actu sed potentia tantum, unde magis est aliquid concreatum quam creatum. Nihilominus tamen materia prima etiam secundum potentiam non est infinita simpliciter sed secundum quid, quia ejus potentia non se extendit nisi ad formas naturales.

articulus 3. utrum aliquid possit esse infinitum secundum magnitudinem

AD TERTIUM sic proceditur:[1] 1. Videtur quod possit esse aliquid infinitum actu secundum magnitudinem. In scientiis enim mathematicis non invenitur falsum, quia *abstrahentium non est mendacium* ut dicitur in II Phys.[2] Sed scientiæ mathematicæ utuntur infinito secundum magnitudinem; dicit enim geometra in suis demonstrationibus, sit linea talis infinita. Ergo non est impossibile aliquid esse infinitum secundum magnitudinem.

2. Præterea, id quod non est contra rationem alicujus non est impossibile convenire sibi. Sed esse infinitum non est contra rationem magnitudinis, sed magis finitum et infinitum videntur esse passiones quantitatis. Ergo non est impossibile aliquam magnitudinem esse infinitam.

3. Præterea, magnitudo divisibilis est in infinitum, sic enim definitur continuum quod est in infinita divisibile ut patet in III Phys.[3] Sed contraria nata sunt fieri circa idem. Cum ergo divisioni opponatur additio et diminutioni augmentum videtur quod magnitudo possit crescere in infinitum. Ergo possibile est esse magnitudinem infinitam.

4. Præterea, et motus et tempus habent quantitatem et continuitatem a magnitudine super quam transit motus ut dicitur in IV Phys.[4] Sed non est contra rationem temporis et motus quod sint infinita, cum unumquodque indivisibile signatum in tempore et motu circulari sit principium et finis. Ergo nec contra rationem magnitudinis erit quod sit infinita.

SED CONTRA, omne corpus superficiem habet. Sed omne corpus superficiem habens est finitum, quia superficies est terminus corporis.† Ergo omnis

---

*Leonine adds *quæ*, at least an ability to understand.
†Leonine adds *finiti*, boundary of limited bodies.
[1]cf 3a. 7, 12 ad 1. Also *Quodlibet* IX, 1, 1; XII, 2, 1 ad 2. *In Physic.* I, *lect.* 9; III *lect.* 7–10 and 13. *In Meta.* XI, *lect.* 10. *In De Cælo* I, *lect.* 9–15
[2]*Physics* II, 2. 193b35
[3]*Physics* III, 1. 200b20
[4]*Physics* IV, 11. 219a12

of an intellectual soul joined to a body, it is at least able to understand independently of bodily organs.

3. Nowhere in the world does ultimate matter exist by itself, for it is not an actually existent thing, but only potential of existence; hence not so much a product as a by-product of creation. And again even the potentiality of ultimate matter is unlimited only in some, not in all, respects; for matter can only assume physical forms.

article 3. can anything be unlimited in size?

THE THIRD POINT:[1] I. It seems that things can be actually unlimited in size. For mathematical concepts are not without foundation: *abstraction*, as Aristotle says, *is not falsification*.[2] Now mathematics employs the concept of unlimited size; for a geometer proving something will say 'Let this line be infinite'. So something of unlimited size is not impossible.

2. Moreover, a thing may have any property which does not contradict its nature. Now limitlessness does not contradict the nature of extension; indeed to be limited or unlimited a thing must first it seems be extended.[a] So something unlimited in extent is quite possible.

3. Moreover, extension is divisible without limit, for Aristotle defines the continuum as *that which is capable of unlimited division*.[3] Now alternatives are substitutable one for the other; and the alternative to division and subtraction is addition and multiplication. So it seems that extension can be multiplied without limit, and thus unlimited size is possible.

4. Moreover, the continuity and extent of both movement and time derive according to Aristotle from the spatial extension movement must traverse.[4] Now conceivably both time and movement could be endless, since any point you choose in time or in circular movement is a beginning as well as an end. Endless extension is therefore also conceivable.

ON THE OTHER HAND all bodies have surfaces, and any body having a surface is limited since surface is the boundary of bodies. All bodies then are

---

[a]St Thomas's words for extension are a little difficult to translate uniformly. His most generic word is *quantitas* which is literally 'muchness', and divides into *quantitas continua*—'unbroken muchness'—and *quantitas discreta*—'broken-up muchness'. Connected with the first kind of quantity are such words as *magnitudo* (magnitude), *continuum* and *quantitas dimensiva* (volume), and I have generally used the word 'extension' in this connection. Connected up with the second kind of quantity are such words as *multitudo* (manyness), *numerus* (number), and I have generally used this last word 'number'. Literally then the translation of the sentence to which this note is appended should read: 'limitlessness does not contradict the nature of extension; indeed to be limited or unlimited a thing must first it seems possess muchness'.

corpus est finitum. Et similiter potest objici de superficie et linea. Nihil est ergo infinitum secundum magnitudinem.

RESPONSIO: Dicendum quod aliud est esse infinitum secundum suam essentiam et secundum magnitudinem. Dato enim quod esset aliquod corpus infinitum secundum magnitudinem, utpote ignis vel aër, non tamen esset infinitum secundum essentiam, quia essentia sua esset terminata ad aliquam speciem per formam et ad aliquod individuum per materiam. Et ideo habito ex præmissis quod nulla creatura est infinita secundum essentiam,[5] adhuc restat inquirere utrum aliquid creatum sit infinitum secundum magnitudinem.

Sciendum est igitur quod corpus, quod est magnitudo completa, dupliciter sumitur: scilicet, mathematice secundum quod consideratur in eo sola quantitas, et naturaliter secundum quod consideratur in eo materia et forma. Et de corpore quidem naturali quod non possit esse infinitum in actu manifestum est. Nam omne corpus naturale aliquam formam habet determinatam. Cum igitur ad formam substantialem consequantur accidentia, necesse est quod ad determinatam formam consequantur determinata accidentia, inter quæ est quantitas. Unde omne corpus naturale habet determinatam quantitatem et in majus et in minus. Unde impossibile est aliquod corpus naturale infinitum esse. Hoc etiam ex motu patet. Quia omne corpus naturale habet aliquem motum naturalem. Corpus autem infinitum non posset habere aliquem motum naturalem. Nec rectum, quia nihil movetur naturaliter motu recto nisi cum est extra suum locum, quod corpori infinito accidere non posset, occuparet enim omnia loca et sic indifferenter quilibet locus esset locus ejus. Et similiter etiam neque secundum motum circularem, quia in motu circulari oportet quod una pars corporis transferatur ad locum in quo fuit alia pars quod in corpore circulari si ponatur infinitum esse non posset. Quia duæ lineæ protractæ a centro quanto longius protrahuntur a centro tanto longius distant ab invicem, si ergo corpus esset infinitum in infinitum lineæ distarent ab invicem et sic una nunquam posset pervenire ad locum alterius.

De corpore etiam mathematico eadem ratio est. Quia si imaginemur corpus mathematicum existens actu oportet quod imaginemur ipsum sub aliqua forma, quia nihil est actu nisi per suam formam. Unde cum forma quanti inquantum hujusmodi sit figura oportebit quod habeat aliquam figuram. Et sic erit finitum, est enim figura quæ termino vel terminis comprehenditur.

1. Ad primum ergo dicendum quod geometra non indiget assumere aliquam lineam esse infinitam actu, sed indiget accipere aliquam lineam* a qua possit subtrahi quantum necesse est, et hoc nominat lineam infinitam.

---

*Leonine adds *finitam actu*, but actually finite lines.

limited. The same argument applies to surfaces and lines. So that nothing extended can be unlimited.

REPLY: To be unlimited in size is not the same thing as to be unlimited in being. For even if there existed bodily things, say fire or air, of unlimited size, these would still be limited in being: limited to a particular species by their form, and to a particular individual of the species by their matter. So although we have already proved that no creature is unlimited in being,[5] we have still to decide whether anything created can be unlimited in size.

We must realize then the two aspects under which bodies, which have all-round extension, can be considered: the mathematical aspect, which takes account only of the extension, and the physical aspect which includes matter and form. That physically a body cannot actually exist without limits is clear. For physical bodies have determinate forms. Now when a substantial form is determinate, the accidents which follow on that form must also be determinate, and extension is one of these accidents. Every physical body therefore has a determinate maximum and minimum size. And so it is impossible for any physical body to be unlimited. Considering movement will confirm this. To any physical body some movement comes naturally.[b] But to an unlimited body no movement could be natural. Not rectilinear movement, because things only move naturally in straight lines when not in their natural place; now this could not happen to an unlimited body, since it would fill all space, and one place would not be more natural to it than another. Neither could it revolve, since in such movement one part of the body changes places with another part, and this would be impossible if the revolving body was unlimited in size. For the further from the centre of a body two lines are produced, the further the distance between them becomes. In an unlimited body they would become infinitely distant from one another, and one line would never be able to reach the place of the other.

For the mathematical body things are no different. For if we imagine a mathematical body in actual existence we shall have to imagine it with a form, for actuality requires form. Now the form of anything extended as such is its shape, so the body will have to have a shape. And it will therefore be limited, because a shape must be contained within a boundary or boundaries.

Hence: 1. Geometers need not postulate lines which are actually infinite, but lines from which they can cut off whatever length they require, and such are the lines they call infinite.

---

[5]cf 1a. 7, 2
[b]cf note *a* on 1a. 6, 3.

2. Ad secundum dicendum quod licet infinitum non sit contra rationem magnitudinis in communi est tamen contra rationem cujuslibet speciei, scilicet contra rationem magnitudinis bicubitæ vel tricubitæ sive circularis vel triangularis et similium. Non autem est possibile in genere esse quod in nulla specie est. Unde non est possibile esse aliquam magnitudinem infinitam cum nulla species magnitudinis sit infinita.

3. Ad tertium dicendum quod infinitum quod convenit quantitati ut dictum est se tenet ex parte materiæ.[6] Per divisionem autem totius acceditur ad materiam nam partes se habent in ratione materiæ, per additonem autem acceditur ad totum quod se habet in ratione formæ. Et ideo non invenitur infinitum in additione magnitudinis sed in divisione tantum.

4. Ad quartum dicendum quod motus et tempus non sunt secundum totum in actu sed successive, unde habent potentiam permixtam actui. Sed magnitudo est tota in actu. Et ideo infinitum quod convenit quantitati et se tenet ex parte materiæ repugnat totalitati magnitudinis, non autem totalitati temporis vel motus, esse enim in potentia convenit materiæ.

articulus 4. utrum possit esse infinitum in rebus secundum multitudinem

AD QUARTUM sic proceditur:[1] 1. Videtur quod possibile sit esse multa infinita secundum actum. Non enim est impossibile id quod est in potentia reduci ad actum. Sed numerus est in infinitum multiplicabilis. Ergo non est impossibile esse multitudinem infinitam in actu.

2. Præterea, cujuslibet speciei possibile est esse aliquod individuum in actu. Sed species figuræ sunt infinitæ. Ergo possibile est esse infinitas figuras in actu.

3. Præterea, ea quæ non opponuntur ad invicem non impediunt se invicem. Sed posita aliqua multitudine rerum adhuc possunt sumi alia multa quæ eis non opponuntur, ergo non est impossibile alia iterum simul esse cum eis et sic in infinitum. Ergo possibile est esse infinita in actu.

SED CONTRA est quod dicitur *Sap.* xi: *omnia in pondere, numero et mensura disposuisti.*[2]

RESPONSIO: Dicendum quod circa hoc fuit duplex opinio. Quidam enim, scilicet Avicenna et Algazel, dixerunt quod impossibile est esse multitudinem actu infinitam per se, sed infinitam per accidens multitudinem esse

---

[6]cf Ia. 7, 1 ad 2
[1]cf Ia. 14, 12; 46, 2 ad 7; 1a2æ. 1, 4; 3a. 10, 3. Also II *Sent.* 1, 1, 5 ad 17, 18 and 19. *De veritate* II, 10.*Quodlibet* IX, 1, 1; XII, 2, 1 ad 2. *In Physic.* III, *lect.* 12. *In Meta.* XI, *lect.* 10. *De æternitate mundi*
[2]*Wisd.* 11, 21

2. Lack of limits may be compatible with the notion of extension in general, but it contradicts the notion of any specific extension: be it two feet, or a yard, or a circle, or a triangle. Now things cannot exist in a genus without existing in some species of the genus. So that because no species of extension can be limitless, all limitless extension is impossible.

3. The limitlessness of extension is as we said the kind of limitlessness associated with matter.[6] Now division breaks a whole down into its matter, for parts have the nature of material elements; whilst addition is a movement towards completion which has the nature of form. And so only unlimited division of extension can occur, not unlimited addition.

4. Movement and time do not exist all at once but bit by bit, and thus their actuality is shot through with potentiality. Spatial extension however exists all at once. So since potentiality characterizes matter, the extensive limitlessness associated with matter is incompatible with space in its entirety, but compatible with time and movement in their entirety.

article 4. can there exist an unlimited number of things?

THE FOURTH POINT:[1] 1. It seems there can actually exist an unlimited number of things. For what potentially exists can be brought into actual existence. Now it is possible to multiply number indefinitely. An unlimited number of things can therefore actually exist.

2. Moreover, any type can be realized in some actual individual of the type. Now there are unlimited types of geometrical figure. So there can actually exist an unlimited number of such figures.

3. Moreover, only things which conflict with one another preclude one another. Now, given any set of things, one can find another set which does not conflict with the first, and can therefore co-exist with it; and so on without limit. So an unlimited number of things can actually exist.

ON THE OTHER HAND we read in the book of *Wisdom*: *By weight, number and measure thou didst order all things.*[2]

REPLY: On this point there have been two opinions. Certain people like Avicenna and Algazel,[a] held that a number of things cannot actually be inherently unlimited, though there can exist a number of things which

---

[a]Avicenna (Ibn Sina, d. 1087). Algazel (Al Gazali, d. about 1111) known to the Scholastics as the *abbreviator* of Avicenna; in fact his abridgement was intended as a preliminary to a refutation.

non est impossibile. Dicitur enim multitudo esse infinita per se quando requiritur ad aliquid quod sit multitudo infinita. Et hoc est impossibile esse, quia sic oporteret quod aliquid dependeret ex infinitis, unde talis generatio nunquam compleretur cum non sit infinita pertransire. Per accidens autem dicitur multitudo infinita quando non requiritur ad aliquid infinitas multitudinis, sed accidit ita esse. Et hoc sic manifestari potest in operatione fabri ad quam quædam multitudo requiritur per se, scilicet quod sit ars in anima et manus movens et martellus. Et si hæc in infinitum multiplicarentur nunquam opus fabrile compleretur, quia dependeret ex infinitis causis. Sed multitudo martellorum quæ accidit ex hoc quod unum frangitur et accipitur aliud est multitudo per accidens, accidit enim quod multis martellis operetur et nihil differt utrum uno vel duobus vel pluribus operetur vel infinitis si infinito tempore operaretur. Per hunc igitur modum posuerunt quod possibile est esse actu multitudinem infinitam per accidens.

Sed hoc est impossibile. Quia omnem multitudinem oportet esse in aliqua specie multitudinis. Species autem multitudinis sunt secundum species numerorum. Nulla autem species numeri est infinita, quia quilibet numerus est multitudo mensurata per unum. Unde impossibile est esse multitudinem infinitam actu sive per se sive per accidens. Item, omnis multitudo in rerum natura existens est creata, et omne creatum sub aliqua certa intentione creantis comprehenditur, non enim in vanum agens aliquod operatur. Unde necesse est quod sub certo numero omnia creata comprehendantur. Impossibile est ergo esse multitudinem infinitam in actu etiam per accidens.

Sed esse multitudinem infinitam in potentia possibile est, quia augmentum multitudinis consequitur divisionem magnitudinis; quanto enim aliquid plus dividitur tanto plura secundum numerum resultant. Unde sicut infinitum invenitur in potentia in divisione continui quia proceditur ad materiam ut supra ostensum est,[3] eadem ratione et infinitum invenitur in potentia in additione multitudinis.

1. Ad primum ergo dicendum quod unumquodque quod est in potentia reducitur in actum secundum modum sui esse: dies enim non reducitur in actum quod sit tota simul sed successive. Et similiter infinitum multitudinis non reducitur in actum ut sit totum simul sed successive, quia post quandam multitudinem potest sumi alia multitudo in infinitum.

---

[3]cf Ia. 7, 3 ad 3
[b]Notice that St Thomas is perfectly prepared to allow infinite time for the work, yet nevertheless complains earlier against an inherently infinite number of causes that 'the job will never get finished'. 'Never' does not mean 'at no time finitely distant', but 'at no time even infinitely distant'. The understanding of this point

just happen to be unlimited. A number of things is called inherently un-limited when its being unlimited is essential in some connection. Now this can never be, for something would then depend necessarily on an unlimited number of other things, and consequently would never finally achieve existence, for no one can traverse the infinite. We say however that a number of things happens to be unlimited, when nothing requires it to be unlimited, and yet in fact it is so. To make the distinction clear: a certain number of things is inherently necessary to carpentry, namely, a hammer, a hand to wield it, and a mind with practical knowledge. And if the number of such things is to be multiplied indefinitely the job of carpentry will never get finished, for it will depend on an unlimited number of causes. But if, in fact, a number of hammers is used, a second being picked up when the first one breaks, then there just happens to be a number of hammers; as it happens many hammers are used for the work, but it makes no difference whether one or two or more, or indeed an un-limited number, if unlimited time is available for the work.[b] In the same way then these people believed that a number of things that happens to be unlimited could actually exist.

This however is impossible. For any set of things one considers must be a specific set. And sets of things are specified by the number of things in them. Now no number is infinite, for number results from counting through a set in units. So no set of things can actually be inherently un-limited, nor can it happen to be unlimited. Again, every set of things existing in the world has been created, and anything created is subject to some definite purpose of its creator, for causes never act to no purpose. All created things must be subject therefore to definite enumeration. Thus even a number of things that happens to be unlimited cannot actually exist.

But an unlimited number of things can exist potentially. For increase in number results from division of a continuum; the more one divides a thing, the greater number of things one obtains. So that, just as there is potentially no limit to the division of a continuum, which we saw to be a breakdown into matter,[3] so, for the same reason, there is potentially no limit to numerical addition.

Hence: 1. Whatever potentially exists is brought into actual existence in accordance with its own way of existing: thus days do not come into existence all at once, but one after another. And in the same way, an unlimited number of things is not brought into existence all at once, but bit by bit, first a certain number, then an additional one, and so on without limit.

---

is vital to St Thomas's numerous remarks about the impossibility of infinite regress. See Appendices 6 & 7.

2. Ad secundum dicendum quod species figurarum habent infinitatem ex infinitate numeri, sunt enim species figurarum trilaterum, quadrilaterum et sic inde. Unde sicut multitudo infinita numerabilis non reducitur in actum quod sit tota simul ita nec multitudo figurarum.

3. Ad tertium dicendum quod licet quibusdam positis alia poni non sit eis oppositum, tamen infinita poni opponitur cuilibet speciei multitudinis. Unde non est possibile esse aliquam multitudinem actu infinitam.

2. There are unlimited types of geometrical figure because number is unlimited, and the figures are typified as three-sided, four-sided and so on. So just as an unlimited number of things cannot be brought into actual existence all at once, neither can the multitude of geometrical figures.

3. Although positing one set of things will not conflict with the positing of another set, nonetheless positing an unlimited number will conflict with each specific number. So one cannot have an actually unlimited number of things.

QUIA VERO INFINITO convenire videtur quod ubique et in omnibus sit, considerandum est utrum hoc Deo conveniat.

Quæstio 8. de existentia Dei in rebus

Et circa hoc quæruntur quatuor:

1. utrum Deus sit in omnibus rebus,
2. utrum Deus sit ubique,
3. utrum Deus sit ubique per essentiam, potentiam et præsentiam,
4. utrum esse ubique sit proprium Dei.

articulus 1. *utrum Deus sit in omnibus rebus*

AD PRIMUM SIC proceditur:[1] 1. Videtur quod Deus non sit in omnibus. Quod enim est supra omnia non est in omnibus. Sed Deus est supra omnia secundum illud psalmi: *Excelsus super omnes gentes Dominus etc.*[2] Ergo Deus non est in omnibus.

2. Præterea, quod est in aliquo continetur ab eo. Sed Deus non continetur a rebus sed magis continet eas. Ergo Deus non est in rebus sed magis res sunt in eo. Unde Augustinus in libro 83 Quæst. dicit quod *in illo potius sunt omnia quam ipse sit alicubi.*[3]

3. Præterea, quanto aliquid agens est virtuosius tanto ad magis distans ejus actio procedit. Sed Deus est virtuosissimum agens. Ergo ejus actio pertingere potest ad ea quæ ab ipso distant, nec oportet quod sit in omnibus.

4. Præterea, dæmones res aliquæ sunt. Nec tamen Deus est in dæmonibus, non enim est *conventio lucis ad tenebras* ut dicitur II ad Cor. vi.[4] Ergo Deus non est in omnibus rebus.

SED CONTRA, ubicumque operatur aliquid, ibi est. Sed Deus operantur in omnibus secundum illud *Isaiæ* xxvi: *omnia opera nostra operatus es in nobis, Domine.*[5] Ergo Deus est in omnibus rebus.

RESPONSIO: Dicendum quod Deus est in omnibus rebus non quidem sicut pars essentiæ vel sicut accidens sed sicut agens adest ei in quod agit. Oportet enim omne agens conjungi ei in quod immediate agit et sua virtute illud contingere, unde in VII Phys. probatur quod motum et movens oportet

---

[1]cf I *Sent.* 37, 1, 1. *CG* III, 67   [2]*Psalms* 112 (113), 4
[3]*Liber 83 Quæst.* 20. PL 40, 15   [4]II *Corinthians* 6, 14   [5]*Isaiah* 26, 12

AN UNLIMITED THING ought it seems to exist everywhere in everything; we must therefore consider whether this is so of God.

Question 8. God's existence in things

This question has four points of inquiry:[a]

1. does God exist in everything?
2. is God everywhere?
3. is God everywhere in substance, power and presence?
4. is being everywhere something that belongs to God alone?

article 1. does God exist in everything?

THE FIRST POINT:[1] 1. God, it seems, does not exist in everything. For one cannot be both in everything and above everything. Yet we read in the psalms that God is above everything: *The Lord is high above all nations, etc.*[2] So he is not in everything.

2. Moreover, one is contained by what one is in. Now God is not contained by things but rather contains them. So things are in God rather than God in things. This is why Augustine says that *he is not in place, but is rather the place of everything else.*[3]

3. Moreover, the more powerful an agent, the more extended is its sphere of action. Now God is the most powerful of all agents. So his action can reach to things far distant from him, and he has no need to be present in them.

4. Moreover, there are certain things called devils. Now God does not exist in devils, for *light hath no communion with darkness,* as St Paul says.[4] So God does not exist in everything.

ON THE OTHER HAND a thing is present wherever it is active. But God is active in everything, according to Isaiah: *thou hast wrought all our works in us, O Lord.*[5] So God exists in everything.

REPLY: God exists in everything; not indeed as part of their substance or as an accident, but as an agent is present to that in which its action is taking place. For unless it act through intermediaries every agent must be connected with that upon which it acts, and be in causal contact with it: compare Aristotle's proof that for one thing to move another the two must

---

[a]See Appendix 15.

esse simul.[6] Cum autem Deus sit ipsum esse per suam essentiam oportet quod esse creatum sit proprius effectus ejus, sicut igniri est proprius effectus ignis. Hunc autem effectum causat Deus in rebus non solum quando primo esse incipiunt sed quamdiu in esse conservantur, sicut lumen causatur in aëre a sole quamdiu aër illuminatus manet. Quamdiu igitur res habet esse tamdiu oportet quod Deus adsit ei secundum modum quo esse habet. Esse autem est illud quod est magis intimum cuilibet et quod profundius omnibus inest, cum sit formale respectu omnium quæ in re sunt, ut ex supra dictis patet.[7] Unde oportet quod Deus sit in omnibus rebus et intime.

1. Ad primum ergo dicendum quod Deus est supra omnia per excellentiam suæ naturæ, et tamen est in omnibus ut causans omnium esse, sicut dictum est.

2. Ad secundum dicendum quod licet corporalia dicantur esse in aliquo sicut in continente, tamen spiritualia continent ea in quibus sunt, sicut anima continet corpus. Unde et Deus est in rebus sicut continens res. Tamen per quamdam similitudinem corporalium dicuntur omnia esse in Deo inquantum continentur ab ipso.

3. Ad tertium dicendum quod nullius agentis quantumcumque virtuosi actio procedit ad aliquid distans nisi inquantum in illud per media agit. Hoc autem ad maximam virtutem Dei pertinet quod immediate in omnibus agit, dum* nihil est distans ab eo quasi in se Deum non habeat. Dicuntur tamen res distare a Deo per dissimilitudinem naturæ vel gratiæ, sicut et ipse est super omnia per excellentiam suæ naturæ.

4. Ad quartum dicendum quod in dæmonibus intelligitur et natura quæ est a Deo et deformitas culpæ quæ non est ab ipso. Et ideo non est absolute concedendum quod Deus sit in dæmonibus, sed cum hac additione: inquantum sunt res quædam. In rebus autem quæ nominant naturam non deformatam absolute dicendum est Deum esse.

articulus 2. utrum Deus sit ubique

AD SECUNDUM sic proceditur:[1] 1. Videtur quod Deus non sit ubique. Esse enim ubique significat Deum† esse in omni loco. Sed esse in omni loco

---

*Leonine *unde*, so that nothing.
†Leonine omits *Deum*, mean being in every place.
[6]*Physics* VII, 2. 243a4   [7]cf Ia. 3, 4; 4, 1 ad 3
[1]cf Ia. 16, 7 ad 2; 52, 2; 3a. 52, 3 ad 3. Also I *Sent.* 37, 2, 1. *CG* III, 68. *Quodlibet* XI, 1, 1
[b]St Thomas here relates the interiority of God to things not to spatial interiority but to the kind of interiority connected with actuality and essence. For anything essentially bound up with the actuality of a thing is said to be intrinsic to that thing.

be in contact.[6] Now since it is God's nature to exist, he it must be who properly causes existence in creatures, just as it is fire itself sets other things on fire. And God is causing this effect in things not just when they begin to exist, but all the time they are maintained in existence, just as the sun is lighting up the atmosphere all the time the atmosphere remains lit. During the whole period of a thing's existence, therefore, God must be present to it, and present in a way in keeping with the way in which the thing possesses its existence. Now existence is more intimately and profoundly interior to things than anything else, for everything as we said is potential when compared to existence.[7] [b] So God must exist and exist intimately in everything.

Hence: 1. The perfection of his nature places God above everything, and yet as causing their existence he also exists in everything, as we have been saying.

2. That in which bodily things exist contains them, but immaterial things contain that in which they exist, as the soul contains the body.[c] So God also contains things by existing in them. However, one does use the bodily metaphor and talk of everything being in God inasmuch as he contains them.

3. However powerful an agent be its action can only reach to distant things by using intermediaries. The omnipotence of God, though, is displayed by his acting in everything without intermediary, for nothing is distant from him in the sense of God not being in it. Nevertheless one does speak of the unlikeness of things to God in nature or grace being distance from him, just as the perfection of his nature places him above everything.

4. When referring to devils one may be thinking either of their nature, which comes from God, or of the disfigurement due to sin, which does not. And so one can only admit that God exists in devils if one adds the qualification: inasmuch as they, too, are things. But no qualification is needed when saying that God is present in things the nature of which is not disfigured.

article 2. is God everywhere?

THE SECOND POINT:[1] 1. God, it seems, is not everywhere. For this would mean that God was in every place. Now it is not fitting for God to be in

---

[c] The word 'contain' does not always refer to surrounding something spatially: compare, for example, the phrase 'to contain oneself'. So St Thomas is saying here that two apparently contradictory metaphors can both be true: actuality and form, though in one sense interior to things (as we saw in the previous note), in another sense contain them or hold them together.

non convenit Deo cui non convenit esse in loco, nam *incorporalia* ut dicit Boëtius in libro de Hebd. *non sunt in loco.*[2] Ergo Deus non est ubique.

2. Præterea, sicut se habet tempus ad successiva ita se habet locus ad permanentia. Sed unum indivisibile actionis vel motus non potest esse in diversis temporibus. Ergo nec unum indivisibile in genere rerum permanentium potest esse in omnibus locis. Esse autem divinum non est successivum sed permanens. Ergo Deus non est in pluribus locis. Ergo non est ubique.

3. Præterea, quod est totum alicubi nihil ejus est extra locum illum. Sed Deus si est in aliquo loco totus est ibi, non enim, habet partes. Ergo nihil ejus est extra locum illum. Ergo Deus non est ubique.

SED CONTRA est quod dicit *Hierem.* xxiii: *cælum et terram ego impleo.*[3]

RESPONSIO: Dicendum quod cum locus sit res quædam, esse aliquid in loco potest intelligi dupliciter: vel per modum aliarum rerum, idest sicut dicitur aliquid esse in aliis rebus quocumque modo, sicut accidentia loci sunt in loco; vel per modum proprium loci, sicut locata sunt in loco. Utroque autem modo secundum aliquid Deus est in omni loco, quod est esse ubique.

Primo quidem sicut est in omnibus rebus ut dans eis esse et virtutem et operationem, sic enim est in omni loco ut dans ei esse et virtutem locativam. Item, locata sunt in loco inquantum replent locum, et Deus omnem locum replet. Non sicut corpora (corpus enim dicitur replere locum inquantum non compatitur secum aliud corpus, sed per hoc quod Deus est in aliquo loco non excluditur quod alia non sint ibi), immo per hoc replet omnia loca quod dat esse omnibus locatis quæ replent loca.

1. Ad primum ergo dicendum quod incorporalia non sunt in loco per contactum quantitatis dimensivæ sicut corpora, sed per contactum virtutis.

2. Ad secundum dicendum quod indivisibile est duplex. Unum quod est terminus continui ut punctus in permanentibus et momentum in successivis. Et hujusmodi indivisibile in permanentibus, quia habet determinatum situm, non potest esse in pluribus partibus loci vel in pluribus locis; et similiter indivisibile actionis vel motus, quia habet determinatum ordinem in motu vel actione, non potest esse in pluribus partibus temporis. Aliud autem indivisibile est quod est extra totum genus continui, et hoc modo substantiæ incorporeæ ut Deus et anima et substantiæ separatæ dicuntur esse indivisibiles. Tale igitur indivisibile non applicatur ad continuum sicut aliquid ejus sed inquantum contingit illud sua virtute. Unde secundum quod virtus sua se potest extendere ad unum vel multa, ad

---

every place, because it is not fitting for God to be in place at all; as Boëthius says, *only bodies are in place.*[2] So God is not everywhere.

2. Moreover, place is related to the permanent in the same way as time to the transient. Now it is impossible for any indivisible instant of action or change to occur at more than one time. It is therefore equally impossible for any indivisible permanent thing to exist in more than one place. Now God's existence is not transient but permanent. He cannot, therefore, exist in more than one place, and thus cannot be everywhere.

3. Moreover, if a thing exists wholly in one place it can in nowise exist outside it. Now wherever God exists he exists wholly, for he has no parts. So none of him exists anywhere else. God then does not exist everywhere.

ON THE OTHER HAND we read in *Jeremiah*: *I fill heaven and earth.*[3]

REPLY: Place is itself a sort of thing, and so there are two ways of understanding 'being in place': firstly, on an analogy with other things, that is to say, in whatever way we understand 'being in' when talking of other things, and the attributes of any place are in the place in this sense; or secondly, in the way peculiar to place alone, namely the way in which things occupying places are in those places. In both these ways there is a sense in which God is in every place, or in other words is everywhere.

First, he is in every place giving it existence and the power to be a place, just as he is in all things giving them existence, power and activity. Secondly, just as anything occupying a place fills that place, so God fills all places. But not as bodies do (for bodies fill places by not suffering other bodies to be there with them, whilst God's presence in a place does not exclude the presence there of other things); rather God fills all places by giving existence to everything occupying those places.

Hence: 1. Only bodies are in place through dimensional contact; other things are in place through causal contact.

2. Indivisibility is twofold. In one sense it characterizes any stopping-place within continuity, such as an instant in the transient, or a point in the permanent. In anything permanent such indivisible points have a set position, and so cannot be in more than one place or part of a place; and similarly in any action or change indivisible instants occur in a set order, and so cannot occur in more than one period of time. But in another sense indivisibility characterizes things outside all kind of continuousness, and in this sense substances like God, the soul and angels, which are not bodies, are called indivisible. Such indivisible things are related to a continuum, not as being part of it, but as being in causal contact with it. And so, according as their sphere of action is small or large and comprehends one

parvum vel magnum, secundum hoc est in uno vel pluribus locis, et in loco parvo vel magno.

3. Ad tertium dicendum quod totum dicitur respectu partium. Est autem duplex pars, scilicet pars essentiæ ut forma et materia dicuntur partes compositi et genus et differentia partes speciei, et est etiam pars quantitatis in quam scilicet dividitur aliqua quantitas. Quod ergo est totum in aliquo loco totalitate quantitatis non potest esse extra locum illum; quia quantitas locati commensuratur quantitati loci, unde non est totalitas quantitatis si non sit totalitas loci. Sed totalitas essentiæ non commensuratur totalitati loci. Unde non oportet quod illud quod est totum totalitate essentiæ in aliquo nullo modo sit extra illud. Sicut apparet etiam in formis accidentalibus quæ secundum accidens quantitatem habent; albedo enim est tota in qualibet parte superficiei si accipiatur totalitas essentiæ, quia secundum perfectam rationem suæ speciei invenitur in qualibet parte; si autem accipiatur totalitas secundum quantitatem, quam habet per accidens, sic non est tota in qualibet parte superficiei. In substantiis autem incorporeis non est totalitas nec per se nec per accidens nisi secundum perfectam rationem essentiæ, et ideo sicut anima est tota in qualibet parte corporis ita Deus totus est in omnibus et singulis.

articulus 3. utrum Deus sit ubique per essentiam, potentiam et præsentiam

AD TERTIUM sic proceditur:[1] 1. Videtur quod male assignentur modi existendi Deum in rebus cum dicitur quod Deus est in rebus per essentiam, præsentiam et potentiam. Id enim per essentiam est in aliquo quod essentialiter est in eo. Deus autem non est essentialiter in rebus, non enim est de essentia alicujus rei. Ergo non debet dici quod Deus sit in rebus per essentiam, præsentiam et potentiam.

2. Præterea, hoc est esse præsentem alicui rei, non deesse illi. Sed hoc est Deum esse per essentiam in omnibus, non deesse alicui rei. Ergo idem est esse in omnibus per essentiam et præsentiam. Superfluum ergo fuit dicere quod Deus esset in rebus per essentiam, præsentiam et potentiam.

3. Præterea, sicut Deus est principium omnium rerum per suam potentiam, ita per scientiam et voluntatem. Sed non dicitur esse in rebus per scientiam et voluntatem, ergo nec per potentiam.

4. Præterea, sicut gratia est quædam perfectio superaddita substantiæ

---

[1]cf Ia. 43, 3; 3a. 6, I ad I. Also I *Sent.* 37, I, 2; 37, exp

or more things, they are present in a small place or a large one, and in one place or more than one.

3. Whole is said relatively to parts. And part may mean either a part of a nature, as the form and matter composing certain things or the generic and differentiating notions composing definitions are called parts; or it may mean an extended part, into which some extended whole has been divided. So what is wholly in a place to its whole extent cannot extend outside that place; for the extent of anything occupying place is measured by the extent of the place, and unless the place were the thing's whole place the extent would not be the thing's whole extent. Wholeness of nature, however, is not measured by wholeness of place, so that what is wholly in something according to its whole nature can yet be in some wise outside it. This is clear even of accidents that happen to be extended; for if wholeness of nature is meant, whiteness is wholly present everywhere on a surface, its full specific nature being realized in every part; but if the wholeness of the extent it happens to possess is meant, then whiteness is not wholly present everywhere on the surface. Now the only wholeness that things which are not bodies either inherently possess, or happen to possess, is the wholeness of their essential nature. And so just as the soul exists wholly everywhere in the body, so God exists wholly in each and every thing.

article 3. is God everywhere in substance, power and presence?

THE THIRD POINT:[1] 1. To say that God exists in things by substance, presence and power, hardly seems a satisfactory classification of the ways God exists in things. For to exist in something by substance is to reside substantially within it. Now God does not reside substantially in things, since he forms no part of their substance. So we ought not to say that God exists in things by substance, presence and power.

2. Moreover, being present is the same as not being absent. Now God, precisely as existing in all things by substance, is not absent from them. So to exist in everything by substance and by presence are the same. It was therefore redundant to say that God exists in things by substance, presence and power.

3. Moreover, just as the source of everything is God's power, so also is it his knowledge and will. Now God is not said to exist in things by knowledge and will; neither then should he be said to do so by power.

4. Moreover, there are many perfections, like grace, added to the

rei, ita multæ sunt aliæ perfectiones superadditæ. Si ergo Deus dicitur esse speciali modo in quibusdam per gratiam, videtur quod secundum quamlibet perfectionem debeat accipi specialis modus essendi Deum in rebus.

SED CONTRA est quod Gregorius dicit *super Cant.* quod *Deus communi modo est in omnibus rebus præsentia, potentia et substantia, tamen familiari modo dicitur esse in aliquibus per gratiam.*[2]

RESPONSIO: Dicendum quod Deus dicitur esse in re aliqua dupliciter. Uno modo per modum causæ agentis, et sic est in omnibus rebus creatis ab ipso. Alio modo sicut objectum operationis est in operante, quod proprium est in operationibus animæ secundum quod cognitum est in cognoscente et desideratum in desiderante. Hoc igitur secundo modo Deus specialiter est in rationali creatura quæ cognoscit et diligit ipsum actu vel habitu. Et quia hoc habet rationalis creatura per gratiam, ut infra patebit,[3] dicitur esse hoc modo in sanctis per gratiam.

In rebus vero aliis ab ipso creatis quomodo sit considerandum est ex his quæ in rebus humanis esse dicuntur. Rex enim dicitur esse per suam potentiam in toto regno suo licet non sit ubique præsens. Per præsentiam vero suam dicitur aliquid esse in omnibus quæ in prospectu ipsius sunt, sicut omnia quæ sunt in aliqua domo dicuntur præsentia alicui qui tamen non est secundum substantiam suam in qualibet parte domus. Secundum vero substantiam vel essentiam dicitur aliquid esse in loco in quo ejus substantia habetur.

Fuerunt ergo aliqui, scilicet Manichæi, qui dixerunt divinæ potestati subjecta esse spiritualia et incorruptibilia, visibilia vero et corruptibilia subjecta esse dicebant potestati principii contrarii. Contra hoc oportet dicere quod Deus sit in omnibus per potentiam suam. Fuerunt vero alii qui licet crederent omnia esse subjecta divinæ potestati tamen providentiam divinam usque ad hæc inferiora corpora non extendebant, ex quorum persona dicitur *Iob* xxii: *circa cardines cæli versatur nec nostra considerat.*[4] Contra hos oportet dicere quod sit in omnibus per suam præsentiam. Fuerunt vero alii qui licet dicerent omnia spectare ad Dei providentiam

---

[2]Actually quoted from the *Glossa ordinaria* on the *Song of Songs* 5, 17 (one of the continuous glosses on Scripture current in the Middle Ages), where it is attributed to Gregory, but without reference.

[3]cf Ia. 43, 3; Ia2æ. 109, 1, 3   [4]*Job* 22, 14

[a]As St Thomas explains in Ia2æ. 110, 1, a grace is a favour freely given. When God bestows his favours on men it is not because they are first good and thus attract his favour, but it is the bestowal of his favour that makes them good. God's love is creative of good in the creature. It is for this reason that Catholic theology not only applies the word 'grace' to the favour as an act of God, but also to the gift of goodness produced in the creature by that favour. It is this grace in the creature that is

substance of things.ᵃ If God then is said to exist in some people in a special way by grace, it seems we ought to acknowledge special ways in which he exists in things corresponding to each perfection.

ON THE OTHER HAND Gregory tells us that *in the ordinary way God exists in all things by presence, power and substance, but he is said to exist in certain things in a more intimate way by grace.*[2]

REPLY: God is said to exist in things in two ways. Firstly, as an operative cause, and in this way he exists in everything he creates. Secondly, as an object attained by some activity exists within the acting subject, and this applies only to mental activities where the known exists in the knower, and the desired in the one who desires.ᵇ In this latter way, therefore, God exists in a special fashion in those reasoning creatures that are actually knowing and loving him, or are disposed to do so. And since we shall see this to be the result of a grace to the reasoning creature,[3] God is said to exist in this way in holy people by grace.

But to grasp the way in which he exists in other created things we must draw an analogy from human affairs. Thus in virtue of his power a king can be said to exist throughout his kingdom, though not everywhere present. Again, in virtue of its presence, a thing exists in everything within its field of view, so that everything in a house is said to be present even to a person not existing substantially in every part of that house. Finally, a thing exists in substance in the place where its substance is.

Now in the past certain people called Manichees declared that immaterial and imperishable things are subject to God's power, but visible and perishable things to some contrary power. As against this we must say that God exists by power in everything. Other people believed everything to be subject to God's power, but yet withdrew things here below from his providence; and these people the book of *Job* represents as saying: *he walks on the vault of heaven and does not see our doings.*[4] As against this we must say that God exists by presence in everything. Yet others said that God's providence oversees everything, but nevertheless asserted that God did not

---

here being referred to by St Thomas, and especially that grace of knowing and loving God which came to men through Jesus Christ.

ᵇAs we saw in note *b* on 1a. 5, 2, St Thomas regards understanding and knowledge as a process of conceiving an idea from a thing which is then given expression in external words. But knowledge is not an exterior action, since it is the symbolic character of the words which is relevant rather than their physical exteriority. The idea, then, which is the thing as conceived, is not exterior to the conceiving process; and this is what is meant by saying that the known exists in the knower. In the same way St Thomas regards love as a process of becoming interiorly adapted. and impelled towards the loved one. cf for fuller information 1a. 27, 1, 4.

tamen posuerunt omnia non immediate esse a Deo creata, sed quod immediate creavit primas creaturas et illæ creaverunt alias. Sed contra hoc oportet dicere quod sit in omnibus per essentiam.

Sic ergo est in omnibus per potentiam inquantum omnia ejus potestati subduntur, est per præsentiam in omnibus inquantum omnia nuda sunt et aperta oculis ejus, est in omnibus per essentiam inquantum adest omnibus ut causa essendi, sicut dictum est.[5]

1. Ad primum ergo dicendum quod Deus est in omnibus per essentiam non quidem rerum, quasi sit de essentia earum, sed per essentiam suam, quia substantia sua adest omnibus ut causa essendi, sicut dictum est.[6]

2. Ad secundum dicendum quod aliquid potest dici præsens alicui inquantum subjacet ejus conspectui, quod tamen distat ab eo secundum substantiam, ut dictum est. Et ideo oportuit duos modos poni, scilicet per essentiam et præsentiam.

3. Ad tertium dicendum quod de ratione scientiæ et voluntatis est quod scitum sit in sciente et volitum in volente; unde secundum scientiam et voluntatem magis res sunt in Deo quam Deus in rebus. Sed de ratione potentiæ est quod sit principium agendi in aliud, unde secundum potentiam agens comparatur et applicatur rei exteriori. Et sic per potentiam potest dici agens esse in alio.

4. Ad quartum dicendum quod nulla alia perfectio superaddita substantiæ facit Deum esse in aliquo sicut objectum cognitum et amatum nisi gratia, et ideo sola gratia facit singularem modum essendi Deum in rebus. Est autem alius singularis modus essendi Deum in homine per unionem, de quo modo suo loco agetur.

articulus 4. utrum esse ubique sit proprium Dei

AD QUARTUM sic proceditur:[1] 1. Videtur quod esse ubique non sit proprium Dei. Universale enim secundum Philosophum est ubique et semper,[2] materia etiam prima cum sit in omnibus corporibus est ubique. Neutrum autem horum est Deus ut ex præmissis patet.[3] Ergo esse ubique non est proprium Dei.

2. Præterea, numerus est in numeratis. Sed totum universum est constitutum in aliquo numero, ut patet *Sap.* xi.[4] Ergo aliquis numerus est qui est in toto universo, et ita ubique.

---

[5]cf 1a. 8, 1   [6]cf 1a. 8, 1
[1]cf 1a. 52, 2; 112, 1. Also 1 *Sent.* 37, 2, 2; 37, 3, 2. *In De div. nom.* 3, *lect.* 1. *Quodlibet* XI, 1
[2]*Posterior Analytics* I, 31. 87b33
[3]cf 1a. 3, 5 and 8   [4]*Wisd.* 11, 21

create everything without intermediaries, but only the first creatures, who then created others. As against this we must say that God exists in substance in everything.[c]

Thus God exists in everything by power inasmuch as everything is subject to his power, by presence inasmuch as everything is naked and open to his gaze, and by substance inasmuch as he exists in everything causing their existence, as we said earlier.[5]

Hence: 1. God exists in all things by substance, not however by their substance as though he belonged to the substance of things, but by his own which, we have said, exists in everything as causing their existence.[6]

2. We can talk of something being present to someone whenever it lies within his field of vision, even if in substance it is far away from him, as we said. Hence the necessity of asserting the two ways, by substance and by presence.

3. It is of the nature of knowledge and volition that the known should exist in the knower and the thing willed in the one willing; and so, by his knowledge and will, things exist in God rather than God in things. But it is of the nature of power to initiate activity in some other thing, so that in virtue of its power an agent is brought into contact and relation with outside things. And this is why an agent can be described as existing in some other thing by power.

4. Grace is the only perfection added to the substance of things which makes God exist in them as a known and loved object; grace alone then makes God exist in things in a unique way. There is, however, another unique way in which God exists in a man, by being one with him, and we will deal with this in its proper place.[d]

article 4. is being everywhere something belonging to God alone?

THE FOURTH POINT:[1] 1. It seems that being everywhere is not something belonging to God alone. For Aristotle says that universals exist everywhere and always,[2] and the ultimate matter in all bodies must also be everywhere. Now we have already made it clear that neither of these is God.[3] Being everywhere then is not something belonging to God alone.

2. Moreover, there is number in all numbered things. Now the book of *Wisdom* declares the whole world to have been created numbered.[4] Some number then exists in the whole world, that is to say, everywhere.

[c]The opinion of the Manichees can be found, for example, in Augustine, *De Hæres.* 46. PL 42, 35. The second opinion in this article is attributed to Aristotle and Averroes in I *Sent.* 39, 2, 2. The third opinion is attributed to Avicenna and to Peter Lombard later in the Summa at 1a. 45, 5.

[d]The reference is to the unity of God and man in Jesus Christ, 'true God and true man'. This is dealt with by St Thomas in 3a. 2.

3. Præterea, totum universum est quoddam totum corpus perfectum ut dicitur in I *Cæli et Mundi*.[5] Sed totum universum est ubique quia extra ipsum nullus locus est. Non ergo solus Deus est ubique.

4. Præterea, si aliquod corpus esset infinitum nullus locus esset extra eum. Ergo esset ubique. Et sic esse ubique non videtur proprium Dei.

5. Præterea, anima, ut dicit Augustinus in VI *de Trin. est tota in toto et tota in qualibet parte ejus*.[6] Si ergo non esset in mundo nisi unum animal anima ejus esset ubique. Et sic esse ubique non est proprium Dei.

6. Item, Augustinus dicit in *epistola ad Volusianum: anima videt ubi sentit, et ubi sentit ibi vivit, et ubi vivit ibi est*.[7] Sed anima videt quasi ubique, quia successive videt etiam totum cælum. Ergo anima est ubique.

SED CONTRA est quod Ambrosius dicit in libro *de Spiritu Sancto: Quis audeat creaturam dicere Spiritum Sanctum qui in omnibus et ubique et semper est, quod utique deitatis est proprium?*[8]

RESPONSIO: Dicendum quod esse ubique primo et per se est proprium Dei. Dico autem esse ubique primo quod secundum se totum est ubique. Si quid enim esset ubique secundum diversas partes in diversis locis existens non esset primo ubique, quia quod convenit alicui ratione partis suæ non convenit ei primo, sicut si homo est albus dente albedo non convenit primo homini sed denti. Esse autem ubique per se dico id cui non convenit esse ubique per accidens propter aliquam positionem factam, quia sic granum milii esset ubique si nullum aliud corpus esset. Per se igitur convenit esse ubique alicui quando tale est quod qualibet positione facta sequitur illud esse ubique. Et hoc proprie convenit Deo. Quia quotcumque loca ponantur etiam si ponerentur infinita præter ista quæ sunt, oporteret in omnibus esse Deum quia nihil potest esse nisi per ipsum.

Sic igitur esse ubique primo et per se convenit Deo et est proprium ejus, quia quotcumque loca ponantur oportet quod in quolibet sit Deus non secundum partem sed secundum seipsum.

1. Ad primum ergo dicendum quod universale et materia prima sunt quidem ubique sed non secundum idem esse.

2. Ad secundum dicendum quod numerus cum sit accidens non est per se sed per accidens in loco. Nec est totus in quolibet numeratorum sed secundum partem. Et sic non sequitur quod sit primo et per se ubique.

3. Ad tertium dicendum quod totum corpus universi est ubique sed non

[5]*De Cælo et Mundo* I, 1. 268b8
[6]*De Trinitate* VI, 6. PL 42, 929
[7]*Epistola* 137 (Letter to Volusianus), 2. PL 33, 518
[8]*De Spiritu Sancto* I, 7. PL 16, 723

3. Moreover, according to Aristotle the whole world is in its way a complete and perfect body.[5] Now the whole world is everywhere, for there can be no place outside it. So not only God is everywhere.

4. Moreover, there would be no place outside of an unlimited body, if such existed. And so it would be everywhere. Being everywhere then need not it seems belong to God alone.

5. Moreover, souls, says Augustine, are *wholly in the whole and wholly in every part of the whole*.[6] If then nothing existed in the world but one animal, its soul would be everywhere. Being everywhere then need not belong to God alone.

6. Again, Augustine says *wherever the soul sees it perceives, and wherever it perceives there it lives, and wherever it lives there it exists*.[7] Now the soul sees everywhere in a sense, for bit by bit it sees the whole heavens. The soul then exists everywhere.

ON THE OTHER HAND Ambrose asks *who would dare to name creature the Holy Ghost who exists always, everywhere, in everything; for this without doubt is something belonging to God alone*.[8]

REPLY: Being everywhere outright and essentially belongs to God alone. By being everywhere outright I mean being everywhere in one's completeness. For to exist everywhere, but with a different part in each different place, is not to be everywhere outright, since any property of a part is not the outright property of the whole: thus the whiteness of a man with white teeth belongs outright to the teeth, not to him. By being everywhere essentially I mean not just happening to be everywhere in certain circumstances, as the grain of wheat would be everywhere if no other bodies existed. When a thing is such that it would exist everywhere in any circumstances, it exists everywhere essentially. Now this belongs to God alone. For no matter how many places one may think up, even infinitely more than now exist, God would necessarily exist in them all, since nothing can exist except he cause it to do so.

And so to be everywhere outright and essentially belongs to God and to God alone, for no matter how many places one may think up God himself will necessarily exist in them, and not just parts of him.

1. Universals and the ultimate matter of things are indeed everywhere but not with one and the same existence.

2. Number, being an accident, is not essentially in place but only happens to be there. Nor is it complete in each numbered thing, but partly exists in each. So one cannot conclude that number is everywhere outright and essentially.

3. The whole body of the world is everywhere piece by piece, not whole

primo, quia non totum est in quolibet loco sed secundum suas partes. Nec iterum per se, quia si ponerentur aliqua alia loca non esset in eis.

4. Ad quartum dicendum quod si esset corpus infinitum esset ubique secundum suas partes.

5. Ad quintum dicendum quod si esset unum solum animal anima ejus esset ubique primo quidem sed per accidens.

6. Ad sextum dicendum quod cum dicitur anima alicubi videre potest intelligi dupliciter. Uno modo secundum quod hoc adverbium 'alicubi' determinat actum videndi ex parte objecti. Et sic verum est quod dum cælum videt in cælo videt, et eadem ratione in cælo sentit, non tamen sequitur quod in cælo vivit vel sit, quia 'vivere' et 'esse' non important actum transeuntem in exterius objectum. Alio modo potest intelligi secundum quod adverbium determinat actum videntis secundum quod exit a vidente. Et sic verum est quod anima ubi sentit et videt ibi est et vivit secundum istum modum loquendi. Et ita non sequitur quod sit ubique.

in every place, and so not everywhere outright. Nor essentially everywhere, for if there were other places it would not be in them.

4. An unlimited body, if it existed, would exist everywhere piece by piece.

5. If only one animal existed, then its soul would indeed exist everywhere outright, but nevertheless only happen to do so.

6. One can interpret the phrase 'wherever the soul sees' in two ways. The first interpretation takes the adverb 'wherever' as determining the object of the seeing. And in this sense it is true that when the soul is seeing the heavens it is seeing in the heavens and thus perceiving in the heavens; but it does not follow that it lives or exists in the heavens because these two verbs do not name actions going out to external objects. The other interpretation takes the adverb 'wherever' as determining the position of the one seeing. And in this sense it is true that the soul lives and exists where it sees and perceives. But then it does not follow that it exists everywhere.

CONSEQUENTER CONSIDERANDUM est de immutabilitate et æternitate divina quæ immutabilitatem consequitur.

Quæstio 9. de immutabilitate Dei

Circa immutabilitatem vero quæruntur duo:

    1. utrum Deus sit omnino immutabilis,
    2. utrum esse immutabile sit proprium Dei.

articulus 1. *utrum Deus sit omnino immutabilis*

AD PRIMUM sic proceditur:[1] 1. Videtur quod Deus non sit omnino immutabilis. Quidquid enim movet seipsum est aliquo modo mutabile. Sed sicut dicit Augustinus VIII *super Gen. ad litt.*: *Spiritus creator movet se sed nec per tempus nec per locum.*[2] Ergo Deus est aliquo modo mutabilis.

2. Præterea, *Sap.* vii dicitur de sapientia quod est *mobilior omnibus mobilibus.*[3] Sed Deus est ipsa sapientia. Ergo Deus est mobilis.

3. Præterea, appropinquari et elongari motum significant. Hæc autem dicuntur de Deo in scripturis *Jac.* iv: *appropinquate Deo et appropinquabit vobis.*[4] Ergo Deus est mutabilis.

SED CONTRA est quod dicitur *Malach.* iii: *Ego Deus et non mutor.*[5]

RESPONSIO: Dicendum quod ex præmissis ostenditur Deum esse omnino immutabilem.

Primo quidem quia supra ostensum est esse aliquod primum ens quod Deum dicimus, et quod hujusmodi primum oportet esse purum actum absque permixtione alicujus potentiæ, eo quod potentia simpliciter est posterior actu.[6] Omne autem quod quocumque modo mutatur est aliquo modo in potentia. Ex quo patet quod impossibile est Deum aliquod modo mutari.

Secundo, quia omne quod movetur quantum ad aliquid manet et quantum ad aliquid transit, sicut quod movetur de albedine in nigredinem manet secundum substantiam. Et sic in omni eo quod movetur attenditur aliqua compositio. Ostensum est autem supra quod in Deo nulla est compositio, sed est omnino simplex.[7] Unde manifestum est quod Deus moveri non potest.

Tertio, quia omne quod movetur motu suo aliquid acquirit et pertingit ad aliquid ad quod prius non pertingebat. Deus autem cum sit infinitus comprehendens in se omnem plenitudinem perfectionis totius esse non

---

[1]cf Ia. 2, 3. Also 1 *Sent.* 8, 3, 1. *CG* I, 13. *In De Trin.* 5, 4 ad 2. *Compendium Theol.* 4

AS A NEXT STEP we must consider God's unchangeableness and consequent eternity.

Question 9. God's unchangeableness

For this question about unchangeableness there are two points of inquiry:

    1. is God altogether unchangeable?
    2. is only God unchangeable?

article 1. is God altogether unchangeable?

THE FIRST POINT:[1] 1. It seems that God is not altogether unchangeable. For anything that moves itself is in some way changeable. Now Augustine says that *the creating spirit moves himself, though not in space and time.*[2] So in some way God is changeable.

    2. Moreover, wisdom is described in the book of *Wisdom* as *more mobile than any moving thing.*[3] Now God is wisdom itself. God then is movable.

    3. Moreover, drawing near and drawing away are descriptions of movements. Yet scripture applies them to God: *draw nigh to God and he will draw nigh to you.*[4] God then is changeable.

ON THE OTHER HAND we read in *Malachy*: *I am God, I change not.*[5]

REPLY: Our findings so far prove God to be altogether unchangeable.

    First, because we have proved that there must be some first existent, called God, sheerly actual and unalloyed with potentiality, since actuality, simply speaking, precedes potentiality.[6] Now any changing thing, whatsoever the change, is somehow potential. So it clearly follows that God cannot change in any way.

    Secondly, because anything in change partly persists and partly passes, as a thing changing from white to black persists in substance. Things in change are therefore always composite. Now God we have shown to be not at all composite, but altogether simple.[7] Clearly then he cannot change.

    Thirdly, because anything in change acquires something through its change, attaining something previously not attained. Now God, being limitless and embracing within himself the whole fullness of perfection of all existence, cannot acquire anything, nor can he move out towards

---

[2]*Super Genesim ad litt.* VIII, 20. PL 34, 388
[3]*Wisd.* 7, 24   [4]*James* 4, 8   [5]*Malachy* 3, 6
[6]cf Ia. 2, 3; 3, 1   [7]cf Ia. 3, 7

potest aliquid a acquirere nec extendere se in aliquid ad quod prius non pertingebat. Unde nullo modo sibi competit motus. Et inde est quod quidam antiquorum quasi ab ipsa veritate coacti posuerunt primum principium esse immobile.

1. Ad primum ergo dicendum quod Augustinus ibi loquitur secundum modum quo Plato dicebat primum movens movere seipsum, omnem operationem nominans motum, secundum quod etiam ipsum intelligere et velle et amare motus quidam dicuntur. Quia ergo Deus intelligit et amat seipsum secundum hoc dixerunt quod Deus movet seipsum, non autem secundum quod motus et mutatio est existentis in potentia ut nunc loquimur de mutatione et motu.

2. Ad secundum dicendum quod sapientia dicitur mobilis esse similitudinarie secundum quod suam similitudinem diffundit usque ad ultima rerum. Nihil enim esse potest quod non procedat a divina sapientia per quamdam imitationem sicut a primo principio effectivo et formali, prout etiam artificiata procedunt a sapientia artificis. Sic igitur, inquantum similitudo divinæ sapientiæ gradatim procedit a supremis quæ magis participant de ejus similitudine usque ad infima rerum quæ minime participant, dicitur esse quidam processus et motus divinæ sapientiæ in res, sicut si dicamus solem procedere usque ad terram inquantum radius luminis ejus usque ad terram pertingit. Et hoc modo exponit Dionysius cap. 1 *Cæl. Hier.* dicens quod *omnis processus divinæ majestatis* venit and nos a Patre luminum moto.*[8]

3. Ad tertium dicendum quod hæc dicuntur de Deo in scripturis metaphorice. Sicut enim dicitur sol intrare domum vel exire inquantum radius eius pertingit ad domum, sic dicitur Deus appropinquare ad nos vel recedere a nobis inquantum percipimus influentiam bonitatis ipsius vel ab eo deficimus.

articulus 2. utrum esse immutabile sit proprium Dei

AD SECUNDUM sic proceditur:[1] 1. Videtur quod esse immutabile non sit proprium Dei. Dicit enim Philosophus in II *Meta.* quod materia est in omni eo quod movetur.[2] Sed substantiæ quædam creatæ sunt sicut angeli et animæ quæ non habent materiam, ut quibusdam videtur. Ergo esse immutabile non est proprium Dei.

2. Præterea, omne quod movetur movetur propter aliquem finem, quod ergo iam pervenit ad ultimum finem non movetur. Sed quædam creaturæ iam pervenerunt ad ultimum finem sicut omnes beati. Ergo aliquæ creaturæ sunt immobiles.

**majestatis.* Leonine *manifestationis*, every emanation in which God is revealed.
[8]*De Cælesti Hierarchia* I, I. PG 3, 120

something previously not attained. So one cannot in any way associate him with change.

And this is why some of the ancient philosophers, bowing to the truth, so to speak, held that the first source of things is unchangeable.[a]

Hence: 1. Augustine is here using a Platonic way of speaking, according to which the first source of movement is said to move itself, meaning by 'movement' any operation at all, even understanding, willing and loving. So since God understands and loves himself, the Platonists said that God moves himself, not however meaning, as we are doing at the moment, the movement and change of something potential.

2. To call wisdom mobile is a metaphorical way of saying that wisdom spreads its own likeness throughout the length and breadth of things. For nothing can exist except it be a sort of reflection deriving from God's wisdom as from its primary operative and formal cause; just as works of handicraft derive from craftsmanship. Inasmuch then as this likeness to divine wisdom is transmitted step by step from the highest things, which share the likeness most, to the lowest, which share it least, we talk of God's wisdom sallying forth as it were and moving into things. It is as though we talked of the sun sallying forth on earth when its light-rays touched earth. And this is the explanation Dionysius gives, when he says that *every emanation of the divine majesty comes to us set in motion by the Father of lights.*[8]

3. The scripture is here talking of God in metaphors. For just as the sun is said to enter or depart from a house by touching the house with its rays, so God is said to draw near to us when we receive an influx of his goodness, or draw away from us when we fail him.

article 2. is only God unchangeable?

THE SECOND POINT:[1] 1. Not only God, it seems, is unchangeable. For Aristotle says that anything in change contains matter.[2] Now there are people who believe that certain created substances, such as souls and angels, exist without matter.[a] So not only God is unchangeable.

2. Moreover, all change has a goal in view, so that things which have already achieved their ultimate goal will not change. Now some creatures such as saints have already achieved their ultimate goal. Some creatures then are unchangeable.

---

[1]cf 1a. 10, 3 & 5; 50, 5; 61, 2 ad 3; 65, 1 ad 1; 75, 6; 97, 1. Also I *Sent.* 8, 3, 2; 19, 5, 3. *De malo* XVI, 2 ad 6. *Quodlibet* X, 2, 1. *In* I *Tim.* 6, *lect.* 3

[2]*Metaphysics* II, 2. 994b25. (In Ross text see critical apparatus)

[a]The reference is probably to Parmenides and Melissus. cf Aristotle, *Physics* I, 2. 184b16.

[a]St Thomas himself teaches this in 1a. 50, 2.

3. Præterea, omne quod est mutabile est variabile. Sed formæ sunt invariabiles, dicitur enim in *libro Sex Principiorum* quod *forma est simplici et invariabili essentia consistens.*[3] Ergo non est solius Dei proprium esse immutabile.

SED CONTRA est quod dicit Augustinus in libro *de Natura Boni: solus Deus immutabilis est; quæ autem fecit quia ex nihilo sunt mutabilia sunt.*[4]

RESPONSIO: Dicendum quod solus Deus est omnino immutabilis, omnis autem creatura aliquod modo est mutabilis.

Sciendum est enim quod mutabile potest aliquid dici dupliciter, uno modo per potentiam quæ in ipso est, alio modo per potentiam quæ in altero est. Omnes enim creaturæ antequam essent non erant possibiles esse per aliquam potentiam creatam cum nihil creatum sit æternum, sed per solam potentiam divinam inquantum Deus poterat eas in esse producere. Sicut autem ex voluntate Dei dependet quod res in esse produxit, ita ex ejus voluntate dependet quod res in esse conservat. Non enim aliter eas in esse conservat quam semper eis esse dando, unde si suam actionem eis subtraheret omnia in nihilum redigerentur, ut patet per Augustinum IV *super Gen. ad litt.*[5] Sicut igitur in potentia creatoris fuit ut res essent antequam essent in seipsis, ita in potentia creatoris est postquam sunt in seipsis ut non sint. Sic igitur per potentiam quæ est in altero scilicet in Deo sunt mutabiles, inquantum ab ipso ex nihilo potuerunt produci in esse et de esse possunt reduci in non esse.

Si autem dicatur aliquid mutabile per potentiam in ipso existentem, sic etiam aliquo modo omnis creatura est mutabilis. Est enim in creatura duplex potentia, scilicet activa et passiva. Dico autem potentiam passivam secundum quam aliquid assequi potest suam perfectionem vel in essendo vel in consequendo finem. Si igitur attendatur mutabilitas rei secundum potentiam ad esse, sic non in omnibus est mutabilitas, sed in illis solum in quibus illud quod est possibile in eis potest stare cum non esse. Unde in corporibus inferioribus est mutabilitas et secundum esse substantiale (quia materia eorum potest esse cum privatione formæ substantialis ipsorum), et quantum ad esse accidentale si subjectum compatiatur secum privationem accidentis (sicut hoc subjectum homo compatitur non album et ideo potest mutari de albo in non album). Si vero sit tale accidens quod consequatur principia essentialia subjecti, privatio illius accidentis non potest stare cum subjecto, unde subjectum non potest mutari secundum illud accidens; sicut nix non potest fieri nigra. In corporibus vero cælestibus

---

[3]*Liber Sex Principiorum* I (opening words). PL 188, 1257. The reputed work of Gilbert de la Porrée, Chancellor of Paris University, Bishop of Poitiers, d. 1154
[4]*De Natura Boni* I. PL 42, 551   [5]*Super Genesim ad litt.* IV, 12. PL 34, 305

3. Moreover, changeable things can vary. Forms, however, are invariable, as the *Book of the Six Principles* says: *form is that which subsists with simple and invariable being*.[3] So not only God is unchangeable.

ON THE OTHER HAND Augustine says *God alone is unchangeable; while the things God makes are made from nothing and therefore changeable*.[4]

REPLY: Only God is altogether unchangeable; creatures can all change in some way or other.

For one must realize that there are two possible grounds for calling a thing changeable, its own[b] potentiality, and something else's power.[b] Before creatures existed their existence was possible not because of any created potentiality, since nothing created exists eternally, but simply because God had the power to bring them into existence. Now just as bringing things into existence depends on God's will, so also preserving them in existence. For he preserves them in existence only by perpetually giving existence to them, and were he therefore to withdraw his activity from them all things, as Augustine makes clear, would fall back into nothingness.[5] So just as before things existed on their own it was in the creator's power for them to exist, so now that they do exist on their own it is in the creator's power for them not to exist. They are thus changeable because of power present in somebody else, namely, God, who was able to bring them into existence out of nothing, and is able to reduce them again from existence to nothingness.

Yet even if we talk of changeableness in things due to their own potentiality, every creature is still changeable in some way. For we must distinguish in creatures both active and passive potentialities. I call 'passive potentiality' the capacity of a thing to be perfected, either in being or by attaining the goal of its action. If we consider then the changeableness consequent upon a thing's potentiality to being, not everything is changeable, but only those things in which possibilities can exist without being realized. Thus bodies here on earth can change substantially in being (for the matter in them can exist without assuming the form of those particular substances), and can change also in such accidental modes of being as the subject can do without (as man can change from white to some other colour because man as subject can do without whiteness). If, however, the accidental mode of being is derivative from the subject's essential nature,[c] the subject cannot do without it, and cannot therefore change with respect to it; thus, snow cannot become black. In heavenly bodies, on the other

---

[b]It will be useful to remember throughout the following argument that the Latin word for potentiality and for power is the same: *potentia*.

[c]Accidents belonging 'by nature' are referred to in note *a* on 1a. 3, 6.

materia non compatitur secum privationem formæ quia forma perficit totam potentialitatem materiæ; et ideo non sunt mutabilia secundum esse substantiale sed secundum esse locale, quia subjectum compatitur secum privationem hujus loci vel illius. Substantiæ vero incorporeæ quia sunt ipsæ formæ subsistentes, quæ tamen se habent ad esse ipsarum sicut potentia ad actum, non compatiuntur secum privationem hujus actus; quia esse consequitur formam et nihil corrumpitur nisi per hoc quod amittit formam. Unde in ipsa forma non est potentia ad non esse, et ideo hujusmodi substantiæ sunt immutabiles et invariabiles secundum esse. Et hoc est quod dicit Dionysius iv cap. *de Div. Nom.* quod *substantiæ intellectuales creatæ mundæ sunt a generatione et ab omni variatione sicut incorporales et immateriales.*[6] Sed tamen remanet in eis duplex mutabilitas: una secundum quod sunt in potentia ad finem, et sic est in eis mutabilitas secundum electionem de bono in malum ut Damascenus dicit;[7] alia secundum locum inquantum virtute sua finita possunt attingere quædam loca quæ prius non attingebant, quod de Deo dici non potest quia sua infinitate omnia replet, ut supra dictum est.[8]

Sic igitur in omni creatura est potentia ad mutationem vel secundum esse substantiale sicut corpora corruptibilia, vel secundum esse locale sicut corpora cælestia, vel secundum ordinem ad finem et applicationem virtutis ad diversa sicut in angelis. Et universaliter omnes creaturæ communiter sunt mutabiles secundum potentiam creantis in cujus potestate est esse et non esse earum. Unde cum Deus nullo istorum modorum sit mutabilis proprium ejus est omnino immutabilem esse.

1. Ad primum ergo dicendum quod objectio illa procedit de eo quod est mutabile secundum esse substantiale vel accidentale, de tali enim motu philosophi tractaverunt.

2. Ad secundum dicendum quod angeli boni supra immutabilitatem essendi quæ competit eis secundum naturam habent immutabilitatem electionis ex divina virtute; tamen remanet in eis mutabilitas secundum locum.

3. Ad tertium dicendum quod formæ dicuntur esse invariabiles quia non possunt esse subjectum variationis, subjiciuntur tamen variationi inquantum subjectum secundum eas variatur. Unde patet quod secundum quod sunt sic variantur, non enim dicuntur entia quasi sint subjectum essendi sed quia eis aliquid est.

---

[6]*On the Divine Names* 4, 1. PG 3, 693
[7]*De Fide Orthodoxa* II, 3. PG 94, 868   [8]cf 1a. 8, 2

hand, the potentiality of the matter is wholly realized by the form, so that the matter cannot exist without that form; and such bodies therefore cannot change substantially in being, though they are able to change place, for the subject can exist without being in this or that particular place. Again, substances which are not bodies but are forms subsisting in themselves, cannot do without existence, even though related to that existence as potentialities to some actualization; for existence follows immediately upon form, and a thing can perish only by losing its form. In a form as such then there is no potentiality of non-existence, and so such substances are unable to change or vary in being. And this is what Dionysius means when he says that *created intellectual substances are free from generation and from all variation, being neither bodies nor material.*[6] In two ways, however, such substances can change: firstly, because of their potentiality to some goal, they can, as Damascene says, change their minds and choose evil rather than good;[7] secondly, they can change place, because, their power being limited, they can bring it to bear on places not previously touched by it— which cannot be said of God who in his limitlessness, as we saw, fills all places.[8]

In all creatures then there exists potentiality of change, either substantially as with perishable bodies, or in place as with the heavenly bodies, or in orderedness to a goal and application of power to different things as with the angels. And in addition there is a changeableness common to the whole universe of creatures, since whether they exist or not is subject to the creator's power. So, because God cannot change in any of these ways, he alone is altogether unchangeable.

Hence: 1. This argument holds for changeableness in being, either substantial or accidental, for that is the kind of change which interests philosophers.

2. In addition to unchangeable being belonging to them by nature, the good angels are endowed by God's power with unchangeable choice;[d] but they can still change as regards place.

3. Forms are called invariable because they themselves cannot be the subjects of variation; but they take part nonetheless in variation, inasmuch as a subject may have now this and now that form. Clearly then they vary in exactly the same way as they exist; for they are said to exist not as subjects of existence, but because things have existence through them.

---

[d] St Thomas teaches that all who enjoy the vision of the supreme good in heaven will have no alternative but to love it. cf 1a. 62, 8.

DEINDE QUÆRITUR de æternitate.

Quæstio 10. de æternitate Dei

Et circa hoc quæruntur sex:

1. quid sit æternitas,
2. utrum Deus sit æternus,
3. utrum esse æternum sit proprium Dei,
4. utrum æternitas differat ab ævo et* tempore,
5. de differentia ævi et temporis,
6. utrum sit unum ævum tantum sicut est unum tempus et una æternitas.

articulus 1. quid sit æternitas

AD PRIMUM sic proceditur:[1] 1. Videtur quod non sit conveniens definitio æternitatis quam Boëtius ponit v de Consolatione dicens quod æternitas est interminabilis vitæ tota simul et perfecta possessio.[2] Interminabile enim negative dicitur. Sed negatio non est de ratione nisi eorum quæ sunt deficientia, quod æternitati non competit. Ergo in definitione aeternitatis non debet poni 'interminabile'.

2. Præterea, æternitas durationem quamdam significat. Duratio autem magis respicit esse quam vitam. Ergo non debuit poni in definitione æternitatis 'vita' sed magis 'esse'.

3. Præterea, totum dicitur quod habet partes. Hoc autem æternitati non competit cum sit simplex. Ergo inconvenienter dicitur tota.

4. Præterea, plures dies non possunt esse simul nec plura tempora. Sed in æternitate pluraliter dicuntur dies et tempora. Dicitur enim Micheæ v: egressus ejus ab initio a diebus æternitatis,[3] et ad Rom. ultimo: secundum revelationem mysterii temporibus æternis taciti.[4] Ergo æternitas non est tota simul.

5. Præterea, totum et perfectum sunt idem. Posito igitur quod sit tota, superflue additur quod sit perfecta.

6. Præterea, possessio ad durationem non pertinet. Æternitas autem quædam duratio est. Ergo æternitas non est possessio.

RESPONSIO: Dicendum quod sicut in cognitionem simplicium oportet nos venire per composita, ita in cognitionem æternitatis oportet nos venire per

---

*Leonine omits ævo et, the 'æon' and.
[1]cf 1 Sent. 8, 2, 1. In De div. nom. 10, lect. 3. In De causis, lect. 2
[2]De Consolatione v, prosa 6. PL 63, 858   [3]Micah 5, 2   [4]Romans 16, 25

WE ASK NEXT about eternity.

Question 10. the eternity of God

For this question there are six points of inquiry:[a]

 1. what is eternity?
 2. is God eternal?
 3. does eternity belong to God alone?
 4. is eternity different from the æon and time?
 5. the difference between the æon and time.
 6. is there only one æon, as there is one time and one eternity?

article 1. what is eternity?

THE FIRST POINT:[1] 1. The definition of eternity given by Boëthius seems unsuitable. He says that *eternity is the instantaneously whole and perfect possession of unending life.*[2] Now 'unending' is a negative term, such as belongs only in the definition of a defective thing. Eternity, however, is not defective. So the word 'unending' should not occur in a definition of eternity.

2. Moreover, 'eternity' names a sort of duration, and duration is connected with existence rather than with life. So we ought to use the word 'existence' rather than 'life' when defining eternity.

3. Moreover, one uses the word 'whole' of something having parts. Now eternity is simple, and therefore has no parts. So it should not be described as 'whole'.

4. Moreover, several days or several times cannot occur instantaneously. Yet in speaking of eternity these words 'day' and 'time' are used in the plural. The prophet Micah says *his goings forth are from the beginning, from the days of eternity,*[3] and in St Paul we read: *according to the revelation of the mystery kept secret through times eternal.*[4] Eternity therefore is not instantaneously whole.

5. Moreover, wholeness is the same as perfection. Given that eternity is whole, then, it is redundant to add that it is perfect.

6. Moreover, possession is unconnected with duration. Now eternity is a sort of duration. It is not therefore possession.

REPLY: Just as we can only come to know simple things by way of composite ones, so we can only come to know eternity by way of time, which

---

[a]See Appendix 16.

tempus, quod nihil aliud est quam *numerus motus secundum prius et posterius.*[5] Cum enim in quolibet motu sit successio et una pars post alteram, ex hoc quod numeramus prius et posterius in motu apprehendimus tempus, quod nihil aliud est quam numerus prioris et posterioris in motu. In eo autem quod caret motu et semper eodem modo se habet non est accipere prius et posterius. Sicut igitur ratio temporis consistit in numeratione prioris et posterioris in motu, ita in apprehensione uniformitatis ejus quod est omnino extra motum consistit ratio aeternitatis. Item, ea dicuntur tempore mensurari quæ principium et finem habent in tempore, ut dicitur in IV *Phys.*[6] et hoc ideo quia in omni eo quod movetur est accipere aliquod principium et aliquem finem. Quod vero est omnino immutabile sicut nec successionem ita nec principium[*] habere potest.

Sic ergo ex duobus notificatur æternitas. Primo, ex hoc quod id quod est in æternitate est *interminabile,* idest principio et fine carens (ut terminus ad utrumque referatur). Secundo, ex hoc quod ipsa æternitas successione caret *tota simul* existens.

1. Ad primum ergo dicendum quod simplicia consueverunt per negationem definiri, sicut punctus est cuius pars non est. Quod non ideo est quia negatio sit de essentia eorum, sed quia intellectus noster qui primo apprehendit composita, in cognitionem simplicium pervenire non potest nisi per remotionem compositionis.

2. Ad secundum dicendum quod illud quod est vere æternum non solum est ens sed vivens. Et ipsum vivere se extendit quodammodo ad operationem, non autem esse. Processio autem durationis videtur attendi secundum operationem magis quam secundum esse; unde et tempus est numerus motus.

3. Ad tertium dicendum quod æternitas dicitur tota non quia habet partes sed inquantum nihil ei deest.

4. Ad quartum dicendum quod sicut Deus cum sit incorporeus nominibus rerum corporalium metaphorice in scripturis nominatur, sic æternitas simul existens nominibus temporalibus successivis.

5. Ad quintum dicendum quod in tempore est duo considerare, scilicet ipsum tempus quod est successivum, et nunc temporis quod est imperfectum. Dicit ergo tota simul ad removendum tempus, et perfecta ad excludendum nunc temporis.

6. Ad sextum dicendum quod illud quod possidetur firmiter et quiete habetur. Ad designandum ergo immutabilitatem et indeficientiam æternitatis usus est nomine possessionis.

---

[*]Leonine adds *aut finem,* cannot have either beginning or end.
[5]cf Aristotle, *Physics* IV, 11. 220a25
[6]*Physics* IV, 12. 221b28

is merely the *numbering of before and after in change*.[5] For in any change there is successiveness, one part coming after another, and by numbering the antecedent and consequent parts of change there arises the notion of time, which is simply this numberedness of before and after in change. Now something lacking change and never varying its mode of existence will not display a before and after. So just as numbering antecedent and consequent in change produces the notion of time, so awareness of invariability in something altogether free from change produces the notion of eternity. A further point: time is said to measure things which begin and end in time, as Aristotle points out,[6] and this is because one can assign a beginning and end to any changing thing. But things altogether unchangeable cannot have a beginning any more than they can display successiveness.

So two things characterize eternity. First, anything existing in eternity is *unending*, that is to say, lacks both beginning and end (for both may be regarded as ends). Secondly, eternity itself exists as an *instantaneous whole* lacking successiveness.

Hence: 1. We often use negations to define simple things, as when we say that a point has no parts. Now this is not because they are negative in their essential nature, but because our mind first of all grasps composite things, and cannot come to know simple things except by denying compositeness of them.

2. In point of fact, that which is eternal is not only existent but living. Now living includes in a way activity, which existence does not. And flow of duration is more apparent in activity than in existence; time, for example, is a numbering of change.

3. Eternity is called whole, not because it has parts, but because nothing is lacking to it.

4. Just as Scripture describes God metaphorically in bodily terms, although he is not a body, so it describes eternity in temporal and successive terms although eternity exists instantaneously.

5. There are two things to be noted about time, namely, that time itself is successive, and that an instant of time is imperfect.[b] To deny that eternity is time Boëthius uses 'instantaneously whole'; to deny temporal instantaneity the word 'perfect'.

6. To possess something is to hold it firmly and immovably. To signify then the unchangeableness and constancy of eternity, we use the word 'possession'.

---

[b]That time is successive means that as a whole it is not actual; that an instant of time is imperfect means that any actualization of time is momentary and not whole.

articulus 2. utrum Deus sit æternus

AD SECUNDUM sic proceditur:[1] 1. Videtur quod Deus non sit æternus. Nihil enim factum potest dici de Deo. Sed æternitas est aliquid factum, dicit enim Boëtius quod *nunc fluens facit tempus, nunc stans facit æternitatem*,[2] et Augustinus dicit in *libro Octaginta Trium Quæst.* quod *Deus est auctor æternitatis*.[3] Ergo Deus non est æternus.

2. Præterea, quod est ante æternitatem et post æternitatem non mensuratur æternitate. Sed Deus est ante æternitatem ut dicitur in *libro de Causis*,[4] et post æternitatem, dicitur enim *Exod.* xv quod *Dominus regnabit in æternum et ultra*.[5] Ergo esse æternum non convenit Deo.

3. Præterea, æternitas mensura quædam est. Sed Deo non convenit esse mensuratum. Ergo non competit ei esse æternum.

4. Præterea, in æternitate non est præsens, præteritum vel futurum, cum sit tota simul, ut dictum est.[6] Sed de Deo dicuntur in scripturis verba præsentis temporis, præteriti vel futuri. Ergo Deus non est æternus.

SED CONTRA est quod dicit Athanasius: *Æternus Pater, æternus Filius, æternus Spiritus Sanctus*.[7]

RESPONSIO: Dicendum quod ratio æternitatis consequitur immutabilitatem, sicut ratio temporis consequitur motum, ut ex dictis patet.[8] Unde cum Deus sit maxime immutabilis sibi maxime competit esse æternum. Nec solum est æternus sed est sua æternitas, cum tamen nulla alia res sit sua duratio, quia non est suum esse. Deus autem est suum esse uniforme, unde sicut est sua essentia ita est sua æternitas.

1. Ad primum ergo dicendum quod nunc stans dicitur facere æternitatem secundum nostram apprehensionem. Sicut enim causatur in nobis apprehensio temporis eo quod apprehendimus fluxum ipsius nunc, ita causatur in nobis apprehensio æternitatis inquantum apprehendimus nunc stans. Quod autem dicit Augustinus quod *Deus est auctor æternitatis* intelligitur de æternitate participata, eo enim modo communicat Deus suam æternitatem aliquibus quo et suam immutabilitatem.

2. Et per hoc patet solutio ad secundum. Nam Deus dicitur esse ante æternitatem prout participatur a substantiis immaterialibus. Unde et ibidem dicitur quod *intelligentia parificatur æternitati*. Quod autem dicitur in *Exodo, Dominus regnabit in æternum et ultra*, sciendum quod æternum accipitur ibi pro sæculo sicut habet alia translatio. Sic igitur dicitur quod Deus

---

[1]cf Ia. 13, 1 ad 3. Also I *Sent.* 19, 2, 1. *CG* I, 15. *Compendium Theol.* 5, 7 and 8
[2]*De Trinitate* IV. PL 64, 1253   [3]*Liber 83 Quæst.* 23. PL 40, 16
[4]*De Causis* 2. ed. Bardenhewer 165, 4   [5]*Exodus* 15, 18   [6]cf Ia. 10, 1
[7]*Athanasian Creed.* Denzinger 39   [8]cf Ia. 10, 1

article 2. is God eternal?

THE SECOND POINT:[1] 1. God, it seems, is not eternal. For one cannot ascribe to God something produced. Now eternity is produced, for Boëthius says that *the flowing instant produces time and the abiding instant eternity*,[2] whilst Augustine says that *God is the source of eternity*.[3] So God is not eternal.

2. Moreover, eternity cannot measure what exists before and after eternity. Now, according to the *book of Causes*, God exists before eternity,[4] and according to *Exodus*, where we read that *the Lord will reign to eternity and beyond*,[5] he also exists after eternity. So eternity cannot be ascribed to God.

3. Moreover, eternity is a sort of measure. But one cannot measure God. One cannot therefore ascribe eternity to him.

4. Moreover, present, past and future do not exist in eternity, which, as we have said, is instantaneously whole.[6] But the Scriptures use verbs in the present, past and future tenses, when talking of God. So God is not eternal.

ON THE OTHER HAND the *Athanasian Creed* proclaims: *Eternal the Father, eternal the Son, eternal the Holy Ghost.*[7]

REPLY: We have shown already that the notion of eternity derives from unchangeableness in the same way that the notion of time derives from change.[8] Eternity therefore principally belongs to God, who is utterly unchangeable. Not only that, but God is his own eternity, whereas other things, not being their own existence, are not their own duration. God, however, is his own invariable existence, and so is identical with his own eternity just as he is identical with his own nature.

Hence: 1. The abiding instant is said to produce eternity according to our way of conceiving the situation. For just as we become aware of time by becoming aware of the flowing instant, so we grasp the idea of eternity by grasping the idea of an abiding instant. Augustine's statement that *God is the source of eternity* must be taken to mean eternity as shared, for just as God shares his unchangeableness with other things, so he does his eternity.

2. And this gives us the key to the second difficulty. For God exists before the eternity shared by immaterial substances. Hence in the same passage we read that *intelligence is co-extensive with eternity*.[a] As to the statement in *Exodus* that *the Lord will reign to eternity and beyond* one must realize that 'eternity' is here a synonym for 'ages', the word used by

---

[a] The background to this statement is to be found in the neo-Platonist hierarchy of beings emanating from a supreme being, which was presupposed by the author of the *De Causis*. 'Intelligence' here stands for an immaterial substance lower in the order of emanations than God. If eternity is defined as the duration in which the intelligence exists, then God must be prior to eternity in this sense.

regnat ultra æternum quia durat ultra quodcumque sæculum, idest ultra quamcumque durationem datam; nihil est enim aliud sæculum quam periodus cujuslibet rei ut dicitur in libro de Cælo.[9] Vel dicitur etiam ultra æternum regnare quia si etiam aliquid aliud semper esset, ut motus cæli secundum quosdam philosophos, tamen Dominus ultra regnat inquantum ejus regnum est tota simul.

3. Ad tertium dicendum quod æternitas non est aliud quam ipse Deus. Unde non dicitur Deus æternus quasi sit aliquo alio* mensuratus, sed accipitur ibi ratio mensuræ secundum apprehensionem nostram tantum.

4. Ad quartum dicendum quod verba diversorum temporum attribuuntur Deo inquantum ejus æternitas omnia tempora includit, non ita quod ipse varietur per præsens, præteritum et futurum.

articulus 3. utrum esse æternum sit proprium Dei

AD TERTIUM sic proceditur:[1] 1. Videtur quod esse æternum non sit soli Deo proprium. Dicitur enim Danielis xii *qui ad justitiam erudiunt multos erunt quasi stellæ in perpetuas æternitates.*[2] Non autem essent plures æternitates si solus Deus esset æternus. Non igitur solus Deus est æternus.

2. Præterea, *Matth.* xxv dicitur: *Ite maledicti in ignem æternum.*[3] Non igitur solus Deus est æternus.

3. Præterea, omne necessarium est æternum. Sed multa sunt necessaria; sicut omnia principia demonstrationis et omnes propositiones demonstrativæ. Ergo non solus Deus est æternus.

SED CONTRA est quod dicit Hieronymus† ad Marcellam:[4] *Deus solus est qui exordium non habet.* Quidquid autem exordium habet non est æternum. Solus ergo Deus est æternus.

RESPONSIO: Dicendum quod æternitas vere et proprie in solo Deo est, quia æternitas immutabilitatem consequitur ut ex dictis patet,[5] solus autem Deus est omnino immutabilis, ut superius est ostensum.[6] Secundum tamen quod aliqua ab ipso immutabilitatem percipiunt secundum hoc aliqua ejus æternitatem participant. Quædam ergo quantum ad hoc immutabilitatem sortiuntur a Deo quod nunquam esse desinunt, et secundum hoc

---

*Leonine *modo*, his being measured in any way.
†mss: *Augustinus*, Augustine.

[9]*De Cælo et Mundo* I, 9. 279a23
[1]cf I *Sent.* 8, 2, 2. IV *Sent.* 49, 1, 2 (3a) ad 3. *In De div. nom.* 10, *lect.* 3. *In De causis, lect.* 2. *Quodlibet* X, 2, 1   [2]*Daniel* 12, 3   [3]*Matthew* 25, 41
[4]*Epistola 15* (Letter to Damasus). PL 22, 357   [5]cf Ia. 10, 1   [6]cf Ia. 9, 2

another translation. So that God is said to reign beyond eternity because he outlasts all ages, outlasts, that is to say, any given duration; for, as Aristotle says, an age is nothing more than the period of a thing's life.[9] Or one can also say that God reigns beyond eternity, because even if something else were to exist for ever, as certain philosophers believed the rotation of the heavens to do, the Lord would still reign beyond it, because his reign is instantaneously whole.

3. Eternity and God are the same thing. So calling him eternal does not imply his being measured by something extrinsic; the notion of measurement arises only in our way of conceiving the situation.

4. Verbs of different tenses are used of God, not as though he varied from present to past to future, but because his eternity comprehends all phases of time.

article 3. does eternity belong to God alone?

THE THIRD POINT:[1] 1. Eternity does not seem to belong to God alone. For Daniel prophesies that *they who turn many to righteousness shall be as the stars in perpetual eternities*.[2] Now if God alone was eternal there could be only one eternity. So not only God is eternal.

2. Moreover, we read in *Matthew*: *Depart, ye cursed, into eternal fire*.[3] Not only God then is eternal.

3. Moreover, what is necessarily so is eternally so. Now there are many necessary things: the first principles of demonstration, for example, and all propositions employed in demonstrations.[a] So not only God is eternal.

ON THE OTHER HAND Jerome writes to Marcella that *God alone has no beginning*.[4] Now whatever has a beginning is not eternal. So God alone is eternal.

REPLY: Eternity, in the true and proper sense, belongs to God alone, for eternity, we said, follows upon unchangeableness,[5] and God alone, as we showed, is altogether unchangeable.[6] Certain things, however, receive from God a share in his unchangeableness, and to that extent they share in his eternity. The unchangeableness some things obtain from God is such that they never cease existing, and so the earth, as we read in Ecclesiastes,

---

[a]Either employed in demonstrations to help demonstrate other propositions, as the form of the Latin adjective would suggest, or employed in demonstrations as being the propositions demonstrated, as the sense of the sentence would seem to tolerate more easily.

dicitur *Eccles.* I de terra quod *in æternum stat.*[7] Quædam etiam æterna in scripturis dicuntur propter diuturnitatem durationis licet coruptibilia sint, sicut in psalmo dicuntur *montes æterni*,[8] et *Deut* xxxiii etiam dicitur: *de pomis collium æternorum.*[9] Quædam autem amplius participant de ratione æternitatis inquantum habent intransmutabilitatem vel secundum esse vel ulterius secundum operationem sicut angeli et beati qui Verbo fruuntur. Quia quantum ad illam visionem Verbi non sunt in sanctis *volubiles cogitationes* ut dicit Augustinus xv *de Trin.*[10] Unde et videntes Deum dicuntur habere vitam æternam, secundum illud *Ioann.* xvii: *hæc est vita æterna ut cognoscant, etc.*[11]

1. Ad primum ergo dicendum quod dicuntur multæ æternitates secundum quod sunt multi participantes æternitatem ex ipsa Dei contemplatione.

2. Ad secundum dicendum quod ignis inferni dicitur æternus propter interminabilitatem tantum. Est tamen in pœnis eorum transmutatio secundum illud *Iob* xxiv: *ad nimium calorem transibunt ab aquis nivium.*[12] Unde in inferno non est vera æternitas sed magis tempus; unde illud psalmi: *erit tempus eorum in sæcula.*[13]

3. Ad tertium dicendum quod necessarium significat quemdam modum veritatis. Verum autem secundum Philosophum VI Metaph. est in intellectu.[14] Secundum hoc igitur vera necessaria sunt æterna quia sunt in intellectu æterno, qui est intellectus divinus solus. Unde non sequitur quod aliquid extra Deum sit æternum.

articulus 4. utrum æternitas differat ab (ævo et) tempore

AD QUARTUM sic proceditur:[1] 1. Videtur quod æternitas non sit aliud a tempore. Impossibile est enim duas esse mensuras durationis simul nisi una sit pars alterius; non enim sunt simul duo dies vel duæ horæ, sed dies et hora sunt simul quia hora est pars diei. Sed æternitas et tempus sunt simul, quorum utrumque quodammodo mensuram durationis importat. Cum igitur æternitas non sit pars temporis quia æternitas excedit tempus et includit ipsum, videtur quod tempus sit pars æternitatis et non sit aliud ab æternitate.

2. Præterea, secundum Philosophum in IV *Phys.* nunc temporis manet idem in toto tempore.[2] Sed hoc videtur constituere rationem æternitatis quod sit idem indivisibiliter se habens in toto decursu temporis. Ergo æternitas est nunc temporis. Sed nunc temporis non est aliud secundum substantiam a tempore. Ergo æternitas non est aliud secundum substantiam a tempore.

---

[7]*Ecclesiastes* I, 4   [8]*Psalm* 75 (76), 5   [9]*Deuteronomy* 33, 15
[10]*De Trinitate* xv, 16. PL 42, 1079   [11]*John* 17, 3   [12]*Job* 24, 19
[13]*Psalm* 80 (81), 16   [14]*Metaphysics* VI, 4. 1027b27

abideth eternally.[7] Other things though perishable are called in the Scriptures eternal because they endure for a long time, and so the psalm sings of *eternal mountains*[8] and *Deuteronomy* of *the fruits of the eternal hills*.[9] Yet others share eternity still more fully, possessing unchangeableness of existence and even of activity, and such are the angels and saints enjoying sight of the divine Word.[b] For, as Augustine says, *eddying thoughts* have no part in the saints' vision of the Word.[10] And this is why those who see God are said to have eternal life, as in *John: this is eternal life to know thee etc.*[11]

Hence: 1. One talks of many eternities because many are the things sharing God's eternity by contemplating him.

2. The fire of hell is called eternal only because it is unending. But the pains of hell include change[c], for we read in *Job* that *they shall pass from waters of snow to excessive heat*.[12] In hell then there is no true eternity, but rather time; hence the psalm saying *their time shall last for ever*.[13]

3. Necessity is a mode of truth. Now truth, according to Aristotle, resides in the mind.[14] So necessary truths are eternal only if they exist in the eternal mind, which is nothing other than God's mind. So it does not follow that anything outside God is eternal.

article 4. is eternity different from (the 'æon' and) time?

THE FOURTH POINT:[1] 1. Eternity seems no different from time. For two measures of duration can only be simultaneous, if one is part of the other; thus two days or hours cannot occur simultaneously, but an hour and a day can for an hour is part of a day. Now eternity and time, both signifying some sort of measure of duration, exist together. So since eternity is not part of time but exceeds and comprehends it, time must seemingly be a part of eternity and identical with it.

2. Moreover, according to Aristotle, the 'now' persists unchanged throughout time.[2] But the nature of eternity seems to consist precisely in remaining unbrokenly the same throughout the whole course of time. Eternity then is identical with the 'now' of time. And since the 'now' of time is in substance identical with time itself, so must eternity be.[a]

---

[1]cf 1a2æ. 31, 2. Also I *Sent.* 8, 2, 2; 19, 2, 1. *De potentia* III, 14 ad 9. *In De div. nom.* 10, *lect.* 3
[2]*Physics* IV, 11. 219b11; 13. 222a15
[b]The joy of the saints in heaven is the vision of God face to face. Since the Word, the second person of the divine Trinity, is the self-revelation of God, the vision is often referred to, especially by St Augustine, as the vision of the Word.
[c]Or alternatively one could translate 'But their pains do change'.
[a]The 'now' of time is the part of time that is actual—the present. As such it is identical with time, in so far as time is actual.

3. Præterea, sicut mensura primi motus est mensura omnium motuum, ut dicitur in IV Phys.,[3] ita videtur quod mensura primi esse sit mensura omnis esse. Sed æternitas est mensura primi esse quod est esse divinum. Ergo æternitas est mensura omnis esse. Sed esse rerum corruptibilium mensuratur tempore. Ergo tempus vel est æternitas vel aliquid æternitatis.

SED CONTRA est quod æternitas est tota simul, in tempore autem est prius et posterius. Ergo tempus et æternitas non sunt idem.

RESPONSIO: Dicendum quod manifestum est tempus et æternitatem non esse idem. Sed hujus diversitatis rationem quidam assignaverunt ex hoc quod æternitas caret principio et fine, tempus autem habet principium et finem. Sed hæc est differentia per accidens et non per se. Quia, dato quod tempus semper fuerit et semper futurum sit secundum positionem eorum qui motum cæli ponunt sempiternum, adhuc remanebit differentia inter æternitatem et tempus ut dicit Boëtius in libro *de Consolatione* ex hoc quod æternitas est tota simul quod tempori non convenit,[4] quia æternitas est mensura esse permanentis, tempus vero est mensura motus.

Si tamen prædicta differentia attendatur quantum ad mensurata et non quantum ad mensuras sic habet aliquam rationem, quia solum illud mensuratur tempore quod habet principium et finem in tempore, ut dicitur in IV *Phys.*[5] Unde si motus cæli semper duraret tempus non mensuraret ipsum secundum suam totam durationem cum infinitum non sit mensurabile, sed mensuraret quamlibet circulationem quæ habet principium et finem in tempore.

Potest tamen et aliam rationem habere ex parte istarum mensurarum si accipiatur finis et principium in potentia. Quia etiam dato quod tempus semper duret tamen possibile est signare in ipso et principium et finem, accipiendo aliquas partes ipsius, sicut dicimus principium et finem diei vel anni, quod non contingit in æternitate.

Sed istæ differentiæ consequuntur eam quæ est per se et primo differentiam, per hoc quod æternitas est tota simul, non autem tempus.

1. Ad primum ergo dicendum quod ratio illa procederet si tempus et æternitas essent mensuræ unius generis, quod patet esse falsum, ex his quorum est tempus et æternitas.

2. Ad secundum dicendum quod nunc temporis est idem subjecto in toto tempore sed differens ratione, eo quod sicut tempus respondet motui, ita nunc temporis respondet mobili. Mobile autem est idem subjecto in toto decursu temporis sed differt ratione inquantum est hic et ibi. Et ista

---

[3]*Physics* IV, 14. 223b18
[4]*De Consolatione* V, prosa 6. PL 63, 859. Boëthius cites Aristotle by name as the author holding that the heavens rotate eternally   [5]*Physics* IV, 12. 221b28

3. Moreover, Aristotle says that the measure of the most fundamental change measures all change;[3] in the same way it seems that the measure of the most fundamental existence should measure all existence. Now eternity measures divine existence which is the most fundamental existence, and so measures all existence. The existence of perishable things, however, is measured by time. So time is either eternity or a part of eternity.

ON THE OTHER HAND eternity is an instantaneous whole, whilst in time there is before and after. So time and eternity differ.

REPLY: Time and eternity clearly differ. But certain people make the difference consist in time having a beginning and an end whilst eternity has neither. Now this is an accidental and not an intrinsic difference. For even if time had always existed and will always exist, as those hold who think the heavens will rotate for ever, there will still remain the difference Boëthius points out between time and eternity: that eternity is an instantaneous whole whilst time is not,[4] eternity measuring abiding existence and time measuring change.

If, however, the suggested difference applies to the things measured rather than to the measures themselves, there is some ground for it; for, as Aristotle says, time measures only things beginning and ending in time.[5] So, even though the heavens rotated for ever, time would measure, not the whole duration of the movement, since the infinite is immeasurable, but each revolution separately as it began and ended in time.

Or again the suggested difference could apply validly to the measures themselves, if we were to talk of potential beginnings and ends. For even though time lasted for ever, it would be possible to mark off beginnings and ends in it by dividing it into parts, and so in fact we talk of the beginning and end of a day or year; and this cannot happen in eternity.

However, these differences are all consequent upon the primary and intrinsic difference that eternity exists as an instantaneous whole, whereas time does not.

Hence: 1. This would be a valid argument if time and eternity were measures of the same type, which clearly they are not if one considers the different things they measure.

2. The 'now' remains unchanged in substance throughout time, but takes on different forms, because, just as time corresponds to movement, so the 'now' corresponds to the thing moving. Now the thing moving remains in substance the same throughout the course of time, but it differs in position, first here and then there, its movement consisting in the

alteratio ejus est motus. Similiter fluxus ipsius nunc secundum quod alternatur ratione est tempus. Æternitas autem manet eadem et subjecto et ratione. Unde æternitas non est idem quod nunc temporis.

3. Ad tertium dicendum quod sicut æternitas est propria mensura ipsius esse, ita tempus est propria mensura motus. Unde secundum quod aliquod esse recedit a permanentia essendi et subditur transmutationi recedit ab æternitate et subditur tempori. Esse ergo rerum corruptibilium quia est transmutabile non mensuratur æternitate sed tempore. Tempus enim mensurat non solum quæ transmutantur in actu sed quæ sunt transmutabilia. Unde non solum mensurat motum sed etiam quietem quæ est ejus quod natum est moveri et non movetur.

articulus 5. de differentia ævi et temporis

AD QUINTUM sic proceditur:[1] 1. Videtur quod ævum non sit aliud a tempore. Dicit enim Augustinus VIII *super Gen. ad litt.* quod *Deus movet creaturam spiritualem per tempus.*[2] Sed ævum dicitur esse mensura spiritualium substantiarum. Ergo tempus non differt ab ævo.

2. Præterea, de ratione temporis est quod habeat prius et posterius, de ratione vero æternitatis est quod sit tota simul, ut dictum est.[3] Sed ævum non est æternitas, dicitur enim *Ecclus.* 1. quod sapientia æterna *est ante ævum.*[4] Ergo non est totum simul, sed habet prius et posterius, et ita est tempus.

3. Præterea, si in ævo non est prius et posterius sequitur quod in æviternis non differat esse vel fuisse vel futurum esse. Cum igitur sit impossibile æviterna non fuisse sequitur quod impossibile sit ea non futura esse. Quod falsum est cum Deus possit ea reducere in nihilum.

4. Præterea, cum duratio æviternorum sit infinita ex parte post, si ævum sit tota simul sequitur quod aliquod creatum sit infinitum in actu, quod est impossibile. Non igitur ævum differt a tempore.

SED CONTRA est quod dicit Boëtius: *qui tempus ab ævo ire jubes.*[5]

---

[1]cf 1a. 61, 2 ad 2; 63, 6 ad 4; 85, 4 ad 1; 1a2æ. 113, 7 ad 5. Also I *Sent.* 8, 2, 2; 19, 2, 1. II *Sent.* 2, 1, 1. *Quodlibet* X, 2, 1

[2]*Super Genesim ad litt.* VIII, 20 and 22. PL 34, 388–9

[3]cf 1a. 10, 1

[4]*Ecclesiasticus* 1, 1

[5]*De Consolatione* III, metra 9. PL 63, 758

[b]The substance of this reply is to be found in Aristotle, *Physics* IV, 11. 219b23. Although, as the previous note says, time in so far as it is actual is identical with the present 'now', nevertheless the present 'now' is a perpetually different part of

change of position. In the same way time consists in the flow of the 'now' changing its form.[b] But eternity remains unchanged both in substance and in form. Eternity therefore differs from the 'now' of time.

3. Just as eternity is properly the measure of existence as such, so time is properly the measure of change. In so far then as any existence falls short of permanence in its existing and is subject to change, so will it fall short of eternity and be subjected to time. So the existence of perishable things, being changeable, is measured by time and not by eternity. For time measures not only the actually changing but also the potentially changeable. It measures, therefore, not only movement but also rest, the state of the movable when not moving.

article 5. the difference between the æon and time

THE FIFTH POINT:[1] 1. 'Æon' seems to be another name for time. For the æon is defined as the measure of immaterial substances. Now Augustine talks of *God moving immaterial creatures through time*.[2] Time and the æon are therefore the same.[a]

2. Moreover, according to their definitions, as we saw, time possesses before and after, whilst eternity is instantaneously whole.[3] Now the æon is not eternity, for according to *Ecclesiasticus* the eternal *wisdom exists prior to the æon*.[4] The æon therefore is not instantaneously whole but possesses a before and after, which makes it the same as time.

3. Moreover, were the æon to lack before and after, then, for things measured by the æon, existing in the present or past would be the same as existing in the future. Such things, consequently, since they cannot not have existed in the past, would not be able not to exist in the future. And this is false, for they can be annihilated by God.

4. Moreover, things in the æon are going to last into an unlimited future. But if the whole æon exists at an instant, the limitlessness of such created things is already actual, which is impossible. So the æon is no different from time.

ON THE OTHER HAND Boëthius writes of him who orders time to go from the æon.[5]

---

time viewed as a potential whole. Aristotle's way of saying this is that the now is perpetually changing in form or in character.

[a]The 'æon' is a term derived by a different route from the same word as 'eternity'. In the early years of Greek philosophy it was in use as a measure of duration, which became distinct from eternity strictly so-called. Lucretius, the early Gnostics, and the neo-Platonists all make use of the term. How St Thomas understands it is clear from the text.

RESPONSIO: Dicendum quod ævum differt a tempore et æternitate, medium existens inter illa.

Sed horum differentiam aliqui sic assignant dicentes quod æternitas principio et fine caret, ævum habet principium sed non habet finem, tempus autem habet principium et finem. Sed hæc differentia est per accidens sicut supra dictum est;[6] quia si etiam semper æviterna fuissent et semper futura essent ut aliqui ponunt, vel etiamsi quandoque deficerent quod Deo possibile esset, adhuc ævum distingueretur ab æternitate et tempore.

Alii vero assignant differentiam inter hæc tria per hoc quod æternitas non habet prius et posterius, tempus autem habet prius et posterius cum innovatione et veteratione, ævum autem habet prius et posterius sine innovatione et veteratione. Sed hæc positio implicat contradictoria. Quod quidem manifeste apparet si innovatio et veteratio referantur ad ipsam mensuram. Cum enim prius et posterius durationis non possint esse simul, si ævum habet prius et posterius oportet quod priori parte ævi recedente posterior de novo adveniat, et sic erit innovatio in ipso ævo sicut est in tempore. Si vero referantur ad mensurata adhuc sequitur inconveniens. Ex hoc enim res temporalis inveteratur tempore quod habet esse transmutabile, et ex transmutabilitate mensurati est prius et posterius in tempore,* ut patet ex IV Phys.[7] Si igitur ipsum æviternum non sit inveterabile nec innovabile hoc erit quia esse ejus est intransmutabile. Mensura ergo ejus non habebit prius et posterius.

Est ergo dicendum quod, cum æternitas sit mensura esse permanentis, secundum quod aliquid recedit a permanentia essendi secundum hoc recedit ab æternitate. Quædam autem sic recedunt a permanentia essendi quod esse eorum est subiectum transmutationis vel in transmutatione consistit, et hujusmodi mensurantur tempore, sicut omnis motus et etiam esse omnium corruptibilium. Quædam vero recedunt minus a permanentia essendi quia esse eorum nec in transmutatione consistit nec est subjectum transmutationi, tamen habent transmutationem adjunctam vel in actu vel in potentia. Sicut patet in corporibus cælestibus quorum esse substantiale est intransmutabile, tamen esse intransmutabile habent cum transmutabilitate secundum locum. Et similiter patet de angelis quod habent esse intransmutabile cum transmutabilitate secundum electionem quantum ad eorum naturam pertinet, et cum transmutabilitate intelligentiarum et affectionum et locorum suo modo. Et ideo hujusmodi mensurantur

---

*Leonine mensura, the before and after of the measure derives.
[6]cf Ia. 10, 4   [7]Physics IV, 12. 221a31 and 220b9
[b]The first opinion mentioned in this article was that of Alexander of Hales (d. 1245); the second that of St Bonaventure (d. 1274).

REPLY: The æon is neither time nor eternity, but lies somewhere between the two.

Certain people express the difference by saying that eternity has neither beginning nor end, the æon has a beginning but no end, whilst time has both beginning and end. But this, as we have seen, is an accidental difference;[6] for even if things in the æon always had existed and always will exist, as some hold, or even if God were to bring them to an end sometime, as he is able to do, the æon would still be distinguishable from both eternity and time.

Others express the difference between the three measures by saying that eternity does not have before and after, time has before and after and also newness and oldness, whilst the æon has before and after but not newness and oldness. But this is self-contradictory. If it is newness and oldness of the measure itself that is meant, the contradiction is obvious. For the before and after of duration cannot be instantaneous; if then the æon has a before and after, as each fore-part moves away an after-part must become newly present, and so there will be newness in the æon just as there is in time. If newness and oldness of the things measured is meant, an inconsistency still arises. For it is due to their changeable existence that temporal things age with time, and, as Aristotle shows, from this changeableness in the thing measured the before and after of time derives.[7] So that if things in the æon cannot be new or old, this will be because their existence is unchangeable. And in that case the measure itself will have no before and after.[b]

We therefore say that as eternity is the measure of abiding existence, the further a thing falls short of abiding existence, the further it falls short of eternity. Now some things fall far enough short of abiding existence to have an existence consisting in or subject to change, and such things time measures; all movements, for example, and in perishable things, even their existence. Other things do not fall so far short of abiding existence that their existence consists in or is subject to change, but nonetheless it is accompanied by some actual or potential change. An example is the heavenly bodies which, whilst existing unchanged in substance, combine with this unchangeable existence a changeableness of place. And for another example, take angels who combine unchangeable existence with changeability of choice at the natural level, and with changeability of thoughts, affections and, in their own fashion, places.[c] These sorts of

---

[c]The heavenly bodies were thought to be free from generation and corruption and the sort of change of quality which occurs in the sublunar world. But they changed their place, of course, in the heavens. The angels, though not in place like bodies because possessing no dimensions, are nevertheless conceived of as in causal contact with bodies which are in place and which change place.

ævo quod est medium inter æternitatem et tempus. Esse autem quod mensuratur æternitate nec est mutabile nec mutabilitati adjunctum. Sic ergo tempus habet prius et posterius, ævum autem non habet in se prius et posterius sed ei conjungi possunt, æternitas autem neque habet prius et posterius neque ea compatitur.

1. Ad primum ergo dicendum quod creaturæ spirituales quantum ad affectiones et intelligentias in quibus est successio mensurantur tempore. Unde et Augustinus ibidem dicit quod per tempus moveri est per affectiones moveri. Quantum vero ad eorum esse naturale mensurantur ævo. Sed quantum ad visionem gloriæ participant æternitatem.

2. Ad secundum dicendum quod ævum est totum simul, non tamen est æternitas, quia compatitur secum prius et posterius.

3. Ad tertium dicendum quod in ipso esse angeli in se considerato non est differentia præteriti et futuri, sed solum secundum adjunctas mutationes. Sed quod dicimus angelum esse vel fuisse vel futurum esse differt secundum acceptionem intellectus nostri, qui accipit esse angeli per comparationem ad diversas partes temporis. Et cum dicit angelum esse vel fuisse supponit aliquid cum quo ejus oppositum non subditur divinæ potentiæ, cum vero dicit futurum esse nondum supponit aliquid. Unde cum esse et non esse angeli subsit divinæ potentiæ absolute considerando, potest Deus facere quod esse angeli non sit futurum, tamen non potest facere quod non sit dum est vel quod non fuerit postquam fuit.

4. Ad quartum dicendum quod duratio ævi est infinita quia non finitur tempore. Sic autem esse aliquod creatum infinitum, quia non finitum puodam alio, non est inconveniens.

articulus 6. utrum sit unum ævum tantum

AD SEXTUM sic proceditur:[1] 1. Videtur quod non sit tantum unum ævum. Dicitur enim in apocryphis *Esdræ* quod *majestas et potestas ævorum est apud te, Domine.*[2]

2. Præterea, diversorum generum sunt diversæ mensuræ. Sed quædam æviterna sunt in genere corporum, scilicet corpora cælestia, quædam vero sunt spirituales substantiæ, scilicet angeli. Non ergo est unum ævum tantum.

3. Præterea, cum ævum sit nomen durationis, quorum est unum ævum est una duratio. Sed non omnium æviternorum est una duratio, quia quædam post alia esse incipiunt ut maxime patet in animabus humanis. Non est ergo unum ævum tantum.

---

[1]cf Ia. 66, 4 ad 3; 3a. 75, 7 ad 1. Also II *Sent.* 2, 1, 2. *Quodlibet* V, 4, 1
[2]III (I) Ezra 4, 40

thing then are measured by the æon, which lies somewhere between eternity and time. Eternity itself measures any existence which is both unchangeable and unaccompanied by changeableness. To sum up, then, time has a before and after, the æon has no before and after in itself but can be accompanied by it, whilst eternity neither possesses a before and after nor can co-exist with it.

Hence: 1. Inasmuch as their thoughts and affections display successiveness, immaterial creatures are measured by time. And so Augustine says in the same passage that to be moved through time is to be moved in affections. But as regards their natural existence they are measured by the æon; and inasmuch as they contemplate God's glory they share in eternity.

2. Although the æon is instantaneously whole, it differs from eternity in being able to co-exist with before and after.

3. There is no difference of past and future in an angel's existence as such, but only consequent upon accompanying changes. But we distinguish between angels existing or having existed or existing in the future, because we talk in the way we think, and we think of the existence of angels by relating it to different periods of time. Now in talking of angels existing or having existed, we incorporate a supposition such that the opposite of what we say is no longer within God's power; but in talking of them existing in the future, we as yet make no such supposition. Absolutely speaking, that angels should or should not exist is within God's power, so God can cause an angel not to exist in future, even if he cannot cause it not to exist while it exists, or not to have existed when it already has.

4. The duration of the æon is unlimited in the sense of not being limited by time. But there is no difficulty about something created being unlimited, if we mean that it is not limited by some particular other thing.

article 6. is there only one æon?

THE SIXTH POINT:[1] 1. More than one æon exists, it would seem. For we read in the apocryphal books of *Ezra* that *the majesty and power of the æons is with thee, O Lord.*[2]

2. Moreover, each kind of thing has its own measure. Now some things measured by an æon are bodies, namely the heavenly bodies, and some, namely the angels, are immaterial substances. There is therefore more than one æon.

3. Moreover, if 'æon' names a kind of duration, everything in one æon will have the same duration. Now not all things measured by an æon have the same duration, for some come into existence later than others; the clearest case is that of human souls. So there is not only one æon.

4. Præterea, ea quæ non dependent ab invicem non videntur habere unam mensuram durationis. Propter hoc enim omnium temporalium videtur esse unum tempus quia omnium* quodammodo est causa primus motus qui primo tempore mensuratur. Sed æviterna non dependent ab invicem.† Non ergo est unum ævum tantum.

SED CONTRA, ævum est simplicius tempore et propinquius se habet ad æternitatem. Sed tempus est unum tantum. Ergo multo magis ævum.

RESPONSIO: Dicendum quod circa hoc est duplex opinio, quidam enim dicunt quod est unum ævum tantum, quidam autem quod multa. Quid autem horum verius sit, oportet considerare ex causa unitatis temporis, in cognitionem enim spiritualium per corporalia devenimus.

Dicunt enim quidam quod est unus tempus omnium temporalium propter hoc quod est unus numerus omnium numeratorum, cum *tempus sit numerus* secundum Philosophum.³ Sed hoc non sufficit, quia tempus non est numerus ut abstractus extra numeratum sed ut in numerato existens; alioquin non esset continuus, quia decem ulnæ panni continuitatem habent non ex numero sed ex numerato. Numerus autem in numerato existens non est idem omnium sed diversus diversorum.

Unde alii assignant causam unitatis temporis ex unitate æternitatis quæ est principium omnis durationis. Et sic omnes durationes sunt unum si consideretur earum principium, sunt vero multæ si consideretur diversitas eorum quæ recipiunt durationem ex influxu primi principii. Alii vero assignant causam unitatis temporis ex parte materiæ primæ quæ est primum subjectum motus cujus mensura est tempus. Sed neutra assignatio sufficiens videtur, quia ea quæ sunt unum principio vel subjecto, et maxime remoto, non sunt unum simpliciter sed secundum quid.

Est ergo ratio unitatis temporis unitas primi motus secundum quem cum sit simplicissimus omnes alii mensurantur, ut dicitur in x *Meta.*⁴ Sic ergo tempus ad illum motum comparatur non solum ut mensura ad mensuratum sed etiam ut accidens ad subjectum, et sic ab eo recipit unitatem. Ad alios autem motus comparatur solum ut mensura ad mensuratum. Unde secundum eorum multitudinem non multiplicatur, quia una mensura separata multa mensurari possunt.

---

*Leonine adds *motuum*, the cause of every other process.
†Leonine adds *quia unus angelus non est causa alterius*, because one angel does not cause another.
³*Physics* IV, 12. 220b8   ⁴*Metaphysics* X, 1. 1053a8
ᵃThe authors of the opinions cited in the text seem to be as follows. Alexander of Hales (an early thirteenth-century theologian) maintained one æon, whilst St

4. Moreover, things unconnected causally do not seem to have the same measure of duration. Thus, one time measures everything temporal, it seems, because time measures first the most fundamental process in the world, and this process is in a way the cause of everything else. Now things measured by æons are not in causal connection. There is thus more than one æon.

ON THE OTHER HAND the æon is simpler than time, and nearer to eternity. But only one time exists. Still more then is there only one æon.

REPLY: There are two opinions on this point, some people saying that there is only one æon, some that there are many. And to decide which is nearer the truth we must ask ourselves why time is one, for we come to understand the immaterial through the material.

Some derive the unity of time in all temporal things from the unity of a number in numbered things, time being, as Aristotle says, *a numbering*.[3] But this is not enough, for time is not a number abstracted from the things it numbers, but a numberedness existing in the things themselves; otherwise it would lack continuity, just as the continuity of ten yards of cloth derives not from the number but from the thing numbered. Now the numberedness in things differs in different things, and is not the same for all.

Others therefore derive the unity of time from the unity of eternity, the source of all duration. All duration, these people say, is one at source, although multiplied according to the differing things receiving duration from this primary source. Others again derive the unity of time from the unity of ultimate matter, the fundamental subject of the changes time measures. Neither derivation seems adequate, however, for things that are one in source or in subject, especially when these are the distant source and subject, are not one simply speaking, but only one in certain respects.

The true ground of time's unity is therefore the unity of the most fundamental process in the world, by which—since it is the simplest—all other processes are measured, as Aristotle says.[4] Time is not only the measure of this process, but also an accident of it, and so receives unity from it. But time is merely a measure of other processes, and so is not diversified by their diversity, for one measure, when independently existent, can measure many things.[a]

Bonaventure (a Franciscan contemporary of St Thomas) maintained more than one. Themistius (one of the early Aristotelean commentators) based the unity of time on the unity of number; Alexander of Hales on the unity of eternity; and Bonaventure on the unity of matter.

Hoc igitur habito sciendum quod de substantiis spiritualibus duplex fuit opinio. Quidam enim dixerunt quod omnes processerunt a Deo in quadam æqualitate, ut Origenes dixit, vel etiam multæ earum, ut quidam posuerunt. Alii vero dixerunt quod omnes substantiæ spirituales processerunt a Deo quodam gradu et ordine. Et hoc videtur sentire Dionysius qui dicit cap. x *Cæl. Hier.* quod inter substantias spirituales sunt primæ, mediæ et ultimæ, etiam in uno ordine angelorum.[5] Secundum igitur primam opinionem necesse est dicere quod sunt plura æva secundum quod sunt plura æviterna prima æqualia. Secundum autem secundam opinionem oportet dicere quod sit unum ævum tantum, quia cum unumquodque mensuretur simplicissimo sui generis ut dicitur in x *Meta.*,[6] oportet quod esse omnium æviternorum mensuretur per simplicius esse primi æviterni, quod tanto est simplicius quanto prius. Et quia secunda opinio verior est ut infra ostendetur,[7] concedimus ad præsens unum esse ævum tantum.

1. Ad primum ergo dicendum quod ævum aliquando accipitur pro sæculo quod est periodus durationis alicujus rei, et sic dicuntur multa æva sicut multa sæcula.

2. Ad secundum dicendum quod licet corpora cælestia et spiritualia differant in genere naturæ tamen conveniunt in hoc quod habent esse intransmutabile. Et sic mensurantur ævo.

3. Ad tertium dicendum quod nec omnia temporalia simul incipiunt et tamen omnium est unum tempus propter primum quod mensuratur tempore. Et sic omnia æviterna habent unum ævum propter primum, etiamsi non omnia simul incipiunt.

4. Ad quartum dicendum quod ad hoc quod aliqua mensurentur per aliquod unum non requiritur quod illud unum sit causa omnium, sed quod sit simplicius.

---

[5] *De Cælesti Hierarchia* 10, 2. PG 3, 273
[6] *Metaphysics* X, 1. 1052b33   [7] cf Ia. 47, 2; 50, 4

Given this foundation, we must note two opinions concerning immaterial substances. Certain people have held with Origen that they all came out from God equal, or with other thinkers that many of them were equal.[b] Other people have held that all immaterial substances came out from God in a certain order and hierarchy. And this seems to be Dionysius's opinion, who says that among such substances some are first, some intermediate and others last, and this even within one order of angels.[5] Holders of the first opinion then must confess more than one æon, corresponding to the many equally primary substances measured by æons. Holders of the second opinion, however, must confess only one æon, for Aristotle says that the simplest thing in a genus measures the other things,[6] so that the simpler existence of the primary thing in the æon—simpler because more primary—will measure the existence of everything in the æon. And because as we shall see later the second opinion is nearer the truth,[7] we shall here admit only one æon.

Hence: 1. 'Æon' sometimes means age, that is to say the period of a thing's duration; and in this sense we talk of many æons, as of many ages.

2. Although the heavenly bodies differ in nature from immaterial things, both kinds of thing agree in existing unchangeably. And as such they are both measured by the æon.

3. Not all temporal things come into existence together, but all nonetheless are measured by one and the same time as the primary temporal thing. In the same way everything in the æon is measured by the same æon as some primary thing, even if they do not come into existence together.

4. In order for one thing to measure others, it does not have to cause them all, but only to be simpler than them all.

---

[b] St Thomas treats of these opinions later in detail in 1a. 50, 4.

POST PRÆMISSA considerandum est de divina unitate.

Quæstio 11. de unitate Dei

Et circa hoc quæruntur quatuor:

1. utrum unum addat aliquid supra ens,
2. utrum opponantur unum et multa,
3. utrum Deus sit unus,
4. utrum Deus sit maxime unus.

articulus 1. utrum unum addat aliquid supra ens

AD PRIMUM sic proceditur:[1] 1. Videtur quod unum addat aliquid supra ens. Omne enim quod est in aliquo genere determinato se habet ex additione ad ens, quod circuit omnia genera. Sed unum est in aliquo genere determinato, est enim principium numeri qui est species quantitatis. Ergo unum addit aliquid supra ens.

2. Præterea, quod dividit aliquid commune se habet ex additione ad illud. Sed ens dividitur per unum et multa. Ergo unum addit aliquid supra ens.

3. Præterea, si unum non addit supra ens idem esset dicere unum et ens. Sed nugatorie dicitur ens ens. Ergo nugatio esset dicere ens unum, quod falsum est. Addit igitur unum supra ens.

SED CONTRA est quod dicit Dionysius ult. cap. de Div. Nom. *nihil est existentium non participans uno,*[2] quod non esset si unum adderet supra ens, quia contraheret ipsum. Ergo unum non habet se ex additione ad ens.

RESPONSIO: Dicendum quod unum non addit supra ens rem aliquam sed tantum negationem divisionis, unum enim nihil aliud significat quam ens indivisum. Et ex hoc ipso apparet quod unum convertitur cum ente. Nam omne ens aut est simplex aut compositum. Quod autem est simplex est indivisum et actu et potentia. Quod autem est compositum non habet esse quamdiu partes ejus sunt divisæ, sed postquam constituunt et componunt ipsum. Unde manifestum est quod esse cujuslibet rei consistit in indivisione. Et inde est quod unumquodque sicut custodit suum esse ita custodit suam unitatem.

---

[1] cf Ia. 30, 3. Also I *Sent.* 8, 1, 3; 19, 5, I ad 3; 24, 1, 3. *De veritate* I, I; XXI, I. *De potentia* III, 16 ad 3; IX, 7. *Quodlibet* X, I, I. *In Meta.* III, *lect.* 12; IV, *lect.* 2; X, *lect.* 3   [2] *On the Divine Names* 13, 2. PG 3, 977–80

WE MUST FOLLOW what we have so far said with a treatment of the oneness of God.

Question 11. The oneness of God

This question has four points of inquiry:[a]

1. does being one add anything to existing?
2. is being one the opposite of being many?
3. is there one God?
4. is God supremely one?

article 1. does being one add anything to existing?

THE FIRST POINT:[1] 1. Being one seems to add something to existing. For being in some determinate genus adds to existing, in itself common to all genera. Now to be one a thing must be in a determinate genus, for unity initiates number which is a species of the genus quantity. Being one therefore adds something to existing.

2. Moreover, subdivisions of a general concept add something to the general concept itself. Now being is subdivided into being one and being many. Being one adds something therefore to being.

3. Moreover, if being one added nothing to existing, the words 'one' and 'existent' would be synonymous. Now it is tautological to say that what exists is existent. It should therefore be tautological to say that what exists is one, which is not so. Being one must therefore add something to existing.

ON THE OTHER HAND Dionysius says that *nothing exists without being somehow one*.[2] But if being one added something to existing, it would narrow its application, and Dionysius would be wrong. Being one therefore adds nothing to existing.

REPLY: Oneness adds nothing real to any existent thing, but simply denies division of it, for to be one means no more than to exist undivided. And from this it is clear that everything existing is one. For everything existing is either simple or composite. Now simple things are neither actually nor potentially divided, whilst composite things do not exist as long as their constituent parts are divided but only after these parts have come together to compose the thing. Clearly then everything's existence is grounded in indivision. And this is why things guard their unity as they do their existence.

---

[a] See Appendix 12 (9–10).

1. Ad primum igitur dicendum quod quidam putantes idem esse unum quod convertitur cum ente et quod est principium numeri divisi sunt in contrarias positiones. Pythagoras enim et Plato videntes quod unum, quia convertitur cum ente, non addit aliquam rem supra ens sed significat substantiam entis prout est indivisa æstimaverunt sic se habere de uno quod est principium numeri. Et quia numerus componitur ex unitatibus crediderunt quod numeri essent substantiæ omnium rerum. E contrario Avicenna considerans quod unum quod est principium numeri addit aliquam rem supra substantiam (alias numerus ex unitatibus compositus non esset species quantitatis), credidit quod unum quod convertitur cum ente addat rem aliquam supra substantiam entis, sicut album supra hominem. Sed hoc manifeste falsum est, quia quælibet res est una per suam substantiam. Si enim per aliquid aliud esset una, quælibet res, cum illud iterum sit unum, si esset iterum unum per aliquid aliud esset abire in infinitum. Unde standum est in primo: sic igitur dicendum est quod unum quod convertitur cum ente non addit aliquam rem supra ens sed unum quod est principium numeri addit aliquid supra ens ad genus quantitatis pertinens.

2. Ad secundum dicendum quod nihil prohibet id quod est uno modo divisum esse alio modo indivisum (sicut quod est divisum numero est indivisum secundum speciem), et sic contingit aliquid esse uno modo unum et alio modo multa. Sed tamen si sit indivisum simpliciter (vel quia est indivisum secundum id quod pertinet ad essentiam rei, licet sit divisum quantum ad ea quæ sunt extra essentiam rei, sicut quod est unum subjecto et multa secundum accidentia; vel quia est indivisum in actu et divisum in potentia, sicut quod est unum toto et multa secundum partes), hujusmodi erit unum simpliciter et multa secundum quid. Si vero aliquid e converso sit indivisum secundum quid et divisum simpliciter (utpote quia est divisum secundum essentiam et indivisum secundum rationem vel secundum principium sive causam), erit multa simpliciter et unum secundum quid, sicut quæ sunt multa numero et unum specie vel unum principio. Sic igitur ens dividitur per unum et multa quasi per unum simpliciter et multa secundum quid. Nam et ipsa multa non continentur sub ente nisi secundum quod aliquo modo continentur sub uno. Dicit enim Dionysius ult. cap. *de Div. Nom.* quod *non est multitudo non participans uno: sed quæ sunt multa partibus sunt unum toto, et quæ sunt multa accidentibus sunt unum subjecto, et quæ sunt multa numero sunt unum specie, et quæ sunt multa specie sunt unum genere, et quæ sunt multa processibus sunt unum principio.*[3]

---

[3]*On the Divine Names* 13, 2. PG 3, 980

[b]Quantity, or extension, is the divisibility of material things, according to St Thomas. That is to say, the parts which result from actual division of an extended thing, are not qualitatively or formally distinct one from the other, but simply

Hence: 1. Two opposing positions have been adopted by those who identify the unity equivalent with existing and the unity initiating number.[b] Pythagoras and Plato, seeing that the unity equivalent with existing adds nothing to existing but simply signifies the existent substance undivided, thought this also true of the unity initiating number. And since number is composed of unities, they believed number to be the substance of all things. Avicenna, on the other hand, seeing that the unity initiating number adds something to substance (for otherwise number composed of unities would not be a species of quantity), believed that the unity equivalent with existing added something to the substance of an existent thing, as whiteness adds something to man. Now this is clearly false, for everything is one of its very substance. If it were one by something else, that something else, being itself one, would be one by something else again, and so on and so on. Better not to embark on such a course, and say, therefore, that the unity equivalent with existing adds nothing to existing, whilst the unity initiating number adds something belonging to the genus of quantity.

2. There is nothing to stop things being divided from one point of view and undivided from another (numerically divided, for example, yet undivided in kind), and they will then be from one point of view one, and from another many. If a thing is simply speaking divided (either because undivided in essentials although divided in non-essentials, as one substance having many accidents; or because actually undivided although potentially divisible, as one whole having many parts), then such a thing will be simply speaking one, and many only in a certain respect. On the other hand, if things are simply speaking divided though in a certain respect undivided (as things divided in substance although undivided in species or in causal origin), then they will be simply speaking many, and one only in a certain respect, as things many in number can be of one species or origin. Now being is subdivided into being one and being many in the sense of one simply speaking and many in a certain respect. For the many as such cannot be said to exist, except in so far as they have a certain unity. Thus, Dionysius says that no *manifold exists without being somehow one: for many parts are one whole, many accidents one in subject, many things one in species, many species one in genus, and many processes one in origin.*[3]

---

factually or materially distinct. Division of extension involves no qualitative change, and as a consequence the parts which result can be imagined already present before division. Measurement of extension exploits this fact, for measuring proceeds by imagined division of extension into parts not further divided, and therefore called units. Unity in general is undividedness of being; unity in the genus of quantity is undividedness of divisible being, is the unit of measurement. St Thomas calls unity in general the unity equivalent with being, and the unity in the genus of quantity the unity that initiates number.

3. Ad tertium dicendum quod ideo non est nugatio cum dicitur ens unum, quia unum addit secundum rationem supra ens.

articulus 2. utrum opponantur unum et multa

AD SECUNDUM sic proceditur:[1] 1. Videtur quod unum et multa non opponantur. Nullum enim oppositum prædicatur de suo opposito. Sed omnis multitudo est quodammodo unum, ut ex dictis patet.[2] Ergo unum non opponitur multitudini.

2. Præterea, nullum oppositum constituitur ex suo opposito. Sed unum constituit multitudinem. Ergo non opponitur multitudini.

3. Præterea, unum uni est oppositum. Sed multo opponitur paucum. Ergo non opponitur ei unum.

4. Præterea, si unum opponitur multitudini opponitur ei sicut indivisum diviso, et sic opponetur ei ut privatio habitui. Hoc autem videtur inconveniens, quia sequeretur quod unum sit posterius multitudine et definiatur per eam, cum tamen multitudo definiatur per unum. Unde erit circulus in definitione, quod est inconveniens. Non ergo unum et multa sunt opposita.

SED CONTRA, quorum rationes sunt oppositæ ipsa sunt opposita. Sed ratio unius consistit in indivisione, ratio vero multitudinis divisionem continet. Ergo unum et multa sunt opposita.*

RESPONSIO: Dicendum quod unum opponitur multis sed diversimode. Nam unum quod est principium numeri opponitur multitudini quæ est numerus ut mensura mensurato, unum enim habet rationem primæ mensuræ et numerus est multitudo mensurata per unum, ut patet ex x Meta.[3] Unum vero quod convertitur cum ente opponitur multitudini per modum privationis ut indivisum diviso.

1. Ad primum ergo dicendum quod nulla privatio tollit totaliter esse, quia privatio est negatio in subjecto secundum Philosophum;[4] sed tamen omnis privatio tollit aliquod esse. Et ideo in ente ratione suæ communitatis accidit quod privatio entis fundatur in ente, quod non accidit in privatione formarum specialium ut visus vel albedinis vel alicujus hujusmodi. Et sicut est de ente ita est de uno et bono quæ convertuntur cum ente, nam

---

*Many early manuscripts omit the argument Sed contra.

[1]cf Ia. 30, 3 ad 3; 85, 8 ad 2: Ia2æ. 17, 4. Also I Sent. 24, I, 3 ad 4. De potentia III, 16 ad 3; IX, 7 ad 7, 14, 15, 17. In Meta. x, lect. 4 and 8

3. There is no tautology in saying that what exists is one, because unity adds to existence conceptually.

article 2. is being one the opposite of being many?

THE SECOND POINT:[1] 1. It seems that being one is not the opposite of being many. For one cannot assert one opposite of the other. Yet the many are always in a certain respect one, as has been said.[2] So being one is not opposed to being many.

2. Moreover, nothing is composed of its opposite. But the many is composed of unities. Unity, therefore, is not opposed to the many.

3. Moreover, one thing has one opposite. Now few is the opposite of many. One, therefore, is not the opposite of many.

4. Moreover, if the one and the many are opposed it must be like indivision and division are, namely, as lack to possession. Now this does not seem right, for unity would then be subsequent as an idea to the many, and defined in terms of it; but in fact the many is defined in terms of unity. We would thus be defining in circles, which will not do. So one and many are not opposed.

ON THE OTHER HAND, things are opposed if their definitions are opposed. Now indivision defines unity, whilst division enters into the definition of the many. So one and many are opposed.

REPLY: One is the opposite of many in differing ways. Thus the unity initiating number is opposed to the manyness of number as a measure opposes what it measures, for unity is by definition the fundamental measure, and number is many measured in ones, as Aristotle says.[3] The unity convertible with existing, however, is opposed to the many as indivision is opposed to division, by lacking it.

Hence: 1. To lack something is not to cease existing entirely, for Aristotle defines lack as the non-existence of some attribute in some subject;[4] but it is to cease existing in some respect. And so it happens that lack of existence is grounded in an existent, existence being a universal attribute, a thing that does not happen when the lack is of some special attribute like sight or whiteness or the like. And what is true of existence is true of

---

[2] cf 1a. 11, 1 ad 2
[3] *Metaphysics* X, 1. 1052b18; 6. 1057a3
[4] *Metaphysics* IV, 2. 1004a15

privatio boni fundatur in aliquo bono, et similiter remotio unitatis fundatur in aliquo uno. Et exinde contingit quod multitudo est quoddam unum, et malum est quoddam bonum, et non ens est quoddam ens. Non tamen oppositum prædicatur de opposito quia alterum est simpliciter et alterum secundum quid. Quod enim secundum quid est ens ut in potentia est non ens simpliciter idest actu, vel quod est ens simpliciter in genere substantiæ est non ens secundum quid quantum ad aliquod esse accidentale. Similiter ergo quod est bonum secundum quid est malum simpliciter, vel e converso. Et similiter quod est unum simpliciter est multa secundum quid, et e converso.

2. Ad secundum dicendum quod duplex est totum, quoddam homogeneum quod componitur ex similibus partibus, quoddam vero heterogeneum quod componitur ex dissimilibus partibus. In quolibet autem toto homogeneo totum constituitur ex partibus habentibus formam totius, sicut quælibet pars aquæ est aqua. Et talis est constitutio continui ex suis partibus. In quolibet vero toto heterogeneo quælibet pars caret forma totius, nulla enim pars domus est domus nec aliqua pars hominis est homo. Et tale totum est multitudo. Inquantum ergo pars ejus non habet formam multitudinis componitur multitudo ex unitatibus, sicut domus ex non domibus; non quod unitates constituant multitudinem secundum id quod habent de ratione indivisionis prout opponuntur multitudini, sed secundum hoc quod habent de entitate, sicut et partes domus constituunt domum per hoc quod sunt quædam corpora, non per hoc quod sunt non domus.

3. Ad tertium dicendum quod multum accipitur dupliciter: uno modo absolute et sic opponitur uni; alio modo secundum quod importat excessum quemdam et sic opponitur pauco. Unde primo modo duo sunt multa, non autem secundo.

4. Ad quartum dicendum quod unum opponitur privative multis inquantum multa sunt divisa. Unde oportet quod divisio sit prius unitate non simpliciter sed secundum rationem nostræ apprehensionis. Apprehendimus enim simplicia per composita, unde definimus punctum cujus pars non est vel principium lineæ. Sed multitudo etiam secundum rationem consequenter se habet ad unum, quia divisa non intelligimus habere rationem multitudinis nisi per hoc quod utrique divisorum attribuimus unitatem. Unde unum ponitur in definitione multitudinis, non autem multitudo in definitione unius. Sed divisio cadit in intellectu ex ipsa negatione entis. Ita quod primo cadit in intellectu ens, secundo quod hoc ens non est illud ens et sic apprehendimus divisionem, tertio unum, quarto multitudinem.

---

[a]To understand this one must compare it with St Thomas's teaching on the stages implicit in the process of understanding a thing. To be knowable a thing must

the unity and goodness convertible with existence: for lack of goodness is grounded in a good, and absence of unity in something one. So the many turn out to be somehow one, the bad thing a sort of good, and the non-existent a kind of existent. Nonetheless there is no contradiction involved for one term is understood simply speaking, the other only in a certain respect. For what is existent in a certain respect is non-existent simply speaking, for example, the potentially existent does not actually exist; and what is existent simply speaking does not exist in a certain respect, for example, a substance will lack certain accidents. Similarly, therefore, what is good in a certain respect is bad simply speaking, or vice versa. And what is one simply speaking is many in a certain respect, or vice versa.

2. A whole can be homogeneous, if composed of similar parts, or hetero-geneous, if composed of dissimilar parts. In homogeneous wholes the component parts share the form of the whole, thus every bit of water is water. And this is the way a continuum is made up from its parts. In heterogeneous wholes the parts lack the form of the whole; thus no part of a house is itself a house, and no part of man a man. The many is this kind of whole. And so because no part of the many has the form of the many, the many is composed of unities, like the house from things not houses; but these unities compose the many inasmuch as they exist, not inasmuch as they are undivided and opposed to the many, just as the parts of a house make up the house inasmuch as they are bodies of a certain sort, not inasmuch as they are not houses.

3. 'Many' can be given two meanings: the straightforward one opposed to unity, and that connoting a certain excess and opposed to few. In the first sense two is many, but not in the second.

4. The one is opposed to the many because it lacks the division possessed by the many. So division must precede unity as an idea in our minds, though not in simple fact. For we grasp the simple things by way of the composite, defining a point as something without parts or as the beginning of a line. Even in our minds, however, the many is subsequent to unity, for we only conceive divided things as many by ascribing unity to each of them. So unity enters the definition of the many, but the many does not enter the definition of unity. Now division arises in the mind simply by negating existence. So that the first idea to arise in the mind is the existent, then that this existent is not that existent and so we grasp division, thirdly unity, and fourthly the many.[a]

---

first be actual (existent); to be able to be judged the principle of contradiction must be applicable to it, so that it cannot at the same time and in the same respect be what it is not (this existent is not that existent); the result of a judgment is certainty which St Thomas defines as the determining of the mind to unity.

articulus 3. *utrum Deus sit unus*

AD TERTIUM sic proceditur:[1] 1. Videtur quod Deus non sit unus. Dicitur enim I *ad Cor.* viii: *siquidem sunt dii multi et domini multi.*[2]

2. Præterea, unum quod est principium numeri non potest prædicari de Deo cum nulla quantitas de Deo prædicetur. Similiter nec unum quod convertitur cum ente, quia importat privationem et omnis privatio imperfectionem, quæ Deo non competit. Non est igitur dicendum quod Deus sit unus.

SED CONTRA est quod dicitur *Deut.* vi: *Audi, Israel, Dominus Deus tuus Deus unus est.*[3]

RESPONSIO: Dicendum quod Deum esse unum ex tribus demonstratur.

Primo quidem ex ejus simplicitate. Manifestum est enim quod illud unde aliquid singulare est hoc aliquid nullo modo est multis communicabile. Illud enim unde Socrates est homo multis convenire potest, sed id unde est hic homo non potest convenire nisi uni tantum. Si ergo Socrates per id esset homo per quod est hic homo, sicut non possunt esse plures Socrates ita non possent esse plures homines. Hoc autem convenit Deo, nam ipse Deus est sua natura ut supra ostensum est.[4] Secundum igitur idem est Deus et hic Deus. Impossibile est igitur esse plures Deos.

Secundo vero ex infinitate ejus perfectionis. Ostensum est enim supra quod Deus comprehendit in se totam perfectionem essendi.[5] Si ergo essent plures dii oporteret eos differre. Aliquid ergo conveniret uni quod non conveniret alteri. Et si hoc esset privatio non esset simpliciter perfectus, si autem hoc esset perfectio alteri eorum deesset. Impossibile est ergo esse plures deos. Unde et antiqui philosophi quasi ab ipsa veritate coacti ponentes principium infinitum posuerunt unum tantum principium.

Tertio ab unitate mundi. Omnia enim quæ sunt inveniuntur esse ordinata ad invicem dum quædam quibusdam deserviunt. Quæ autem diversa sunt in unum ordinem non convenirent nisi ab aliquo uno ordinarentur. Melius enim multa reducuntur in unum ordinem per unum quam per multa, quia per se unius unum est causa et multa non sunt causa unius nisi per accidens inquantum scilicet sunt aliquo modo unum. Cum igitur illud quod est primum sit perfectissimum et per se non per accidens, oportet quod primum reducens omnia in unum ordinem sit unum tantum. Et hoc est Deus.

---

[1]cf Ia. 103, 3. Also I *Sent.* 2, 1; II *Sent.* 1, 1, 1. *CG* I, 42. *De potentia* III, 6. *In De div. nom.* 13, *lect.* 2 and 3. *Compendium Theol.* 15. *In Physic.* VIII, *lect.* 12. *In Meta.* XII, *lect.* 12

article 3. *is there one God?*

THE THIRD POINT:[1] 1. God is not one, it seems. For St Paul says *there are indeed many gods and many lords.*[2]

2. Moreover, the unity with which number begins cannot be attributed to a God to whom quantity cannot be attributed. Nor can the unity convertible with existence because it implies lack and lack imperfection, which cannot exist in God. So we cannot talk of one God.

ON THE OTHER HAND *Deuteronomy* proclaims: *Hear, O Israel, the Lord our God is one God.*[3]

REPLY: That there is one God can be shown in three ways.

First, because God is simple. For clearly no individual can share with others its very singularity. Socrates can share what makes him man with many others, but what makes him this man can belong to one alone. So if Socrates were this man just by being a man, there could no more be many men than there can be many Socrates. Now in God this is the case, for as we showed God is himself his own nature.[4] So to be God is to be this God. And it is thus impossible for there to be many Gods.

Secondly, because God's perfection is unlimited. For God, as we have seen, embraces in himself the whole perfection of existence.[5] Now many Gods, if they existed, would have to differ. Something belonging to one would not belong to the other. And if this were a lack the one God would not be altogether perfect, whilst if it were a perfection the other God would lack it. So there cannot be more than one God. And this is why philosophers in ancient times, bowing, so to speak, to the truth, held that if the source of things was unlimited it could not be many.[a]

Thirdly, because the world is one. For we find all existent things in mutual order, certain of them subserving others. Now divers things only combine in a single order where there is a single cause of order. For unity and order is introduced into a plurality of things more perfectly by a single cause than by many, unity producing unity essentially whilst the many produce unity only incidentally in so far as they too are somehow one. So the primary source of unity and order in the universe, namely, God, must be one himself, for the primary is always most perfect and not incidental but essential.

[2] *1 Corinthians* 8, 5 [3] *Deuteronomy* 6, 4
[4] cf 1a. 3, 3 [5] cf 1a. 4, 2
[a] Perhaps St Thomas is thinking of Aristotle's remarks in the *Physics* III. 4. 203b4–14.

1. Ad primum ergo dicendum quod dicuntur *dii multi* secundum errorem quorundam qui multos deos colebant, æstimantes planetas et alias stellas esse deos, vel etiam singulas partes mundi. Unde subdit, *nobis autem unus Deus Pater etc.*

2. Ad secundum dicendum quod unum secundum quod est principium numeri non prædicatur de Deo, sed solum de his quæ habent esse in materia. Unum enim quod est principium numeri est de genere mathematicorum quæ habent esse in materia, sed sunt secundum rationem a materia abstracta. Unum vero quod convertitur cum ente est quoddam metaphysicum, quod secundum esse non dependet a materia. Et licet in Deo non sit aliqua privatio, tamen secundum modum apprehensionis nostræ non cognoscitur a nobis nisi per modum privationis et remotionis. Et sic nihil prohibet aliqua privative dicta de Deo prædicari, sicut quod est incorporeus, infinitus. Et similiter de Deo dicitur quod sit unus.

articulus 4. utrum Deus sit maxime unus

AD QUARTUM sic proceditur:[1] 1. Videtur quod Deus non sit maxime unus. Unum enim dicitur secundum privationem divisionis. Sed privatio non recipit magis et minus. Ergo Deus non dicitur magis unus quam alia quæ sunt unum.

2. Præterea, nihil videtur esse magis indivisibile quam id quod est indivisibile actu et potentia, cujusmodi est punctus et unitas. Sed intantum dicitur aliquid magis unum inquantum est indivisibile. Ergo Deus non est magis unum quam unitas et punctus.

3. Præterea, quod est per essentiam bonum est maxime bonum, ergo quod est per essentiam suam unum est maxime unum. Sed omne ens est unum per suam essentiam, ut patet per Philosophum in v *Meta.*[2] Ergo omne ens est maxime unum. Deus igitur non est magis unum quam alia entia.

SED CONTRA est quod dicit Bernardus quod *inter omnia quæ unum dicuntur arcem tenet unitas divinæ Trinitatis.*[3]

RESPONSIO: Dicendum quod unum cum sit ens indivisum, ad hoc quod sit maxime unum oportet quod sit et maxime ens et maxime indivisum. Utrumque autem competit Deo. Est enim maxime ens inquantum est non habens aliquod esse determinatum per aliquam naturam cui adveniat, sed est ipsum esse subsistens omnibus modis indeterminatum. Est etiam

---

[1]cf Ia, 6, 3 ad 1; 76, 7; 3a. 2, 9 ad 1. Also I *Sent.* 24, 1, 1. *In De div. nom.* 1, *lect.* 2.; *lect.* 3

Hence: 1. The words *many gods* allude to the mistaken beliefs of those who worshipped many gods, thinking the planets and the other stars and even each separate part of the world to be divine. And so the passage continues, *yet there is for us one God and Father*, etc.

2. The unity with which number begins is not attributed to God but only to material things. For it is studied in mathematics which treats of entities existing in matter but defined without reference to matter. The unity convertible with existence, on the other hand, is a sort of metaphysical entity which can exist outside of matter. And although God cannot lack anything, yet because of our ways of understanding things, he cannot be known by us except we conceive him as lacking or excluding certain attributes. And so there is nothing wrong with describing God as lacking things: being without a body, for example, or without limits. And in the same way we call God one.

article 4. *is God supremely one?*

THE FOURTH POINT:[1] 1. God, it seems, is not supremely one. For unity is absence of division. Now for something to be more or less absent is impossible. So we cannot say God is more one than other things.

2. Moreover, nothing seems more indivisible than things like points and units which are indivisible both actually and potentially. Now the degree of unity we ascribe to a thing depends on its degree of indivisibility. So God is not more one than points and units.

3. Moreover, just as the supremely good is good of itself, so the supremely one must be one of itself. Now Aristotle tells us that everything that exists is one of itself.[2] So everything is supremely one. God is therefore no more one than anything else.

ON THE OTHER HAND Bernard says that *among all the things we say are one the unity of the divine Trinity takes pride of place.*[3]

REPLY: Since to be one is to exist undivided, anything supremely one must be both supremely existent and supremely undivided. Both characteristics belong to God. He exists supremely, because he has not acquired an existence which his nature has then determined, but is subsistent existence

---

[2]*Metaphysics* IV, 2. 1003b32
[3]*De Consideratione* V, 8. PL 182, 799. St Bernard of Clairvaux, d. 1153

maxime indivisum inquantum neque dividitur actu neque potentia secundum quemcumque modum divisionis, cum sit omnibus modis simplex, ut supra ostensum est.[4] Unde manifestum est quod Deus est maxime unus.

1. Ad primum ergo dicendum quod licet privatio secundum se non recipiat magis et minus, tamen secundum quod ejus oppositum recipit magis et minus etiam ipsa privativa dicuntur secundum magis et minus. Secundum igitur quod aliquid est magis divisum vel divisibile vel minus vel nullo modo, secundum hoc aliquid dicitur magis et minus et maxime unum.

2. Ad secundum dicendum quod punctus et unitas quæ est principium numeri non sunt maxime entia cum non habeant esse nisi in subjecto aliquo. Unde neutrum eorum est maxime unum. Sicut enim subjectum non est maxime unum propter diversitatem accidentis et subjecti, ita nec accidens.

3. Ad tertium dicendum quod licet omne ens sit unum per suam substantiam non tamen se habet æqualiter substantia cujuslibet ad* unitatem quia substantia quorumdam est ex multis composita, quorumdam vero non.

itself, in no way determined. He is also supremely undivided, because as we have seen he is altogether simple, not divided in any way, and this neither actually nor potentially.[4] Clearly then God is supremely one.

Hence: 1. Although there cannot be more or less absence as such, a thing can be said to have more or less of a lack inasmuch as it has less or more of the opposite attribute. So a thing is called more or less or supremely one, inasmuch as it is less or more or not at all divided or divisible.

2. The point and numerical unity are not supremely existent, since they only exist as accidents in a subject. Neither of them then is supremely one. For just as no subject is supremely one because of the heterogeneity of subject and accident, so also no accident.

3. Although everything that exists is one in substance, not every substance has the same relation to unity, for certain substances have many component parts and some not.

---

*Leonine adds *causandam*, the same causal relation to unity.
[4] cf 1a. 3, 7

Appendix 1

THE OPENING QUESTION

1. AFTER SKETCHING the plan of the *Summa* St Thomas straightway proceeds to the topic of God's existence. The treatment occupies a single question, and this, he begins by remarking, can be divided into three articles, three moments or points in the prosecution of the one inquiry. For perhaps it is self-evident that God exists (a possibility discussed in article 1), or perhaps, on the other hand, there is no possible means of making it evident (a possibility discussed in article 2). Only if God's existence can and should be made evident is it sensible to try to do so (as in article 3).

Each article takes the form of resolving an apparent conflict between opinion and fact. Thus the first article starts with a conflict about God's hiddenness or unhiddenness. Some people say that a God who exists cannot possibly hide the fact (the three opening arguments, hereafter called the 'objections'); but 'on the other hand', *sed contra* (the part of the article I shall call the suggestion to the contrary), we have the phenomenon of atheism, witnessed to by the Bible itself. The main body of the article (the 'reply') is given over to resolving this conflict, and any loose ends remaining are tidied up with reference to each objection separately (the 'answers to the objections').

The aim of the comments which follow is simply to reveal this structure in each article; difficulties requiring fuller explanation will be dealt with in later appendices.

2. *Article 1: is it self-evident that there is a God?* It would seem impossible for God to exist and yet hide the fact, though apparently this is what happens: here is the conflict of the article. It is not merely that God must throw his shadow over the whole world, so that the substance of our experience (argument 3) and the very cast of our own natures (argument 1) will tell us of God, but also that God in himself, the fount of all meaning, must be an utterly obvious mental necessity (argument 2). And yet from some people, brusquely called fools in the Bible, he manages to hide (suggestion to the contrary).

In resolving this conflict St Thomas remarks that it depends *from whom* God's existence is hidden. Will sticks and stones, for example, though they fall under God's shadow, *know* that they do? Man's very nature and man's very knowledge may witness to God's existence, but will he *know* his knowledge witnesses it? Man's eyes and ears open immediately upon the bodily world, and his mind penetrates immediately only the broader significance of such a world. To define this significance more closely, and to bring to light its implications, especially when they lead further away from the bodily, is a process which can build up in man only slowly. However much God is the centre of light and meaning in himself, he can only be brought to light for man through the bodily world.

'God in himself,' St Thomas writes, 'is utterly intelligible, and does not have to wait for man to bring him to light as material objects do. But God as man sees him is not self-evident. There are reflections of God which are self-evident (thus the existence of truth, which is a reflection of God), but that there is a God existing separate from the bodily world with a nature of his own is not self-evident. The only things self-evident to us are things we know immediately by way of sense-experience; thus, once we have seen wholes and parts, we know immediately and without any argument that wholes are greater than parts. But to arrive at God from sense-experience, we must first recognize that what we see is caused, that this implies a cause, and that the ultimate cause transcends this bodily world. So we can arrive at God only by argument, and anything that must be argued is not self-evident.'[1]

There may be elements in our experience, like the tendency of our natures to pursue happiness, which reflect God; that the element exists may be self-evident, but that it reflects God will require proof. 'To be aware of somebody approaching is not to be aware of Peter, even should it be Peter approaching.' Again, to accept that if a thing exists perfectly it exists in fact may be an obvious mental necessity, but that there actually is such a being requires argument from effect to cause.

The vocabulary in which the above arguments are presented in the *Summa* is the accepted logical vocabulary of the age—'subject', 'predicate', etc. It is discussed in the next appendix.

3. *Article 2: can the existence of God be made evident?* The inquiry now swings round to the opposite pole. It seems that God must be so hidden an implication of the bodily world that he can never be brought out into the light. For how can natural reason discern the supernatural (argument 1), or define the infinite (arguments 2 and 3)? Yet the Bible again witnesses to the contrary. St Thomas answers that we can at least discern that there is something we cannot discern, can define that there exists something we cannot define. The answer distinguishes coming to see *that* God is from coming to see *what* he is. Coming to see God as implied in this bodily world is not coming to see him in himself (which is impossible to man in this life); it is coming to see that someone we do *not* see in himself nevertheless exists.

In the answers to the objections it is this distinction which is applied. That there is a God of faith who talked with Abraham, Isaac and Jacob is a matter of revelation; but this is because God's talking to Abraham is revelation, not because God's existence is. The infinite cannot be defined, but, by way of its effects, it can be named, and the name proved to be not devoid of reference.

Again the argument is presented in logical terms to be discussed in the next appendix.

4. *Article 3: is there a God?* Although the book of *Exodus* says that God exists, he is difficult to fit into one's picture of the world. The difficulty is

---

[1] *I Sent.* 3, 1, 2

connected with the 'total' character of God: his existence makes no 'difference' to the world because it makes the 'totality' of the world. This seems to be the converging point of both the objections in this article: the first stresses the difficulty of conceiving God to exist in the same world as 'otherness'; the second asks whether the whole really adds anything to the parts.

But the same difficulty that militates against God as an element in the world counts for him as the cause of the world. For every negative statement designed by an objector to thrust God out of existence is accepted by a defender of God's existence as proving the ultimacy and transcendence of God's causal activity. A cause does not rival its effects, but is rather their greatest patron; and the ultimate cause expresses itself in the very variety of secondary causes that it initiates.

The whole article revolves, therefore, round the notions of ultimate and non-ultimate causality, and the five ways of proving God's existence should be thought of as five ways of disclosing ultimate causality within non-ultimate causality.

Much has been written in the last seven centuries about these five ways; at present I wish to make only a few points.

i. The plan of each of the ways is that of an argument from effect to cause, as described in article 2 in the answer to the second objection. Starting only with a knowledge of what the word 'God' is to mean, and without possessing or acquiring any knowledge of what God is in himself, we discover that he is implied by the world we observe, in a manner analogous to that in which effects imply a cause.

ii. The world 'God' is taken to mean what it ordinarily means, namely a universal providence, and not in any narrower philosophers' sense that needs filling out in later questions and articles.

iii. The five ways are not attempting 'extra' support for the ordinary human conviction that a God or gods exist, but rather attempt to put into words the process by which such a conviction arises, and to reveal its validity.

iv. The first four ways are not arbitrarily chosen from many other possible ways, but correspond with precision to the fourfold way in which St Thomas conceives the presence of God's ultimate activity in creatures' secondary activities.[2]

v. The fifth way is not arguing that a world is a harmony of notes, when it might have been discordant, but rather that each note is deftly and surely sounded. The proof points rather to the occurrence of definite tendencies in the world than to their concurrence.

---

[2] Cf Appendix 11, *The Single Causal Origin*

Appendix 2

LOGICAL PRELIMINARIES

'Simple Apprehension'

I believe there is a primary need in man, which other creatures probably do not have, and which actuates all his apparently unzoölogical aims, his wistful fancies, his consciousness of value, his utterly impractical enthusiasms, and his awareness of a 'Beyond' filled with holiness. . . . *This basic need, which certainly is obvious only in man, is the need of symbolization.* . . . [Symbol-making] is the fundamental process of his mind, and goes on all the time . . .; [it is] an act *essential to thought,* and prior to it. . . . It is only natural that a typical human function should require a typically human form of overt activity; and this is just what we find in *the sheer expression of ideas.* This is the activity of which beasts appear to have no need. And it accounts for just those traits in man which he does not hold in common with the other animals—ritual, art, laughter, weeping, speech, superstition and scientific genius.[1]

1. ST THOMAS could have said this. For him man is an animal, but a unique animal; man is the rational or the logical animal. Man resembles other animals in his bodily structure; he depends, like them, upon sense-experience and instinct; the world is present to him, as to other animals, not only in physico-chemical immediacy, but also in recognizable patterns of space and time, of usefulness and harmfulness. But besides all this, the world is present to man in its logical pattern. Within human sense-experience, and aided by the symbolic transmutation this experience undergoes in human imagination, man grasps the sense and significance of what he sees.

For 'symbols' are not simply 'signs', as Miss Langer explains. A sign provokes the sort of overt reaction that the presence of the object signified would provoke: if the bell is rung for dinner, the mouth begins to water. A sign substitutes in the world of overt activity for its object; but symbols are used to transmute objects into significant objects, and reveal their point.

Symbols are not proxy for their objects, but are vehicles for the conception of objects. To conceive a thing or a situation is not the same thing as to 'react toward it' overtly, or to be aware of its presence. In talking about things we have conceptions of them . . .; and it is the conceptions, not the things, that symbols directly 'mean'.[2]

2. That man employs symbols as well as signs, that he can grasp the significance and point of the things and situations he experiences, does not

---

[1]*Philosophy in a New Key.* Suzanne K. Langer. 1942, Harvard University Press. 1948, New York (Mentor Books, pp. 32–4)
[2]op cit, p. 49

follow from the fact that he can think. Rather the fact that he can think (that is to say, can explicitly connect and relate the parts of his experience) follows from the fact that his experience is initially conceived by him in its logical and significant pattern. Symbol-making, as Miss Langer says, is 'an act essential to thought and prior to it'. And the same is true of the conception of objects that occurs within the symbol-making.

> The power of understanding symbols, i.e. of regarding everything about a sense-datum as irrelevant except a certain form that it embodies, is the most characteristic mental trait of mankind. It issues in an unconscious, spontaneous process of abstraction, which goes on all the time in the human mind: a process of recognizing the concept in any configuration given to experience. . . . That is the real sense of Aristotle's definition of man as 'the rational animal'. Abstractive seeing is the foundation of our rationality, and is its definite guarantee long before the dawn of any conscious generalization or syllogism.[3]

3. One must not think of man as first of all inserted into a spatially patterned world, and then beginning consciously to weave a pattern of logic into that world by means of thought. Man is from the beginning inserted into the logical pattern of the world; he is from the beginning present to the definite sense and significance of the things around him; the space he lives in, so to speak, is a logical space. This is why he finds it difficult to make room in his world for experiences that do not make sense, and indeed often meets them with deep fear and loathing. This is why his action or his failure to act is influenced by the significance of the action even when it is not influenced by conscious thought: no one needs to think in order not to offer a cigarette to one who is already smoking. From the beginning man is present to the sense and significance of things; abstractive seeing precedes conscious generalization and syllogism; or, in the language of St Thomas, 'simple apprehension' precedes 'judgment'.

Judgment: 'compounding and dividing'

4. Judgment is the beginning of explicit thought, of conscious reflection upon one's 'simple' apprehension of the sense of things. When a man makes a judgment it is as though the 'simple' contact of his mind with reality was first broken by an explicit awareness of his own mind as different from the reality it conceives; and was then welded together again in a new and complex seeing, which pronounces that the mind is nevertheless 'true' to reality. Judgment reconstructs in a complex fashion the 'simple' contact of conception; mind is no longer engaged in a simple apprehension of reality, but in a complex comprehension of mind and reality together. And with this complexity there enters into man's mind for the first time the quality of truth or falsity.

---

[3]op cit, p. 58

5. Of course, the mind can be said to be 'truly' knowing even when simply apprehending, if there exists conformity between mind and thing; just as the eye can be said to seeing 'truly' if its vision is not deformed. But to know truth is not just to know truly; it is not just to be conformed to reality, but to know one's own conformity. And this the mind does for the first time when it judges that reality is just as it appears to be in simple apprehension. St Thomas usually calls the operation of judging by the name 'compounding and dividing', for 'in every proposition the mind either applies some apprehended form signified by the predicate to some thing signified by the subject (i.e. *compounds*), or disconnects the two (i.e. *divides*)'.[4] It is important to realize that the complexity symbolized by this compounding of subject and predicate is not just a complexity of apprehension, a conception of a complex object; but is precisely the complexity of apprehension plus thing, of conception plus object, of mind plus reality, yet comprehended by that very mind itself. It is this complexity which defines human judgment over against the 'simplicity' of even complex apprehensions.

Subject and Predicate

6. The words 'subject' and 'predicate' as used above must not be over-technically interpreted. A predicate is simply what is predicated, *prædicatum* in Latin, where the verb 'to predicate' is only a more solemn form of the verb 'to say'. The predicate is what we say about the subject, and the subject is what we say it about. The subject is the thing presupposed to the saying, because presupposed to the original apprehension; the predicate is the compounding of that apprehension with the thing.

The difference of subject and predicate is best brought out by examining the difference of nouns and verbs. Nouns differ logically from verbs in that what a noun signifies is conceived as though it was a thing existing on its own; whilst what a verb signifies is conceived as though it was an action, proceeding out of a thing and yet belonging to the thing. Now all subjects have, so to speak, a noun-quality, in that they are conceived as already there, presupposed to the coming predicate; whilst all predicates have a verb-quality, in that they are conceived as applying to or belonging to the subject. Indeed, the simplest and clearest case of predication (to which all other cases bear an analogy, and which we might therefore call the paradigm case of predication) is the attribution of some action, signified by some single verb, to some thing, signified by some single noun: for example, 'George laughs'.

'Categories'

7. To say that the attribution of an action to a thing is the paradigm case of predication, means that other things than action can be predicated of other things than things, but that nevertheless all such predications will bear some

---

[4] Ia. 16, 2

analogy to the attribution of an action to a thing. In the terminology of St Thomas the thing signified (*res significata*) by a predicate will not always be an action, but the way in which it is signified (*modus significandi*) will always be that of an action. Now action, as St Thomas says and as we shall try further to explain in the next appendix, belongs to a thing as proceeding out of it into other things; and as such it holds a sort of middle position between properties wholly intrinsic to a thing and mere denominations of a thing by reference to wholly exterior circumstances. The analogy of action can therefore be extended in two different directions: towards the predication of more and more external descriptions of the subject, like being in a certain place, or at a certain time, being in a certain posture, or having certain things on; or, alternatively, towards the predication of more and more intrinsic quasi-actions (or 'actualities') of the subject, like being acted upon, or related to, or being of this sort or of that amount, or simply being what one is. These are the ten types of predication, or 'categories', or 'predicaments', which Aristotle and St Thomas distinguish, all of which, so to speak, extend the predication of action inwards or outwards.

'Being'

8. But, of course, if A bears an analogy to B, then B also bears an analogy to A. If all the categories bear an analogy to action, to *doing*, including at one end the very extrinsic 'having pyjamas on', and at the other end the very interior 'being a man', then all the categories will also bear analogies to *having*, and all again bear analogy to *being*. The analogy to *having* emerges in such phrases as 'having a certain quality' or 'having a certain relation', and in the fact that all the categories can be called properties of things. The analogy to *being* emerges in the use of the word 'is' to help construct any predication whatsoever. Of these three 'universal' verbs, St Thomas gives pride of place to the verb 'to be', for a reason which will only become clear in Appendix 3. Thus the categories are not only called modes of predication, but also modes of being; and he says that the verb 'to be' (*esse*) is the word which signifies the act-character or actuality-character of anything whatsoever.

9. And thus there arises in St Thomas the doctrine of the 'analogy of being', the doctrine, namely, that the word 'being' has no once-for-all sense, but a whole gamut of senses. Indeed it has such a universal gamut of senses that it can be used for anything at all. But the gamut of senses is nevertheless an organized gamut. 'Being' means first of all 'being a substance' (the most interior of the categories distinguished above); then it has all the different meanings of the other nine categories, which can be summarized as 'belonging to a substance', 'being in'; then it has all the different meanings that 'coming to be' may have (for there *are* such things as changes), and these will also be as numerous as the categories are; further, it has all the different meanings that 'not being' can have (for there can *be* lack of being), again to the number of the ten categories; and finally, there is the 'being'

attributed to any combination of previously mentioned beings (for if there are men, and the men are white, then there are white men).

Reference and meaning (suppositio and significatio)

10. Just as it is possible to predicate other things than actions, so it is possible to have as a subject other things than things; but nevertheless whatever is capable of being the subject of a predication will have the *modus significandi*, the way of being signified, of a thing. Another way of saying this is to say that the subject of a predication must have a noun-quality, where a noun is defined as a word which signifies 'substance with quality'; but then it must be added that the subject only needs to be *signified* in this way, it does not have to *be* a substance with a quality. Thus 'smoking' is a noun and can be the subject of a predication.

To understand the description of nouns as signifying 'substance with quality', let us remember for a moment that a predication is not a complex apprehension, but a complex application of an apprehension to the reality it is truly or falsely apprehending. The subject, unlike the predicate, is not in the predication to *signify* the apprehension, but to *refer to* the reality. Properly speaking, then, the subject does not signify 'substance' but refers to it; to signify substance describes the job of a predicate in what we have called the most interior category. However, the subject *refers to* some reality or 'substance' by *signifying* some quality of this reality; and this is what is meant by saying that a subject (or a noun) signifies 'substance with quality'.

11. At first sight, this is altogether too complicated. Why not simply say that just as the predicate simply signifies an apprehension, so the subject simply refers to a reality? There is an argument in Whitehead's *The Concept of Nature* which, while recognizing the 'practical impossibility' of pure reference, nevertheless argues that it is 'the ideal of thought'. The word he uses is not 'reference', but 'demonstration', and the argument goes as follows:

> Suppose that the expositor . . . is speaking in the college hall and he says, 'This college building is commodious'. The phrase 'this college building' is a demonstrative phrase. Now suppose the recipient answers, 'This is not a college building, it is the lion-house in the Zoo.' . . . The expositor sticks to his original proposition when he replies, 'Anyhow, *it* is commodious.' . . . The '*it*' of this final statement presupposes that thought has seized on the entity as a bare objective for consideration.[5]

Now this is clearly an over-hasty conclusion; for the substitution of 'lion-house' for 'college building' has not entirely bared the entity to a pure 'it'; the entity is still a building. Not only over-hasty, but false; for if the recipient had said 'This is not a college building, it is a blue and white dish-cloth', one could perhaps guess that the expositor would not have stuck to his original

---

[5] *The Concept of Nature.* A. N. Whitehead, Cambridge, 1920, pp. 7 ff

proposition with an 'Anyhow . . .' Without some degree of clothing of the subject-reference the predication will simply not make sense; '*it* is commodious' only makes sense if *it* can be commodious, if *it* is a building. The impossibility of pure reference is not only practical, therefore, but logically necessary, because pure reference will not suffice for sense. There must be what Whitehead calls 'auxiliary complexes' within which the 'it' is set; the 'substance' must be signified with 'quality'.

'Predicables'

12. An alternative way of putting these remarks about reference and meaning is as follows: if a proposition is to make sense, then the predicate must be appropriate to the subject. The scholastic theory of the predicables is a theory that there are five different ways in which a predicate can be appropriate to a subject.[6] The most common way is the one exemplified by Whitehead's sentence earlier, for in that sentence the predicate ('commodious') is appropriate to the subject ('a building') in such a way that the contrary predicate ('not commodious') would be equally appropriate: the scholastic name for this relation of appropriateness of predicate to subject is 'belonging by accident' (*accidens*). We must be careful here of not confusing the predicable 'by accident' with the predicament 'accident'; for the nine categories other than substance are often referred to as accidents. But these accidents—such actualities as qualities, relations, actions, etc.—sometimes 'belong by accident' to the subject, and then it would make equal sense for them not to belong, and sometimes 'belong by right' or 'properly' (*proprium*). This is the second of the scholastic predicables. In a predication in which the predicate 'belongs properly' to the subject, it would not make equal sense for the contrary predicate to belong to the subject. To understand this we must look back again for a moment at our example of the building and the dish-cloth. The reason why dish-cloths cannot be commodious is not because they are uncommodious; they cannot be uncommodious either. The reason is connected with what kind of a thing a dish-cloth is. Now if we were to state simply what kind of a thing a dish-cloth was we would be stating a rule, so to speak, which would tell us which predicates could or could not belong by accident to a dish-cloth. And such a statement of a rule would necessarily be a new kind of predication about the dish-cloth, a second-order predication which could not *not* be true about dish-cloths. As a matter of fact, there might be more than one such rule that I could frame. For example, in ruling about possible predicates of George I might try 'George is an artistic animal', 'George is a religious animal', 'George is an animal with free will', 'George is a rational animal'. But I would find that certain of these rules were more far-reaching than others, and possibly I would decide that 'George is a rational animal' was the most far-reaching of the lot. I would

---

[6]Acknowledgments are paid to Fr Herbert McCabe, O.P., for this idea from *Categories* (*Dominican Studies*, VII, 1954, p. 147), as also for some other ideas in this appendix

have then arrived at the third scholastic predicable: the predicable of 'belonging by definition' (*species*) which describes the most fundamental of those predications that can be called 'belonging by right'. The fourth and fifth scholastic predicables simply refer to the parts of this definition: so that 'George is an animal' is said to predicate something 'belonging generically' (*genus*), and 'George is rational' predicates that which 'belongs as differentiating' (*differentia*).

Definition and Demonstration

13. The 'definition' of a thing is therefore the predication which displays the *sense* of all other possible predications about the thing, it states the point of all other predications, it declares a unity among the manifold properties a thing has, whether these properties belong 'by accident' or belong 'by right'. Definition is, so to speak, the immediate predication about a thing which allows of all other mediate predications. And it is this quality of definition which makes it the mediating predication in a demonstration. In Aristotle's sense of the word a demonstration is first and foremost the deduction of a *proprium* from a definition, that is to say, the deduction of less far-reaching rules about what can belong to a subject from the most far-reaching of such rules. Thus it is demonstrable that George must be a religious animal with free will from the definition of George as a rational animal. What are incapable of demonstration in this way are all predicates that 'belong by accident'. All that can be said about them is that it will make sense to assert them of such and such a subject; but it will also make sense to deny them.[7]

---

[7]The logical principles touched on in this appendix run throughout the treatise translated. In particular they come to the surface at the following points: *judgment*, 1a. 3, 3 ad 1; *subject and predicate*, 1a. 2, 1; *being*, 1a. 3, 4; *reference and meaning*, 1a. 2, 1 ad 1; 3, 3 & 7; *predicables*, 1a. 3, 5; *definition and demonstration*, 1a. 2, 2 ad 2

Appendix 3

EXISTENCE AND CAUSALITY

1. ANY PHILOSOPHY that thinks of logic as imposed on experience, and overlooks the logic in things themselves, will not get very far with the concepts of existence and causality. These concepts, while not purely empirical, are not purely logical either, but belong to that real 'logical space' in which things exist. For there is a sense in which meanings are 'out there' more primitively than external sense-data are.

To think of significance as superimposed upon experience is akin to the error of believing abstract notions to be 'diluted and starved', and generalities to be mere approximations to the truth. All these beliefs stem from a false theory of generalization and abstract thought, which has been put as follows:

> Experience tells us only of individual things . . . [But] we are ever grouping and discriminating, measuring and sounding, framing cross classes and cross divisions, and thereby rising from particulars to generals, that is from images to notions. . . . [The notion of] 'man' is no longer what he really is, an individual presented to us by our senses, but . . . he is attenuated into an aspect, or relegated to his place in a classification. Thus his appellation is made to suggest, not the real being which he is in this or that specimen of himself, but a definition. If I might use a harsh metaphor, I should say he is made the logarithm of his true self, and in that shape is worked with the ease and satisfaction of logarithms.[1]

The humanity of a man is here thought of as though it was a composite photograph of many different men, approximating in likeness to all, but accurately portraying none. Whereas it should be thought of far more as an original model of which many different photographs have been taken. Abstraction is not a process consequent upon sense-experience producing a sort of mental précis of what is experienced; rather abstractive seeing is the conception within sense-experience of the sense and significance of whatever is experienced. The mind does not begin with unconnected experiences which it must then weave together into a logical pattern by thought; from the beginning the experienced world presents itself to us in logical pattern (in logical space), but in a broad pattern which needs closer definition. This, of course, is why we engage in procedures of grouping and discriminating and dividing and classifying: in order to proceed not from the particular to the general but from the wider generalities to more differentiated ones.

> What is to us plain and obvious at first is rather confused masses, the elements and principles of which become known to us later by analysis. Thus we must advance from generalities to particulars. . . . Similarly a

---

[1] *A Grammar of Assent.* J. H. Newman, ch. 3

child begins by calling all men 'father' . . . but later on distinguishes each of them.[2]

Significance then, is not imposed upon experience; it is from the very beginning presupposed to it.

2. This does not mean to say that our concept of a cow exists in the cow itself. But it does mean to say that what is conceived in the concept of a cow is the cow itself. For in a concept of cow we must distinguish the *res significata* (the thing signified) and the *modus significandi* (the way in which it is signified). What is signified or conceived is a significant unity in multifarious cow-activity: we apprehend the 'nature' of cow. Now, cows really have the nature of cows. But they have it as cows have it (by being cows), not as minds have it (by conceiving cows). Cows have the nature of cows, but they do not have the concept of cows. The *res significata* of the concept of cow is in the cow, but not the *modus significandi*. This is what we mean when we say that the world has logical pattern, and that, in a sense, the meaning we apprehend in things is more fundamentally 'there' than the sense-data we observe. Nevertheless it is not apprehensions as such that exist in things, but the apprehended sense and significance of those things themselves.

Indeed, the very notion of a thing is the notion of a significant unity (or nature) expressed in multifarious experienced activity. And similarly, the notion of a community between things (of existential and causal relevance) is the notion of a significant relevance of unities expressing itself in a community of activity. What prevents us seeing this much of the time is the taking-for-granted of the logical space in which things exist as though it were a sort of universal receptacle. The actual relating of things to one another significantly and relevantly is then done surreptitiously by this assumed receptacle, rather like the actual relating of things to one another spatially is often done surreptitiously by an assumed receptacle called 'space'. But simply to assume that there is a space in which things exist is to dodge the difficulties of spatial relations, for space itself cannot exist except it exists in things. Similarly, there can be no 'logical space' for things to commune in unless things have sense and significance in themselves even before the mind gets at them, unless they have natures such as can be disclosed in concepts, unless a real community of nature in things precedes the logical community of concepts in our minds.

3. It is in this real logical space, so to say, that we must look for existence and causality, the concepts of which are neither purely empirical nor purely logical. They are not *purely* empirical because, though exemplified in experience, they generally remain unobserved; and this because they are never *un*exemplified.

> We habitually observe by the method of difference. Sometimes we see an elephant, and sometimes we do not. The result is that an elephant, when present, is noticed. . . . The metaphysical first principles can never fail

---

[2]Aristotle, *Physics*, I, I. 22–184a22—184b13. Translated by R. P. Harvie, Oxford, 1930

of exemplification. We can never catch the actual world taking a holiday from their sway.[3]

Whitehead, who wrote these words, suggested that the true method of discovering metaphysical concepts was to make use of 'imaginative generalization.'

> Factors which are constantly present may yet be observed under the influence of imaginative thought. Such thought supplies the differences which the direct observation lacks.[4]

But this suggestion could be misunderstood. It might be thought that the difference between existents and elephants was an unfortunate consequence of the narrowness of human experience, so that whilst direct experience was wide enough to comprehend both the presence and absence of elephants, it had to be widened by imagination in order to comprehend both the presence and absence of existents. But however much experience is widened, by imagination or by any other means, one can never entertain an experience free from existence. It does not just happen to be generally present; its area of commonness does not just happen to coincide with the area of our experience. Its commonness is a commonness in principle, infinitely flexible, always and necessarily coinciding with experience.

4. Metaphysical generality, therefore, is not an abstractive generality; the concept of existence is not like the concept of cow. It is not the concept of some undifferentiated sense and significance that all things have, for in fact there is no undifferentiated significance attaching to all things. Metaphysical generality is rather an analogy of things in their very differentiation, of elephants in their elephantness and concepts in their conceptness. Metaphysical generality is similar to what Wittgenstein called 'family resemblance' when he was discussing the kind of commonness attaching to the concept of 'game' or of 'number'.

> For instance, the kinds of number form a family. . . . Why do we call something a 'number'? Well, perhaps because it has a—direct—relationship with several things that have hitherto been called number; and this can be said to give it an indirect relationship to other things we call the same name. And we extend our concept of number as in spinning a thread we twist fibre on fibre. And the strength of the thread does not reside in the fact that some one fibre runs through its whole length but in the overlapping of many fibres.[5]

To say that things exist, for example, is to move from thing to thing following out an endless analogy, an analogy which never gives out however differentiated the forms it takes on. To extend an analogy in this way we need imagination, as Whitehead suggested, but we are not isolating some concept

---

[3]*Process and Reality*. A. N. Whitehead. Cambridge, 1929. pp. 5–6
[4]loc cit
[5]*Philosophical Investigations*, I. 67. Translated by E. Anscombe. Oxford, 1953. p. 32

common to all experience, we are not tracking down some common nature that all things have.

5. In the previous appendix we have already seen several examples of this generality by analogy, or by family resemblance. The verbs 'being', 'doing' and 'having' we called 'universal' verbs, because their use could be extended by continual analogy to all the different categories of predication. Now although these verbs have, so to speak, the same universe of application, so that '*having* pyjamas on' can also be described as 'the *action* of wearing pyjamas' or '*being* clothed in pyjamas', nevertheless they break into that universe at different points. 'Having' starts as a description of a thing's relations to utterly exterior things, and is gradually applied to more interior relations. 'Being', on the other hand, starts as a description of the most immanent activity one could conceive, the most interior having: namely, 'doing' or 'having' oneself.

And from this starting-point the notion of being is extended to more and more exterior relations. The meaning of interiority and exteriority here, of course, is not spatial, but connects with such statements as that simple apprehension occurs *within* sense-experience, or that there is a unified significance *within* the multifarious activity of things. Existence is interior to activity, it is the 'action' of having a nature and significance, an action exercised, so to speak, within the total variety of exterior-looking actions in which a thing is engaged. Action is exterior to existence, it is an 'existing' out into the world of other things, the playing out in public of what a thing is.

6. Indeed, action, if one considers it carefully, does not take place in the thing of which it is the activity, but takes place in other things: a bunsen-burner placed under a beaker of water may be said to be heating the water, but what we call the bunsen-burner heating the water is nothing more than the water being heated by the bunsen-burner. The activity of the bunsen-burner (we might call it the 'cause') is nothing more than the change in existence in the water (we might call it the 'effect') due to the bunsen-burner. The existence of the cause expresses itself in activity, but that activity is the coming to existence of the effect. Causality, then, should not be given its modern reading as involving a sequence of two changes: it is one change in the effect seen as from the cause.

7. St Thomas's reply to the question, what kind of causality is implicit in the notion of goodness?[6] provides us with the best text for meditating on this concept of causality. He writes, 'within anything caused there is, firstly, its form which gives the thing existence; second for consideration is the thing's operative power through which it achieves perfect existence . . .; and finally, the thing realizes the idea of good . . .' The 'form' here referred to as the 'first' element in a thing, is nothing more than the interior sense and significance of a thing, its 'point'. Existence is actually having form, or the quasi-action of exerting form. But created things exert their significance by exerting a multifarious activity; and this is why St Thomas goes on to say

---

[6] Ia. 5, 4

that form only *achieves* itself in operation, that existence is *perfected* in operative power. Finally, one must grasp the meaning of 'achievement' or 'perfection' here, if one is to have a full grasp of what a thing is. These words attempt to express *how* action contributes to making the thing what it *is*, how action contributes to existence itself; namely, by completing it, by giving it finish, by ending what the form began. This concept of being an end or completion of existence is the concept of 'being good', for St Thomas, as can be seen in the earlier articles.[7]

8. The analysis here given is the analysis of a caused thing from the standpoint of existence, from the standpoint of interiority. But there is another analysis of the same phenomena from the standpoint of causation and activity. For the *existence* of the effect *is* the *action* of a cause. So St Thomas goes on to consider this: 'In the act of causation we begin at the end or good, which influences the agent to act, then follows the action of the agent eliciting the form, and finally there arises the form. . . . The opposite order is found within the caused thing.'[8] In other words, the act of causing is the same act as the existing of the effect but seen in reverse. The act of existing is seen *within* something (and the fact that it must derive *from* something is neglected); the act of causing is this very act now seen as *from* something (and the fact that it must be exerted *within* something is neglected). Existence, operation and achievement, seen as *within* something are seen in that order: existence being the starting 'point' of a thing, and operation leading it to final achievement. But when the thing is seen as the effect of some cause in the process of producing the thing, then it must first be seen as contributing to the perfection and completion of the cause in some way, and so, secondarily, requiring action of the cause, an action which, finally, turns out to be existence when seen within the effect. When one restricts one's gaze to any particular existent thing, then everything in it derives from its starting 'point' or form; but when one widens one's gaze to the world at large, one sees that its having 'point' is precisely achieving the 'point' of some earlier thing, called its cause.

9. For St Thomas therefore the notions of existence and causality are not sheerly empirical notions. Existence is not observable, but it is the immediate significance of the observable, immediately open to mind working within sense-experience. Causality, too, is an immediate significance of the observable, and of the same observable. Existence is a unification of the multifarious activity observable in the world in some starting 'point' within reality, which gives it 'substance'; causality is that unification of activity towards an end, for existence can never be satisfied merely to begin but requires to pour out its substance in search of achievement and fulfilment.[9]

---

[7]1a. 5, 1, 2, 3

[8]1a. 5, 4

[9]For the four genera of causes, and for final causality as the spring of efficient causality, see Appendix 11.

Appendix 4

THE MEANING OF THE WORD 'GOD'

1. 'WHEN WE argue from effect to cause,' St Thomas says, 'the effect will take the place of the definition of the cause in the proof that the cause exists; and this especially if the cause is God. For when proving anything to exist the central link of the argument is not what that thing is (we cannot even ask what it is until we know that it exists). The central link is rather what we are using the name of the thing to mean. Now when demonstrating from effects that God exists, we are able to start from what the word "God" means, for, as we shall see, the names of God are derived from these effects.'[1] What is meant is that in proving men to be mortal, say, it is possible to start from a grasp of what existent men are, from a grasp of the nature of man arrived at through experience. But to prove that men exist, one could not use such a starting-point, for it already begs the question; one would start rather with a notion of how to use the word 'man', and search experience for traces of creatures to which the name could apply.

St Thomas also says, 'Because they observe that the course of nature follows fixed laws, and that law depends upon a lawgiver, men as a rule perceive that the things they observe have a lawgiver; but from such general considerations it is not immediately obvious who or what the lawgiver of nature is, or whether he is only one. So too when we observe a man moving and performing actions, we perceive that there must exist in him a cause of this behaviour different from that existing in other things; and we call this cause a "soul", though as yet we do not know what the soul is (whether it be a body), or how it causes the observed behaviour.'[2]

2. We shall expect then that the ways of proving God to exist will start from experience and examine it for traces of such a being as could be called 'God', where 'God' ought to have the meaning it has in ordinary everyday language. Now we do in fact find that the structure of the 'ways' is one of argument from experience: 'Some things in the world are certainly in process of change: this we plainly see', 'In the observable world causes are found to be ordered in series', 'Some of the things we come across can be but need not be', 'The fourth way is based on the gradation observed in things', 'An orderedness of actions to an end is observed in all bodies obeying natural laws'. Again, when these observable beginnings have been identified as traces of some newly-disclosed being, we appeal to everyday ordinary language for the name of this being: 'this is what everybody understands by God', 'to which everyone gives the name "God" ', 'and this we call "God" '.

3. It has sometimes been felt that the being disclosed would not have been recognized by the ordinary man as his 'God', and that St Thomas is guilty

---

[1] Ia. 2, 2 ad 2   [2] CG III, 38

of jumping the gun. Some commentators suggest in fact that only at the end of question 11, when there has been proved to be only one God, shall we be at liberty to give what we have proved to exist the name 'God'. St Thomas, a little more realistically, connects the giving of the name with such general considerations as are referred to in the quotation above from the *Contra Gentes*, considerations which do not yet make it obvious, as he says, 'who or what the lawgiver of nature is, or whether he is only one'. For the ordinary man is not in fact usually clear as to whether there is one God or many, and it is only the ordinary man overawed by Christianity that now takes it for granted that there is one.

4. Another cause of difficulty is that the name 'God' is given in the first 'way' to 'some first cause of change', in the second to 'some first cause', in the third to 'the cause that other things must be', in the fourth to 'something which causes in all other things their being . . .', and in the fifth way to 'someone with understanding (directing) everything in nature to its goal'. It has been suggested that here we have five different ways of assigning the name 'God'; none of them, moreover, 'ordinary', but all rather philosophical. And yet one finds it difficult to distinguish the 'different' modes of assignation in the first four ways; and as regards the fifth way one would have said it showed forth a very 'ordinary' way of conceiving God. The first four ways are obviously concerned to trace the existence of *ultimate* causality, a cause behind *everything*, and the fifth way adds the note of intelligence which transforms that 'first cause' into a 'providence'.

5. It is fairly clear that this is what St Thomas thought most people meant by the word 'God': a providence at the causal beginning of the world we see. 'For everybody who talks of God uses the word to name that which exercises a universal providence over things. . . . It is used to signify something transcending all things, at the beginning of all things, separate from all things: it is this to which people using the word 'God' wish to refer.'[3] And however undeveloped this is as a notion, it is not difficult to see that all five ways arrive at it, and that it provides the basis for the further developments of the questions that follow. When considering them in later appendices (11-16) we shall see that the notion of God as a first origin, *primum principium*, the fount of being, becomes very quickly the ruling notion of the whole treatise, a fact to which St Thomas himself draws our attention later, when discussing the Trinity: 'Creatures can lead us to God only as effects to a cause. So natural reason can know about God only that which must belong to him as the first beginning of everything that exists; and this was the basis we used when considering God earlier.'[4]

---

[3] Ia. 13, 8 c. & ad 2
[4] Ia. 32, 1

Appendix 5

THE FIVE WAYS

1. THESE FIVE arguments, the *quinque viæ*, are reasoned ways which open out the prospect of the world caused by God. Their starting-points are distinct, yet how soon they converge is a matter of some debate. Some see them, as it were, as marking traffic-lines on the same road, from the composite to the simple, from the many to the one, from the parts to the whole, and, looking back from an insight they feel no need to analyse, may doubt the value of mapping them separately: indeed an early manuscript is content to speak of a passage by five modes or manners, *quinque modis*. Others, more deliberative in discovery and more attentive to the letter of the text, delay over the distinct conclusions that are reached.

That all five amount to the same thing is shown later, notably in the following question which meditates on the simplicity of God.[1] Then, as it is meant to be, preceding ratiocination is stilled in understanding, like motion in rest and choosing in enjoying;[2] a single recognition that the world as a whole depends on God succeeds reflection about its parts. Remember, too, that the philosophical theism which is developed in the *Summa*, though as thoroughgoing as that of Plotinus and using no substitute where reason can serve, is subsumed, according to its opening promise,[3] in the *sacra doctrina* of faith responding to God's revelation of himself in Christ.

2. We are tempted either to overstate or understate the force of the arguments. It is a temptation to the temper of philosophical mechanics that prevailed before Hume woke Kant from his dogmatic slumbers, and that still persists where flatly-conceived logic provides a board on which solidified metaphysical entities can be moved like chessmen, to treat them as though they offer brisk and quasi-geometrical demonstrations for anybody, except a complete empiricist, who is prepared to think hard. On the other hand, the contemporary feeling that rationalism lies outside a truly religious approach is prone to write them off—all very well as providing an admissible hypothesis for the theist mentality that asks their sort of question, but for the rest profane exercises that have little or nothing to do with our cleaving to the living God.

Kant says that it is very necessary that we should be convinced of God's existence, but not so necessary that we should prove it. St Thomas would agree. All the same he thinks that divine truth can be proved, and for some of us should be proved by the theoretic reason; it is not merely a postulate of the practical reason. Admittedly rational theory is no more than penul-

---

[1] 1a. 3. cf Appendix 12
[2] 1a. 79, 8; 83, 4. *In De Trin.* VI, I
[3] 1a. I, I, 3, 7, 8

188

timate, all the same, as appears in the introductory question to the *Summa*, it is an intrinsic part of *sacra doctrina* and neither irrelevant nor irreverent to the Christian mysteries. The arguments about to be considered display his characteristic combination of modesty and confidence; the power of reasoning is not overloaded to bear more than it will carry nor relegated to a rhetoric of religion.

They display a philosophical effort of construction, or of road-making towards what lies behind appearances. Inevitably the job is not complete, but it has to be done, and while a fideist may be excused if personally he finds the work unnecessary, so also an agnostic if he finds it too perplexing and the results unsatisfactory, a dogmatic atheist may well be challenged to show equal stamina of reason in sustaining his negation.

3. Before looking at the common build-up of the five proofs let us take from earlier works two parallel passages on what may be called inchoate theism. The first refers to the general observation that natural things follow a set order and the inference that therefore they are ordered by something. 'But who or what this is, or whether it be one or not, cannot be gathered from this initial general appreciation. Thus when we observe a man moving and functioning we judge there is a cause in him of this activity, and this we call *soul*, without yet knowing what it is, whether it be a body or not, or how it effects the activity.'[4]

The next passage, which acknowledges its debt to Avicenna, carries the same caution. God's existence is self-evident in itself but not to us, for though somehow implicit in all our knowledge, since every truth reflects and shares in the exemplar truth of God, *secundum suam similitudinem et participationem*, what we first recognize is truth manifested in things of sense, not in God's own substantial being. 'We observe sense-objects and do not reach God except by advancing from them as things which are caused and therefore require an efficient cause, and this ultimately cannot be a body. So we do not arrive at God except by process of argument, which is never demanded for the self-evident.'[5]

4. In these two portmanteau arguments are compressed the four stages that are more clearly marked in the *quinque viæ*. They are: (1) a reading from what we experience through our senses, namely that things are changing, dependent, temporal or contingent, limited, and directed; (2) that something else is implied; (3) which turns out to be itself unchanging, independent, eternal or necessary, unlimited, and not directed by another; (4) and this we call 'God'.

5. Before commenting on each in turn, remark that the ways can be taken in two manners, directly as they are discovered, *in via inventionis*, and reflexively as interpreted, *in via judicii*.[6] To start with they point to something far beyond our experience, yet what this is, or rather what this is not,

---

[4]*CG* III, 28. That the vague ideas men have about God are not enough for happiness. Note also the next chapter, that demonstrative knowledge takes us only a little further   [5]I *Sent.* 3, 1, 2   [6]Ia. 79, 8, 9

still remains much in the dark, and, though we give it the name 'God', is not manifested as the God we worship. Then later, when they are drawn together and the mind contemplates the qualities of uncreated and created being,[7] their evidence grows wider and yet more formed, deeper and yet clearer.

This goes to explain a difference among the commentators. Some, keeping close to the history of the arguments and their position in the *Summa*, do not move far from the context of medieval science and are content with a limited objective. Others, fearing distraction from the true bearing of the dialectic, take it into an ampler metaphysical setting, and, for instance, would free the first argument from ballistics, the second from our consciousness of being acted on, the third from existence in time, the fourth from degrees of physical extensity and intensity, and the fifth from a designed pattern in things: they may even feel that the article does not show St Thomas writing at the top of his form.

The opposition, which goes back earlier than to the age of High Thomism of Cajetan and Bañez in the sixteenth century and will reappear in the following appendices, is about where and when to lay the emphasis in commenting on the *Summa*; it will be seen in proportion if we allow that all the qualifications of an argument need not appear at the outset so long as they are made during the course of development. For the arguments can be set in three periods, of *scientia* which discovers a conclusion, of philosophical *sapientia* which takes a more total view and judges the conclusion in its highest rational causes, and finally of the wisdom of *sacra doctrina* when the highest cause is *veritas prima* accepted by divine faith.[8] These periods are abstractions which can be distinguished, not separable situations for someone who, like St Thomas in the *Summa*, is a Christian thinking single-mindedly about God.

Note that the second reading does not represent the argumentations, for all their display of logical analysis, as directed to pure concepts, forms, or essences, but as searching, throughout, into an existing world, and beyond to the being who supports it. The natural theology that results does not compose a system merely of meanings; it is about things as they are, and in the *Summa* it is an overture to the study of God's revelation in history. In St Thomas's mind the thought rises from living experience, and its translation into our minds has to accept some embarrassments from its original exemplification. From these it can escape, yet without finding refuge among the ideas of Descartes or Leibniz or Wolff.

T. G.

---

[7] Ia. 2–13; 44–9
[8] cf Ia. 1, 6, 7; 79, 9. Ia2æ. 57, 2

Appendix 6

THE FIRST WAY

1. PLATO, THE father of philosophical theology, writes in the *Laws* as an old man who regards atheism as a piece of youthful extravagance and has hardened in his condemnation of the crime of false theological tenets issuing from the theories of Ionians and Sophists. Arguing for the divine government of the world, he discovers motions of soul, ψυχή, behind the unintelligent motions of the corporeal universe. His proof, which elaborates the *Phædrus* on immortality, turns on the examination of motion, κίνησις. This is divided into communicated motion and its source in spontaneous motion, which last is alive, ἔμψυχον. Soul or mind is the cause of all cosmic movement, but although this may culminate in the perfectly good soul, ἀριστή ψυχή, the reasoning disregards the question, rarely felt by the Greeks to be capital, whether there be only one God or many.[1]

Aristotle gets behind self-initiated movement to a still more ultimate cause, the unmoved first mover of others, ἀκίνητον κινητικόν δ᾽ ἕτερον. The steps of the argument are worked out in the *Physics*,[2] and are more theologically presented in the twelfth book of the *Metaphysics*, which has the appearance of having been composed as a separate work:[3] both places are systematically studied in St Thomas's commentaries.[4] Aristotle's theology is Plato's, but written in the terms of a physicist, not a moralist. As to whether his God moves as a final or an efficient cause, it is enough here to remark that these are not alternatives,[5] and that the ultimate object of desire is treated as a present force, not merely an anticipated ideal.

2. The theology seems to be committed to a particular astronomical theory, that of Eudoxus, and can be regarded, not unfairly, as an appendix to physics. The same could be said, in a preliminary and partial sense, of the argument presented by St Thomas. He took it in the first place from the Arabic Aristoteleans; when genetically isolated it can be criticized, as it was by the Scotists, for its adoption of a middle term from physics. Two classical commentaries are much exercised on this point; Ferrariensis twists and turns,[6] and Cajetan resigns himself to the immediate conclusion that the first mover is no more immobile than the human soul.[7] Set the argument, however, in its complete background, against the overhanging questions on God's immutability and eternity,[8] and charged with the metaphysics of actuality and potentiality at the heart of created beings, then one agrees with Bañez that the middle term

---

[1] *Laws* x, 896A   [2] VII–VIII. 241b24–267b26   [3] XII, 6–7. 1071b3–1073a14
[4] *In Physic* VII, lect. 1–9; VIII, lect. 1–23. *In Meta*, XII, lect. 5–8
[5] cf 1a. 103, 1, 5; 105, 3, 4, 5
[6] *Summa Contra Gentiles, cum commentariis* I, 13. Paris, 1552
[7] Commentarii. In 1am. 2, 3. Venice, 1508.   [8] 1a. 9–10

covers all motion, even the application of spiritual power to activity and the attraction of final causes.[9] As such it moves on a plane where it is neither confirmed nor impugned by theories about projectiles or by the laws of thermodynamics.

3. The *prima via*, described by St Thomas as the most open, *manifestior*, of the five, though for us it has become congested with traffic-blocks, starts from Aristotle's faithfulness to fact: movement cannot be regarded as illusory, and if we seek to explain it we arrive at something itself exempt from movement. 1. It examines what is meant by movement; 2. reflects that what is in movement must be set in movement by another, and furthermore that 3. no explanation is reached by infinitely prolonging the series of movers and moved; 4. and infers that a first mover exists which is not subject to movement, and this is what everybody understands by 'God'. These four steps call for separate examination.

4. The *Summa* sometimes uses *motus*, movement or motion, in the widest sense to include life and spontaneous activity, and the term is applied to God and the immanent acts of knowing and loving.[10] As such, the *actus perfecti existentis*, it is contrasted with what is dead, inert, potential and non-actual.[11] Here, however, it is restricted to change, *mutatio*, the transition or process from one condition to another.[12] Change is taken according to Aristotle's resolution of the opposition between Heraclitus and Parmenides, ἡ τοῦ δυνατοῦ, ᾗ δυνατόν, ἐντελέχεια, or in St Thomas's words, *actus imperfecti scilicet existentis in potentia inquantum hujusmodi*, which can be rendered, incomplete actualization, namely of something still as such really potential.[13] The clumsiness of the description is recognized and unavoidable, for perhaps movement can be movingly expressed only by metaphor, but it brings out the composition within change of dual principles, the potential and the actual. There is a being not yet completed but able to be completed (*ens in potentia*) with respect to a being completed (*ens in actu*). These two are already joined in a process of becoming, which, as it were, is a flow of being half-potential, half-actual. The thing in movement is a subject, *motum et patiens*, of what is really going on because of the presence of a force, *movens et agens*. The process is indicated rather than defined, since rational terms arrest meanings, and we tend to speak of a state of motion which, etymologically at least, is a contradiction in terms, since state implies stability and motion the reverse.

Motion so understood is not confined to local motion, but applies also to transformation of substance, as when one kind of thing becomes another, to instantaneous changes of accidents, as when a man is converted from

---

[9]*Scholastica Commentaria*. In 1am. 2, 3. Salamanca, 1588
[10]1a. 9, 1 ad 1; 14, 2 ad 2; 18, 3 ad 1; 58, 1 ad 1. 1a2æ. 31, 2 ad 1. *In De anima* III, *lect.* 12 (Aristotle 431a6)
[11]1a. 9, 1 ad 2; 18, 1–3   [12]cf 1a. 45, 2 ad 2; 3
[13]*Physics* III, 1–2. 201a10, 201b4, 202a7. *In Physic.* III, *lect.* 2–3. *Metaphysics* XI, 9. 1065b5–1066a35. *In Meta.* XI, *lect.* 9

non-loving to loving, as well as to successive changes, such as the alteration of qualities, the addition or subtraction of quantities, and the movement from one place to another.[14] Consequently the argument does not hinge on debated questions of celestial mechanics, though they may be involved for the historian of science and philosophy, but abstracts the universal implications of change as such, that is of *fieri* or becoming in terms of *esse* or being.[15]

5. Next, by reduction to the principle of contradiction it is impossible for the potential as such to be the actual as such, or for the becoming fulfilled to be the being fulfilled at the same time at the same spot. Hence you look outside the being in motion for the principle imparting the motion, or rather, since the analysis transcends the ordinary common-sense image of space, you conclude that the moving principle is 'other' than the principle in motion, according to the formula, *omne quod movetur ab alio movetur*, ἅπαν τὸ κινούμενον ὑπό τινος κινεῖσθαι.[16] Note that this should be taken with formal precision; it means that the passive is not as such the active, not that one and the same thing or substance may not initiate its own movement within a particular system of reference, as is the case with living things. Nor at this preliminary stage does it suppose or state, as has sometimes been thought, the numerical diversity of things: were the world one substance and it was agreed that change was real you would still have to posit somewhere a principle for change which is exempt from change.

6. The argument now enlarges its depth of focus. What is being looked at is movement as a single situation where *actio-passio* are conjoined in one thing or one real universe, not as a transmission of particles along a line of units or a tide of waves of energy. Moreover, this situation is not confined to the initial passage, but extends to the whole condition of being in motion. The full argument performs a kind of 'lumping-together', so that the entire universe is considered as in motion: this will appear later in the *Summa*, and also during appendices that follow.

What we are looking for is the principle into which the change can be resolved, and if many factors are involved then they must be arranged in essential subordination, thus chisel, muscles, nerves, senses, artist, Michelangelo. What we should not look for is the first mover within a series of things each giving and receiving the same sort of movement, thus chisel number one, number two and so forth. Such a series is said to be in accidental subordination, for though the units follow one another they do not depend on one another for their movement. We shall return to this point in considering the argument from causality in the next appendix.

In the meantime let us refer to the question of a series of items stretching endlessly backwards. There are problems about infinite magnitudes and numbers,[17] but whichever way they are solved bears no relation to the need

---

[14]We neglect here the questions of creation (1a. 45, 2) and transubstantiation (3a. 75, 3-7)   [15] cf 1a. 2, 3 ad 2; 79, 4; 105, 5. 1a2æ. 9, 4
[16]*Physics* VII, 1. 241b24. *In Physic.* VII, *lect.* 1. *In Meta.* V, *lect.* 14
[17]1a. 7, 3-4

of having to stop, ἀνάγχη στῆναῖ, at the first mover of the world in process of change. St Thomas himself held that it was impossible for the reason to demonstrate that the world had started once upon a time. In other words the concept of an infinite series is admissible: a closely reasoned process of elimination shows that created reality and everlasting reality are not mutually exclusive concepts.[18] So in the *prima via* he is not attempting to follow a chain of movers-in-motion to the end. The first mover he arrives at is not number one of the series, but outside it. As you watch a long train of goods wagons clattering past your surmise is that they are being pulled by some other force, not a leading wagon, and you will still require something like a locomotive even if it is suggested that the train of trucks needs neither to have had a beginning nor to be going to have an end. The mover-moved relationship, then, is understood not by a repetition of antecedents before consequents keeping always at the same level, but by rising above it; hence any being in motion will serve to take us directly to the being which is not in motion. This will appear more clearly when movement is explicated in causality, and the first cause is seen to be immediately operative in every effect.[19]

7. The argument leads to a first mover which is not itself in motion, *primum movens immobile*. Notice the moderation of the conclusion, which claims no insight into God's own existence, but merely says that there is source of motion, ἀρχη κινήσεως, and this we understand to be God.

Lest a contradiction be suspected here, namely that what commences to move another cannot itself be immobile, observe that the mover-moved relationship is taken according to what is essentially implied, and is not defined by a transference of energy from one thing to another or by our experience of particular kinds of movement. That the mover itself should have been moved by another is incidental, *per accidens*; as such and *per se*, as Aristotle notices, the mover is immobile.[20] For to move another is to actualize, and therefore as such to be actual and not to be potential.

Also lest such an immobile principle be thought of as too inhuman for devotion, and too static to bear any resemblance to the living God, reflect that its stillness is that of pure activity. If Aristotle's God may seem remote, especially if νόησις νοήσεως is translated a thinking on thinking,[21] in St Thomas, heir to the Christian humanism of Chartres and therefore to the gracious spirit of Plato, this *actus purus* is invested with the nobility of every perfection,[22] and holds the unbounded life of eternity,[23] sought in every desire and exemplified at the heart of every delight.[24] But this is to anticipate. Let us return to the mover and the moved, and end with the echo of the psalm.

---

[18]Opusc. De *æternitate mundi contra murmurantes*. cf Ia. 46, 1–3. *CG* II, 31–8
[19]Appendices, 3, 7, 11
[20]*Physics* VIII, 5. 256a3–257a33. *In Physic.* VIII, *lect.* 9. Action as such is motionless; cf Ia. 41, 1 ad 2; 53, 1 ad 2. The strength of God is his immutability; 1a2æ. 61, 5
[21]*Metaphysics* XII, 9. 1074b34. *In Meta.* XII, *lect.* 11
[22]cf Appendix 13
[23]cf Appendix 16   [24]1a2æ. 30, 4; 31, 2

APPENDIX 6. THE FIRST WAY

The heavens declare the glory of God,[25] when St James looks beyond the revolutions of the heavenly bodies and tells us that *every good gift and every perfect gift is from above, and cometh down from the Father of lights, with whom there is no variableness, neither shadow of turning.*[26] The text in effect is a packed comment on the *prima via,* and how warm it is and how accurate.

T. G.

---

[25]*Psalm* 18 (19)
[26]*James* I, 17

Appendix 7

THE SECOND WAY

1. HERE ST THOMAS, one may hold, comes more into his own, for the middle term is now enlarged from motion, as in the *prima via*, to the sustained dependence of the activity evident in our surroundings. The argument turns on things being operative, productive, or effective, rather than on things undergoing a process of change, and on producing, *actus motoris*, rather than on becoming produced, *actus mobilis*: these notes, while not representing diverse elements, are at least distinct enough to provide grounds for two discussions.[1]

In both cases, however, the course of the argument goes through the same stages. Accordingly we shall look at 1. experience and causality; 2. indicate that the 'cause' which is correlative to the 'effect' (from *ex-facere*, to work out) is other than it; 3. that an infinite causal series is impossible; and 4. the conclusion that a first uncaused cause exists, to which everybody gives the name 'God'.

2. The second way begins, 'In the world of sense we find there an order of efficient causes': note the implication that a causal order is discovered in experience, not there disclosed. As we shall soon see, causality in the full sense is a metaphysical conclusion, not an extremely abridged account of empirically registered facts. The later Alexandrian sceptics denounced the search for 'causes', and their criticism finds famous expression in Hume—register your facts, induct your laws, and then remember that as a philosopher you have reached your goal. That events follow a pretty regular course is accepted and that they will continue to do so is expected; hence the sciences, concerned with the co-ordination of items in their own respective systems, rightly rely on some sort of necessary succession of antecedents and consequents, and will want a system of prediction for the operation of apparently random factors.

This, however, does not amount to the causality considered by St Thomas. The critique of science, more aware of the difference between 'plain facts' and 'scientific facts', and of the construction that has gone into the latter, is nowadays less inclined than formerly to accept the old empirical account of scientific method, and even to admit that 'theory' must come in before any 'observation' can be made, and that some sort of deduction is prior to argumentative induction. Nevertheless we can risk over-simplification and say

---

[1]Note in anticipation that creatures are not wholly active or productive, since their substance or being is not identical with their activity. cf 1a. 44, 1, 2

For diversity and distinction see Appendix 13 (5). For the distinction between causality as it appears in the *prima via* and in the *secunda via* see Appendix 11 (2, 3). For causality and experience cf Appendix 3

that if philosophy is ruled out then causality does little more than promulgate a general law, written in a kind of shorthand and often in mathematical notation, summing up the results of induction from cases of 'this' constantly following after 'that'. Afterwards an *ad hoc* explanation for this happening may be attempted by a scientific hypothesis, which, however, will be regarded less as true or false than as good or bad, that is as likely or far-fetched, neat or inelegant, timely or out-moded, useful for advance or unpromising.

All the same the scientist is a man, and man is an animal who hunts for real reasons, and so is driven ever deeper to find explanations; he begins to think of 'things', not merely of 'happenings'. And then, as soon as he begins to ask 'why?', and answer 'because', he is entering philosophy and warming to the idea of 'cause'. True, he may shy off when told that he is thinking metaphysically, partly perhaps because he has learned a lesson from the unfortunate history of metaphysicians intruding their own concepts into a field where, though not unexemplified, they offer no substitute for the proper concepts of the particular science concerned, and possess no heuristic value. Professional metaphysicians do not stand alone in venturing such spurious terms, for all scientists except the closest and narrowest specialists seek wisdom by breaking out into the widest views,[2] and qualify as metaphysicians, if with an amateur status. Indeed controlled imagery is the due tribute we pay to the analogy of being, and it can be doubted whether terms are spurious so long as they do not displace the proper terms for the discipline in question and are not too stiffly applied—and we are aware of transferring their specific meaning from one subject to another.

Let us admit, after all, that thinking about the general comes easier to us than thinking about the particular, if thinking means theory: Aristotle and St Thomas say as much. The more abstract the interest the simpler it is; inasmuch as it is less complicated the difficulties offered call more for subtlety than for hard work, for understanding at depth more than for calculating, for discerning the essential conditions of being more than for systematizing its diverse and heterogeneous manifestations in phenomena.

3. Some such sort of preface serves to lead into the meaning causality has for the *Summa*. It is not concerned with two events, nor even with two diverse things, pictured as one here and the other there in space, the first, as it were, firing into the second and scoring hits that can be registered and recorded. Causality is discerned as a transaction within one being as motion or change is discerned within its subject;[3] and this being caused, like the being changed, though found not to be self-explanatory, is not escaped from, but remains the object of interior examination.[4] Moreover this is inspected, not in its pure idea, but in a judgment that refers to an existing thing: in the case of the *secunda via* to an active thing.

All the same if real and active in itself the thing is not so of itself. Judged

---

[2] cf Ia2æ. 57, 2
[3] cf Appendix 6
[4] cf Appendix 2 (7, 8). Also Vol. I, Appendix 9 (34–6)

to be neither simply self-existing nor wholly self-acting, in both respects it is inferred to depend on an existing and acting 'other', which is its cause.

A cause is a real and positive principle from and on which another proceeds and depends for what it actually is and does. There are four types of causes, final, efficient, material, and formal;[5] here in the *secunda via* the argument immediately engages only the efficient cause. This is the *agens*, the active and executive principle producing the effect, to which it is prior in nature though not necessarily in time, and into which it does not enter as a component part. Efficient cause is a stronger term to a philosopher than to a scientist, who may require no more than an antecedent map-reference or a condition favouring the appearance of an *event*, without thinking of it as exerting and maintaining influence on the inner nature of an *effect*. It is also a stronger term than 'occasion', or juncture of opportune circumstances for something to be done or made. Furthermore its meaning is more 'universal' in philosophy than in a particular science, since it is translated into the abstract medium of 'being'; there it belongs to a full efficient cause to produce and conserve a thing completely, both as to its *esse* and to its *agere*.

4. For an effect to be intelligible (or, to use a terminology later than St Thomas, to have 'sufficient reason') we have to look into its being and activity, and then through and beyond its spring of being and activity, that is to its cause. Now in a series of causal dependents you cannot go back indefinitely. The text of the argument is clear, perhaps too clear, for when you read that without a first cause you cannot have an intermediate cause (or intermediate causes) and a last cause (namely the one posited as present), you might presume that the clause refers to causes linked together in the same chain or to a series of agents of the same kind, starting with 1, going on to 2, 3, 4, &c., and ending, let us say, with 55, taken to stand for the last effect (namely the one confronting us).

Such a causal series is said to be in accidental subordination, that is to say, such causality as 1 exerts on 2 is incidental, *per accidens*, to such causality as 2 exerts on 3, and 3 on 4, and so forth. Such is the case with human generation, when, as St Thomas says, a man begets a child because he is a man, not because he is the son of his father.[6] In this type of series you cannot infer from the present existence of the last the present existence of the first; what is more, and no less a disqualification for philosophical theism, you cannot infer a first cause at all. For human genealogy, St Thomas adds, can possibly stretch back indefinitely.[7] If a halt in the past has to be called it will not be in the name of causality; it may be because of problems involved in natural science by infinite magnitudes or multitudes,[8] and for Christians it will be because of faith. That things started once upon a time is admissible and to be believed, but not capable of proof, *credibile, non autem demonstrabile vel scibile.*[9]

The first cause the argument is seeking is therefore of another kind. If

---

[5]Appendix 11 (1) [6]Ia. 46, 2 ad 7 [7]Ibid
[8]cf Ia. 7, 3, 4 [9]Ia. 46, 2

human generation be the starting-point, this causal origin will not be our first parents but a reality outside the series, like the mover with respect to things in motion.[10] Outside, but not remote, for the prime will be as close to any subsequent generation as to the inaugural generation, and closer to the generating now than this is to the generating then.[11] The series in question is of causes in essential subordination or related *per se*, namely when one exists actively in virtue of the active existence of another and therefore 'higher' being.

The continuity is along the line—if that is not too thin a word—of causation, not of objects that happen in succession, which so far as causality may be concerned may march without beginning in the past or end in the future. When, however, we are resolving a properly causal series, and are faced with a dependent or derived action, we may in the first place uncover another dependent or derived action to account for it, and then go on to uncover more of the same sort, yet eventually we must come to a stop and conclude that there exists an action which is neither dependent nor derived, though what the agent is we do not as yet know. We shall gather during later developments of the argument that the sequence is not prolonged through a great number of factors; accordingly to speak about extending the series is here better avoided. If causation be taken metaphysically, that is purely in terms of *esse* and *agere*, then the highest or the deepest cause (the *causa altissima* judged by wisdom) is swiftly reached from any one exemplification of causation. St Thomas does not treat causation as a number of successive changes strung together, but as the co-presence of effect and cause in one proceeding; he is forming a whole, not searching for the first of a class, and so he looks, not from one action to the previous action, but deeper and deeper into one action within which a higher principle contains a lower. The origins are soon found to lie as deep as divinity.

The world is caused because now it depends on God, not because it was started in the past. He is not another world but of the same sort as ours; then there would be no truly causal dependence, for, though according to popular speech like causes like, if the likeness is univocal, as between members of the same species, one individual may indeed cause another individual to come about (*causa secundum fieri*) but does not cause its nature nor conserve its being (*causa secundum esse*):[12] a full cause is an *agens æquivocum*, and the likeness between it and the effect is analogical.[13]

God might then be supposed to be another world, but of a higher kind than ours, indeed of the highest and best kind. Although at first sight the *quinque viæ* might appear to carry us no further than to such a pantheon, reflection shows that they are not concerned with another world at all—if that means an order of things that bears sufficient resemblance to our world

---

[10] cf Appendix 6 (6, 7)
[11] cf Appendices 15 (2) & 16 (3)
[12] Ia. 104, 1
[13] Ia. 4, 2, 3; 6, 2. *CG* I, 29, 31

to enable us to deal with it in something of the same way and ask its cause. They all point to something of which the question, 'what caused it?' cannot be asked. The commentators may differ about the speed at which they should be taken, but not about the implications of their conclusions, or, when they have met together, of their common conclusion. Then a broader way leads us to the conclusion that God is not a kind of thing at all; he is not in a genus since he is pure being and the fount of all being, *principium totius esse*; he is outside and beyond every genus and can consequently cause every kind of thing, *extra omne genus et principium omnium generum*.[14]

5. The opening argument, St Albert remarks, proves only that God exists in the manner of a cause.[15] The religious appeal of the conclusion is limited, but not inconsiderable. God is named from our universe, and we are not told what God is in himself, though soon we are told a lot about creatures and how in some ways they are like him.[16] Later St Thomas will try to show that in speaking about God we can surpass this creaturely reference, so that when we declare that he is good we mean more than that he is the cause of goodness:[17] an effort that will become easier when, writing specifically as a Christian theologian, his understanding is founded on faith in God's revelation of himself.

T. G.

---

[14]Ia. 3, 5; 4, 3 ad 2
[15]*Summa Theologiæ*, I, 3, 18
[16]Ia. 4, 3
[17]Ia. 13, 2, 6

Appendix 8

THE THIRD WAY

1. CAUSALITY RUNS through all five arguments. The first has taken the actualizing of the effect, the second the acting of the cause; now attention shifts and deepens to the finite being of the effect, considered in its duration by the third, and in its sharing, *participatio*, in existence by the fourth: the fifth can be expanded to consider all finite being as tending to an end.

2. Plato reasons that were nothing deathless nothing now would be alive;[1] Plotinus and St Augustine pick up the same theme.[2] The distinction between necessary and contingent predication is essential to Aristotle's logic, and the existence of ungenerated and indestructible heavenly bodies is cardinal to his natural philosophy, yet for the conclusion that there exists a metaphysical ground of reality that cannot be otherwise St Thomas owes more to the Arabic philosophers than to him, or to Boëthius and the *Liber de Causis*. His wording echoes Maimonides, who took the proof from Avicenna.[3] Everything that is exists either as a 'bound to be' or as a 'possible', this last seeming to signify, for Avicenna and also for Averroes, an essence to which existence is added as an incidental predicate.

3. The difficulty is that existence, *esse*, is not strictly speaking a predicate. Though some may be of the opinion that the *Summa* text lays itself open to the charge of treating existence as a predicate, St Thomas elsewhere makes it evident that his distinction between essence and existence is not between the conceivable and the real, but between the potential and the actual within real created substance: the tenor of the third argument should be read accordingly.

The meaning of three terms he commonly uses may be touched on, namely *ens*, *esse*, and *essentia*. *Ens*, or being, can be treated, like *studens*, either as a noun or as a participle. As a noun it is applied to anything, and signifies that which is, *id quod est*; as such it can be treated as an essential predicate only of a necessary or *per se* being. As a participle it signifies primarily existence, *esse*, that whereby a thing is, *quo est*, and secondarily the subject or essence, the what which a thing, *res*, is, *quod quid est*, hence *quidditas*, an abstract construction like *entitas*, and also *realitas*, not one of St Thomas's terms.[4]

4. The *tertia via*, given in the *Contra Gentes* as an argument for divine eternity,[5] follows the order of the first and second ways, and starts from the plain fact that things are born and die away. Yet were everything perishable,

---

[1]*Phædo* 72. *Phædrus* 245-247
[2]*Enneads* IV, 7. *Confessions* XI, 4
[3]*The Guide of the Perplexed*. Ed. M. Friedländer. London, 1925, Part II, p. 152. Aristotle argues to the same effect for an indestructible 'heaven' in *De cælo* I, 11 sqq
[4]For *esse* also see Appendix 12 (7)
[5]*CG* I, 15

without anything to keep it from perishing, once there would have existed nothing at all, and consequently nothing would exist now. Instead we must posit a necessary being, which exists of itself, *per se*, and possesses what the Latin translator of Avicenna called the *vehementia essendi*.

5. A thing's necessity is either caused by another or not. If not, then we have the conclusion; if caused, then to explain that causes recede *ad infinitum* is like taking refuge in the old myth that the earth is supported by a giant who stands upon a great tortoise who squats on the back of a great elephant whose legs reach all the way down. Therefore a being exists necessary of itself, which has no cause for its necessity but is the cause of the necessity of other things.

6. Three comments on the argument. First, there are various kinds of necessity. The main distinction lies between absolute and conditional necessity.[6] This last ranges from fact to theory; if something has happened, however contingently, it achieves the necessity that now it cannot be otherwise;[7] again the rules of logic admit no alternative, for instance a valid conclusion drawn from a negative premise is bound to be negative; again, a hypothetical necessity invests means if an end is to be obtained; then again, our thoughts may reflect the unchangeable reasons for things in the divine mind, as when we judge that the whole is greater than the part, reality obeys the law of contradiction, friendship is fair in itself, and lying is always wrong.

Many modern philosophers hold that 'necessary' applies only to statements, but it is perfectly sensible to talk, as St Thomas does, about necessary beings, that is things not liable to go out of existence. His argument is about things, and points to the absolutely necessary existent, which requires no condition at all for its necessity, and is implied in every other necessity in things and in statements about them. In brief, if God does not exist nothing is possible.

7. Next, despite some similarity with the Anselmic argument,[8] fallacious reasoning from the conceptual to the real is absent. Existence is not regarded as a predicate that can be inferred from another predicate. (Note that non-existence can be inferred about an object to which incompatible predicates are assigned.) From the beginning and throughout the *Summa*, arguments are about things, and proceed from one manner of existence to another. Here the middle term of the argument is not the notion of beings that conceivably can be or not be, but the existence of such beings. In working from the world to God it works from one existent to another.

8. Finally, like the others, you can take this proof both directly from the beginning or reflexively from the end, or like a prelude about creatures of time and like a coda about creatureliness in a duration beyond time.[9] At first it is enough, Cajetan cautiously observes, that it introduces prime

---

[6]1a. 19, 3, 8; 82, 1; 116, 3. *CG* 1, 67
[7]1a. 25, 4. cf 1a. 16, 8 ad 4
[8]1a. 2, 1 obj. 2
[9]cf Appendix 16

necessary being, without bothering whether this be one or many, though it is evident from the argument itself that it cannot be a collection of contingent things, and from the *prima via* that it is not a steady flow underlying phenomena. Nor would a mental 'law of necessity' meet the case, for what is sought is basic being, not a notional reflection of it.

If, however, you read on and then return to the proof, enjoying a deeper insight into the perfection implied where essence is existence,[10] you will then concentrate on the inherent inadequacy of contingency to explain itself, be less involved with time and less hampered by the difficult third and fourth sentences of the text, and conclude to one single necessary being. Whereas at first the 'possible not to exist' will be read as the 'possible to go out of existence in time', as in the latter of the text and in the knotty argument, closely analysed by St Thomas, in Aristotle's cosmology where he tries to show that something which always existed and will exist is something which must exist,[11] later the *possibile* will be related to *esse* and *non esse* as such, not to *esse tale* and *non esse tale*, this or that kind of existence possessed by things subject to generation and corruption. While the human mind in its present condition starts the argument from looking at ordinary things perishable in time, the blessed in heaven could turn to their timeless yet profoundly contingent surroundings and frame the same metaphysical argument—if they cared to.

T. G.

---

[10]Ia. 4, 4; 4, 2. *CG* I, 28
[11]*De Cælo* I, 11–12. 281a–283b26. St Thomas *in loc. lect.* 25–6

Appendix 9

THE FOURTH WAY

1. THIS ARGUMENT, which appears more imaginative than the last as gazing not at the duration but at the perfection of things in existence, notably at the 'good' that is in them, a good that promises the 'best', is anticipated by Plato,[1] St Augustine,[2] and St Anselm.[3] Elements of it appear in Aristotle.[4] St Thomas stresses the factor of causal dependence in the texture of existing things, not merely of ideas: this is its sterngth.[5]

The stages are similar to those taken by the preceding proofs: 1. the observation of degrees of being; 2. the reflection that 'more or less' implies a 'most'; 3. that the most and noblest being is cause of all other being and good; 4. and this we call God.

2. 'More or less' is taken by analogy for quantity to signify the comparative gradation of forms and perfections;[6] form may be taken to represent any sparkle of being for knowledge, and perfection any attraction for love.

Either quality or substantial being may express perfection. In the first case it can vary by extent or by intensity; extensive growth is measured by the objects covered, intensive growth by the depth of rooting in the subject, thus we can understand or love more and more things and we can grow more and more understanding or loving. Substantial being may be signified by the specific or generic nature of a thing, and in this narrow typological sense perfections do not vary; cats and catmint exhibit the same essentials of vegetable life, and all men are equal not as persons, but as specimens of human nature. Addition here or subtraction changes the species, for species, Aristotle often tells us, are like numbers. Such a formal perfection is predicated univocally, or in the same sense, of all who possess it, and for such a form, bound up with matter, there is not a 'most', still less a causal 'most';[7] as already noticed, a full cause is above or beyond the species of the effect.[8]

If, however, the perfection is not such as to be definable specifically by genus and difference it can be shared in or 'participated' with a constancy of meaning that admits differences of degree.[9] Thus the transcendental attributes of being—truth, unity, goodness, and perhaps beauty. These perfections are called analogical, that is they can be predicated variously of diverse subjects, and it is with these, despite the possibly misleading reference to 'the greatest hot thing' that the argument is concerned.[10] Recall the distinc-

---

[1] cf *Phædo* 75, 77, 93, 100. *Republic* v, 476; vi, 506–7
[2] *De Trinitate* viii, 3. cf *De civitate Dei* xi, 16
[3] *Monologium* 1–4
[4] *Metaphysics* iv, 5. 1008b31–1009a5. St Thomas *in loc. lect.* 9
[5] cf Appendices 3 & 11   [6] 1a2æ. 52, 1. For 'perfection' cf Appendix 13
[7] 1a. 44, 3 ad 2   [8] cf Appendix 7 (4)   [9] 1a. 13, 3 ad 1
[10] cf 1a. 6, 2 ad 3. *CG* ii, 15, for fire as the hottest of things and the cause of heat

tion we have drawn between two periods for the *quinque viæ*, namely when they lead out of a particular cosmological background and when they are retraced in the light of what has been learned. At this second or metaphysical period St Thomas is spared the embarrassment of Platonists who do not distinguish between univocal and analogical perfections; he is not looking for a 'most' horse, but for a 'most' being, not for the best of a kind, but for the best being above all kinds.[11]

3. That 'more or less' implies a 'most' does not remain with the grammar of comparatives and superlatives but is drawn into philosophical insight. Where a perfection is found in diverse things and at various strengths then it is involved *a.* with multiplicity, because it is repeated, and *b.* in composition, because it is not pure. When the same perfection is possessed by things of themselves diverse then all cannot possess it of themselves.[12] Where a perfection is possessed but with a limitation or qualification there it is received in the potentiality of a subject. On these counts we ascend *a.* from the many to the One possessing the perfection of itself, and *b.* from the composite to the Simple, where the perfection is sheerly actual without admixture of potentiality.[13]

4. The argument, which is not an unattached piece of conceptual analysis, hinges on perfections really existing, and opens to the existing of their cause. Though the temper of the dialectic is Platonic, it is content to indicate how the world about it is charged with a strength not its own, or rather not from itself, without proposing an escape to another world of pure forms.

5. All perfections referred to are ultimately resolved into the perfection of existence, *esse*. This is not taken according to its meaning in the logic of statements, as when we say that this is that; nor vaguely and generally to indicate being at one or two removes from non-existence, as when we say that something merely is, but to refer to the actuality of every form or nature, the culmination of every perfection.[14] The way is prepared for the next question, on the existential essence or essential existence of God, who alone is pure act and *ipsum esse subsistens*.[15]

6. Other arguments exemplify this ascent from participated being to pure being and sometimes in a warmer atmosphere; they can be regarded as applications of the *quarta via*. Thus the inference from intelligence to first intelligence,[16] and from truth to eternal truth,[17] dear to St Augustine, suggested here and there in the *Summa*, and kindled by the oratory of Bossuet and Fénelon. Thus also the inference from the good and desirable to the best and supreme object of desire, τὸ ἄριστον, τὸ πρῶτον ὀρεκτον,[18] and from law to the Eternal Law.[19]

T. G.

---

[11]*In Meta.* II, *lect.* 2 (993b25–30). 1a. 13, 5, 6, for analogy of terms used of creatures and God

[12]*De potentia* III, 5   [13]1a. 3, 7; 65, 1. *CG* II, 15. *De potentia* III, 8

[14]1a. 3, 4; 4, 1 ad 3; 2 ad 1. *CG* I, 28   [15]1a. 3, 4

[16]1a. 14, 4; 16, 2; 79, 4   [17]*CG* II, 84. 1a. 16, 6, 7

[18]1a. 60, 5. 1a2æ. 1, 4, 6; 2, 8; 3, 1, 8; 5, 8   [19]1a2æ. 19, 4; 91, 1, 2

Appendix 10

THE FIFTH WAY

1. SINCE TELEOLOGY is so conspicuous a feature of Aristotle's theory of the structure and history of nature, you might expect from him the conclusion that things move towards the fulfilment of some divine plan. Despite a few traces here and there of this line of thought, for instance when the order of the universe is compared to a household or army and is assigned to the head or general, or when a providential activity for the maintenance of species is allowed, or when Anaxagoras is praised for introducing reason as the cause of the ordered disposition of things, unlike Plato he never speaks of foresight or providence, πρόνοια, in God. His concept of purpose relates to ethics and deliberate choice, whereas τὸ ἕνεκά, 'that for the sake of which', or the final cause, corresponds rather to the biological concept of function in the light of the whole organism. As a biologist he is mainly interested in the 'internal directedness' of organic development. Sometimes he contrasts the works of thought and of nature. And though without a mind somewhere directedness is at most unconscious purpose, and unconscious purpose is no purpose at all, his language suggests that, like many modern thinkers, he does not feel the difficulty.[1]

2. In approaching the question St Thomas's mind was of course informed by the Christian doctrine of divine Providence. This is a matter of biography, not of philosophy: the student might expect him to strain the rational evidences, but may well conclude that in fact he does not.

His starting-point, as with the other arguments, is an observed composition, this time of means and ends, not of the changeable and the changing, of the able to act and the acting, of the possible to be and the being, of being partial and not wholly perfect. Like the other arguments, too, it can be taken in two manners, initially as it appears in the text, and reflexively in the context of the metaphysics of final causality. In the first manner it might almost seem to be the argument from design, perhaps not too well compressed, which proves at most that there is some sort of directing mind in the universe: this, for Cajetan, is sufficient at this early stage. In the second manner it need not be based on an observed scheme of associated things nor be restricted unconscious action which seems directed to a purpose, but can proceed, like the other arguments without pursuing a series of subordinates,[2] from any one example of a thing or things where activity as a function of being can be explained only in relation to an end not yet achieved, or a more complete whole not yet disclosed. As such it is read in the light of the four preceding proofs, all of which are variations on the principle that

---

[1] cf Appendix 11 (6). *Physics* II, 8. 198b10–199b34. St Thomas *in loc. lect.* 12–14
[2] Appendices 6 (6), 7 (4), 8 (5)

the potential is causally actualized only by the actual, and notably in the light of the fourth proof, in which all 'desire' is interpreted as a response to the ultimate object of desire. This may be the reason why St Thomas puts this argument last, though of all its appeal is the most popular.

3. It turns on the truth that means cannot be directed to ends except by an intelligent cause. How is the means-end composition brought about? The terms are not yet united, otherwise we should not see things acting as they do, 'questing' as it were, or at least not yet at rest. Yet the terms are related. Where then if not in some sort of prevision? This implies intelligence. Consequently, since we find things without intelligence related to ends, we infer a directing intelligence outside them. The text of the *quinta via* confines itself to these limits, but the argument can be amplified to refer to all functions that need to be resolved into a deeper whole than they constitute taken alone and apart: the scientist here goes some of the way, but not so deeply as the philosopher. Hence the argument applies to all things that do not of themselves possess their ends, that is to all creatures.[3] To appeal to chance instead of purpose is to take a blinkered view, to appeal to blind necessity is to take no view at all.[4]

4. Note first that St Thomas does not say that things are for an end, and so, though he abounded with the medieval humour of accounting for things by reasons *ex convenientiis*, or recommendations from the analogies running through a Christian world-view, his argument is spared the necessity of answering the question why mosquitoes exist. His formula is that activity is for an end, *agere est propter finem*.

Note secondly the implied distinction between external and internal finality.[5] External finality lies, outside the relationship of an activity to its own proper end, in a combined operation by different and diverse things achieving an ordered plan, pattern, or design. This is not finality as such, the inner motion of the partial towards the more complete which concerns the fulfilment of being or substance through activity, or to *esse* as expressing itself in *agere*, but the collective tendency, often presumed, of a group of beings or substances which may override their own particular inclinations; it may be credited with greater social importance, yet is not granted the same metaphysical status, for the *bonum commune* of a group is not the true *bonum universale*.[6]

A group of substances is an accidental unity (not that it has come about by accident, or even merely by convention, but that it consists in an arrangement of diverse substantial unities), and to base the argument for finality on

---

[3]Ia. 103, I. Ia2æ, I, 8. *CG* III, 16
[4]Ia. 49, 3. *Physics* II, 8. 199b19–26. 9.200a30–68. *CG* I, 13. *De veritate* V, 2. *In Physic.* II, *lect.* 12–15. *In Meta.* VI, *lect.* 3
[5]Ia. 65, 2
[6]The *bonum commune* can be a collective notion of the good within the group; in its strongest sense it is the *bonum separatum*, the 'outside' universal good which is the cause of good in each and all together. cf *In Meta.* XII, *lect.* 12. Ia. 103, 2. Ia2æ 109, 3. *CG* III, 17

this incurs the same weakness that attends argument from a series of accidentally subordinate movers or causes.[7] We may well be at a loss to assign the purposes of many things within the world-order; in fact the bleak strength of argument from finality has been damaged by its association with anthropomorphic evocations, both humanist and religious, of a universe organized for man's comfort, dignity, or salvation.

Internal finality is the relation of an acting thing to its own completion; it is easier to see how mosquitoes are organized for their own conservation and reproduction than to appreciate their place in the scheme of things. The fifth argument is about internal finality, and therefore can begin wherever *potentia* is found ordered to *actus*. We need not consider whether the pattern exists for the benefit of any one type of its components; until we can quote with conviction the text that *all things work together for good to those that love God*,[8] the argument does not prove that the teleological universe is particularly good for man.

5. Whenever there is activity there is reason for activity, and therefore intelligence. The argument shows that tendency is 'intended', and that the *opus naturæ* is the *opus intelligentiæ*.[9] St Thomas would have us see love running through the universe; though properly speaking only present with intelligence, love enters also into things which lack even sense-awareness, for these can be said 'not to know naturally, but to love and desire naturally'.[10]

This is not a flower of speech, an example of the pathetic fallacy of reading our emotions into non-human things, but a conclusion from the metaphysics of potentiality and actuality applied to all active being. Love supposes an adaptation and fitting together, *adaptatio, co-aptatio*, of distinct things, an adjustment that springs from direction, not chance.[11] There is a natural setting towards completion even behind our conscious volitions and choices which quickens all we do; we are not responsible for this inborn purpose, but only for the modifications and applications we give it.[12] That ultimately this desire is communicated by one supreme good and intelligent will awaits later proof,[13] as also does the conclusion that all purposes conspire in one ordered universe ruled by a single providence.[14] The fifth argument is not complete until, placed in its total theological context, it is seen to promise the disclosure of a lover.

T. G.

---

[7]cf Appendices 6 (6) & 7 (4)
[8]*Romans* 8, 28
[9]I *Sent.* 25, I, I
[10]III *Sent.* 27, I, 4 ad 13
[11]Ia2æ. 27, 4. *De potentia* I, 5
[12]Ia2æ. 10, I. *De veritate* XXII, 5, 6
[13]Ia. 6, 2, 4; 11, 3; 19, 4; 20, 2; 44, 4. Ia2æ. I, 8
[14]Ia. 22, 2; 47, 3; 103, 3

Appendix 11

THE SINGLE CAUSAL ORIGIN

1. ST THOMAS combines two conclusions, that God is the universal cause of every existing and every acting and that creatures in themselves are real and active, in his theory of the subordination of secondary causes to the first cause: they are not just occasions for higher activity, not channels, as it were, through which cosmic energy is funnelled, not even mere instruments set in motion by divine action without principle or, in the case of rational beings, responsible causality of their own. This responsibility, however, should not be represented as an exclusive little patch in which they are alone, and from which they can co-operate or not at choice with divine causality. Their inner immunity from outside interference relates only to other particular causes; the mastery exercised over them by the first or universal cause is in no sense an interference, still less a compulsion.[1] God does not wait on their assent; he is pure existence and activity, the complete and efficacious cause of all that is and acts, and even the mode of freedom itself is of his making and its determination both to act and to act so issues from his premotion.[2]

2. When inquiring whether God acts in all the operations of nature and in every acting thing, St Thomas examines the four manners in which the first cause bears upon a secondary cause's action,[3] and in doing so brings home the single causal origin to which the *quinque viæ* lead.

These four manners consist in 1. giving the power to act; 2. preserving the power to act; 3. applying the power to act; and 4. entering into the action itself. The headings of this bare, though complete, division are hints that have to be flushed together if we are to appreciate how pervasive is the possession by the first cause of the secondary cause, a possession, however, that is without detriment to its integrity and own proper action as a principle, for the absolutely first cause or universal cause transcends all categories, and is not a particular 'kind' of thing to impose its own specific form of action on another.[4]

3. Each of these manners might be expected to provide a way of argument from creaturely activity to God as *primum principium* or causal origin. So they do, when St Thomas's theory of causality is taken at depth. At the beginning of the *Summa*, before he has contributed his own metaphysics of creation of beings by pure being,[5] his aim is to broach the question of

---

[1]1a2æ. 6, 4; 9, 4 & 6
[2]1a. 83, 1 ad 3. 1a2æ. 10, 3 & 4. *CG* III, 69 & 89. *De veritate* XXII, 8. *De malo* III, 2 ad 4
[3]*De potentia* III, 7—a long but rewarding debate. 1a.105, 5. *CG* III, 67
[4]*CG* I, 14, 25; III, 70, 72, 73. 1a. 105, 4. 1a2æ. 109, 6; 112, 3
[5]1a. 44–6

God's existence by employing the instruments that lie to hand in the writings of Greek, Latin, and Arabic philosophers.

The *prima via* corresponds to the third manner indicated above, the initiation by God of the actual activity (*actus secundus*) of creatures, while the *secunda via* corresponds to the fourth manner, the sharing of the actual activity (*actus secundus*) of creatures in God's causal activity: these two notes, respectively of 'premoving', *divina præmotio*, and of 'running in with', *divinus concursus*, indicate the distinction between the first and second arguments. The *tertia via* corresponds to the second manner, in that God causes the power of acting (*actus primus*) in creatures, not only as begetting but also as maintaining them in being, *non solum quantum ad fieri sicut generans sed etiam quantum ad esse*,[6] while the *quarta via* corresponds to the first manner in that the power of acting (*actus primus*) in all creatures whatsoever derives entirely from God who is the first principle of every perfection.[7]

The *quinta via* argues immediately from the 'intentions' present in unconscious activity, not from created activity as such, and therefore its immediate conclusion is some sort of governing providence, not one ultimate final cause comprehending all good. This last is implied in the dialectic of love, and it will be indicated later how the final cause is the first of the causes and the reason for any activity.

4. St Thomas accepts Aristotle's fourfold division of causes. Cause, αἰτία, can signify 1. that from and in which a thing comes into being which corresponds to its matter, *materia*, ὕλη; 2. its own intrinsic form or species, εἶδος, corresponding to μορφή as the inner shaping principle of matter, and the exemplar, παράδειγμα, in the mind of the maker as a reason, λόγος; 3. the originator of its production, *causa movens, efficiens, agens*, ὅθεν ἡ κίνησις πρῶτον; and 4. that for the sake of which it is, ἕνεκα, or the end, τέλος.[8]

The first of these, namely the material cause, is not an active principle but the subject receiving the effect of action, and therefore does not enter into our present consideration.[9] St Thomas expressly shows that God is free from any potentiality, or composition. He scouts the fancy that in any sense God can be the stuff from which things are made, and excludes the theory that he is the intrinsic forms of things or the soul of the world.[10]

5. Yet divine causality works intimately throughout all activity of creatures as final, efficient, and formal. 'First, according to the significance of *end*. Since all activity is for some good, either genuine or apparent, and nothing can be good or appear so unless it shares some likeness with the supreme good which is God, it follows that God himself is the final cause of

---

[6]*De potentia* III, 7
[7]*CG* III, 67 Ia. 45, 2; 104, 2
[8]*Metaphysics* V, 2. 1013a24–b28. St Thomas *in loc. lect.* 2 & 3. *Physics* II. 3. 194b15–195b30. St Thomas *in loc. lect.* 5, 6
[9]Ia. 105, 5
[10]Ia. 3, 1, 2, 7, 8

any activity whatsoever. Second, given subordinate efficient causes, the secondary acts in the power of the first always, for the first moves the secondary to act; hence all things act in the power of God himself, and he is the *efficient cause* of all actions of active things. Third, consider that God not only moves things to act, as it were applying their forms and powers to activity, like a carpenter using a saw, but also gives active creatures their forms and preserves them in being. . . . And since the form is within the thing, and the more deeply the more primary and comprehensive it is, *prior et universalior*, and since God is the proper cause in all things of their whole very 'isness', *ipsius esse universalis in rebus omnibus*, than which nothing is more intimate or interior, *magis intimum*, it follows that he innermostly acts in all things.'[11]

6. Final, efficient, and exemplar causes compenetrate; ends and agents and forms, at last analysis, are not diverse and separable, as though the first were a thing that pulled, the second another thing that pushed, and the third another thing that stamped a shape: as we have noticed, causality is not to be broken up into units in succession.[12] It is a pity that end, *finis*, so strongly marks a terminal condition, so that we forget the end is in the beginning. Implicit in the first moving cause is the first loving cause; and in the divine loving of the universe the philosophical theologian will recognize the divine ideas,[13] and the Christian theologian the Word born of the Father, the Image to which all things are made.[14]

As for the effects, although the end is the last to be realized there as the outcome, *in ordine executionis*, it comes first as a governing direction, *in ordine intentionis*. The end is prior to all effective activity, and present throughout.[15] Put in a time-scheme and then Aristotle's teleology is not the prediction of the future from the present, but rather of the about-to-be-present from the future, this being future to a particular thing's yet unresolved activity, not to the scientist who sees the organic whole and interprets the function within it. No doubt St Thomas's mood was more prophetic, yet put his teleology, where it properly belongs, beyond a time-scheme and then it is not the projection of observed activity into some idealized completion, or the attachment to one real act of a second and succeeding act not yet real, but the understanding, *intellectus* (*intus legens*), or insight into a function, not an inspired guess about how it serves some outside pattern according to a politically or religiously conceived cosmology. It expresses the conclusion that there would be no activity there for us to consider without the causal presence of a good, and no causal presence of a good without the causal presence of *the* good and best.[16]

---

[11]1a. 105, 5. cf 1a. 8, 1; 44, 1, 3, 4
[12]cf Appendices 3 (5–9), 6 (6), 7 (3–4)
[13]1a. 15, 1, 3
[14]1a. 34, 3; 35, 2; 93, 1, 2, 9
[15]1a. 5, 4. 1a2æ. 1, 2. *In Meta.* XII, *lect.* 7
[16]Appendices 9 & 13 (3)

When efficient or moving causes are detached from final causes they become unintelligible. Teleology is not imposed on biology but rises from it, much as natural theology is not imposed on natural philosophy—and as Christian theology itself is no stranger to, but at home with philosophical theology. Moving causes should be imagined less in terms of mechanics than of biology, and the 'desire' running through them should be recognized, a desire that is natural or inborn, not artificial or credited to them by a convention.[17] And the underlying reason why anything at all comes into being is that the Good is generous, *bonum est diffusivum sui esse*.[18]

7. As separate introductions to the existence of God the five arguments serve well enough so far as they go, but their full strength appears only after they are fused together, and distinct ratiocinations about distinct manifestations of the world's insufficiency are stilled in a single understanding of its essential creatureliness, taken as a distributive whole, and of divine causality that creates, sustains, and contains all other than divine *esse* and *agere*:[19] *upholding all things by the word of his power*.[20] See this truth of continued creation, and you will see that natural theology throughout is a paraphrase, despite their ambiguous predication, of two statements, that God causes *is*, and that he is *is*.

T. G.

---

[17]Appendix 10 (4, 5)
[18]Ia. 5, 4 ad 2. *In De div. nom.* IV, *lect.* 3
[19]Ia. 45, 4; 104, 1, 2
[20]*Hebrews* 1, 3

Appendix 12

SIMPLICITY AND UNITY
(1a. 3 & 11)

1. THE THIRD question introduces the treatise on the divine attributes; as St Thomas's preface to this section more flexibly puts it, 'having recognized that a certain thing exists, we have still to investigate the way it exists, that we may come to understand what it is that exists'. No conceptual system can be constructed to enclose God, or for that matter any real substance, and he warns us that what we can understand is rather what he is not than what he is. Later, however, he argues carefully that while some terms predicated of God are negative or relative, thus 'infinite' removes limitations from him, and 'Lord' indicates our subjection to him, other terms are used positively and absolutely, thus 'good' means more than 'not evil' or the 'cause of the good' observed in the world, but the very heart of goodness. Hence the term is predicated primarily, *per prius*, of God, and derivatively of creatures. He grants that we start in the first place by using it of them, and only afterwards of him, but this priority in discovery, *in ordine inventionis*, does not establish a priority in nature and meaning, *in ordine judicii*.[1] When such terms are applied to God their meanings are purified from implications of a creaturely mode of existence; they are heightened to represent sheer perfections, *per modum eminentiæ*, and particularity or limitation to a subject is eliminated, *per modum negationis*.[2]

2. The attributes considered in this volume are those of God's being. After discussing the logic of predicating terms of God,[3] St Thomas then turns to the attributes of operation, the knowledge, will, and power of divine activity.[4] After that he considers the mystery of the Blessed Trinity.

The attributes of God's being are taken in seven questions, simplicity (3), perfection and goodness (4–6), infinity and omnipresence (7–8), immutability and eternity (9–10), and unity (11). 'Candidly speaking,' William James asks, 'do such qualities as these make any definite connection with our life?' There is no doubt that they enter into St Thomas's life of devotion. Reasoning is part of our living, and religious experience, moral earnestness, intuition, and even faith offer no substitute; theology remains kerygmatic when fostering the effort to reason about divine things. The effort may seem to offer notions from which all relish of sense has evaporated, but at least it is more disinterested than some preaching, and freer from the criticism that can be levelled at 'using' God. In fact, however, the argumentation, though drily

---

[1]cf Appendix 5 (5)
[2]1a. 13, 2, 3, 6
[3]1a. 12–13. Vol. 2
[4]1a. 14–18, 19–26. Vols. 4 & 5

expressed by St Thomas, is calculated to move the hearts of those who have mastered the vocabulary and style.

3. Divine simplicity, the first of these attributes, is studied in a series of closely interlocking arguments, which bring together the *quinque viæ*, and lay the foundation of the questions that follow. The key discussion is the fourth, on the complete identity of essence and existence in God.[5] 'Simplicity' is a poor word for a rich idea; it may somewhat drably suggest sameness and monotony, for lack of inner variety is not attractive to the sensibility. Unity, too, with its shade of being but a unit, also has to be lifted out of an imagined mode of significance. To be simple is to be pure and unalloyed, to be wholly actual without composition with potentiality, and the absence of parts does not spell not possessing the manifold perfections of all other things: indeed they are possessed at fuller strength.[6] Similarly to be one, also a negative notion, does not mean being a unit in a class of many, but to be undivided in oneself and, in the case of a simple being, to be indivisible. We may feel warmer to the notions if we reflect that the more the being the greater the simplicity and unity; so it is in art and nature, for a schooner is more closely knit and more highly one than a lugsail dinghy, so is a turnip compared to a stone, a horse to a turnip, a man to a horse.

4. The eight articles of the question rule out the various types of composition in turn. First, the *integral* composition of a whole possessing quantitative parts, for God is not a body. Second, the *essential* composition of matter and form in physical things, for God is pure act without element of potentiality. Third, the *numerical* composition signified by having a specific nature and being an individual of that nature, as when we say that Peter is a man, but not that he is humanity; God, however, is all godhead, so that although the name 'God' when first introduced is a general term or *nomen naturæ*, admissibly communicable to man, it is now used uniquely of one. Fourth, and most important, there is no composition in God between what he is and his 'is', namely between his essence and his existence, for he is his subsistent nature and his nature is *esse*. Such simplicity (or the absence of what is called *entitative* composition, is proper to God alone; we shall return to the question later. Fifth, he is not composed of generic or specific principles, so that he cannot be classified or placed under a general heading. Sixth, he is not composed of substance and accidents, for there is no real distinction in him between his being and his modes of being; his existing is his acting. Seventh, these conclusions are then recapitulated and developed, and eighth, the rider to this complete simplicity is God's transcendence and 'otherness'; he is not an interior part of the universe, even as a dominant.

5. It is by this analysis that St Thomas rejects monism or pantheism. Being as pure act is completely other than being as participated, and for this reason there is no more being when creatures come into existence, nor even, strictly speaking, more things, for uncreated being is not to be added to or to be reckoned in the same class with created beings.[7] At the same time the

---

[5] Ia. 3, 4   [6] Ia. 4, 2   [7] cf Appendix 14

analysis promises a metaphysical status to composition and plurality by reading the 'potential' in terms of being itself; distinct participations of being are not regarded as flickers on the surface of a single sea of reality; they are diverse things, not merely different modes of one thing. St Thomas, unlike Spinoza, does not think of substance as *causa sui*, and later he will extend his metaphysical pluralism, and show that the universe itself is not one substance or organism.[8]

6. Yet God's transcendence does not spell that he is an absentee from the world, the remote and uncaring deity of some Aristoteleans, for, as already indicated, the first origin and last end is causally closer to secondary causes and effects than they are among themselves:[9] *in him we live and move and have our being.*[10] And a new presence is added when God dwells in us by his grace and is the immediate object of our knowing and loving.[11]

7. Of all the types of simplicity enumerated the identity of essence and existence is the most profound, so that if this be affirmed all the others must follow. For existence is the consummate act of all being and of every mode of being; 'nothing is more intimate and profound, since it is formal and actual with respect to all things in reality'.[12]

Esse has no exact English equivalent, and to translate the term we make do with 'existence'. In any case the verb *est* involves some ambiguity, as in the statements 'this tree is', and 'that tree is dead': 'is' applies to existents and also to privations or absences of due form.[13] *Esse* sometimes expresses the copula 'is' in a judgment joining predicate to subject,[14] and as such is in the mind, not the thing.[15] It can also stand for an underlying condition of being contrasted with more determinate forms.[16] Here it indicates the very act or perfection of being, *actus essendi*.

As for the vexed question of the real distinction of essence and existence in any created thing, *ens*, that which is, *quod est*, it will be enough to say that St Thomas saw nature or essence there as the potential principle of its being, that by which it is what it is, and existence as the actual principle of its being, that by which it is, *quo est*.[17] A shift, at least of emphasis, can be observed in his explanation. At first, as in the early work *De ente et essentia*, written before he received his master's degree at Paris in 1256, and when he was closer to the thought of Avicenna, the distinction seems prompted by the questions, *an sit?* and *quid sit?* and by the answers as to the 'that' and the 'what', namely that the thing is and that this is what it is. As somehow enter-

---

[8]Ia. 47, 1, 2, 3   [9]Appendices 3 (8), 6 (6), 7 (4), 9 (5), 10 (4), 11 (5, 6)
[10]*Acts* 17, 28   [11]Appendix 15 (5)
[12]Ia. 4, 1 ad 3; 8, 1. cf Appendix 8 (3)   [13]Ia. 48, 2 ad 2
[14]Ia. 3, 4 ad 2   [15]*CG* I, 12 *De potentia* VII, 2 ad 1.*Quodl.* IX, 11, 3
[16]*CG* I, 26. cf Ia. 65, 3
[17]It would be helpful to be able to record a text where St Thomas speaks of essence as *quo est*, united with existence, also *quo est*, in a single *quod est*. It is perhaps worth noticing that he attributes the conjunction of *quod est* and *quo est* to others, including Philip the Chancellor and Hugh of St Cher, e.g. Ia. 50, 2 ad 4; cf 75, 5 ad 4

ing the logic of proposition τὸ εἶναι and τὸ τί ἐστιν are distinct terms, especially as the first is found to be contingent and the second to possess a sort of necessity. Later on, however, the distinction is deepened into the heart of things; *essentia* then is less a meaning, concept, or 'quiddity' than a real nature or kind of thing made actual by existence,[18] and therefore really distinct from it, not as a diverse thing, but as the potential from the actual within one thing; *esse* too on its side is then seen less as an exclamation into reality than as the 'most form' in things.[19] Essence is sometimes compared to the *recipiens*,[20] and the crudity of imagining it as a vessel has to be corrected by the reflection that it possesses no anterior being, not even in the sense that the *materia prima* in a physical thing, the subject of substantial change, has pre-existed under a previous form. An essence is, but only by existence; an existence is, but only in essence.

8. God is not an essence nor an existence. He is the godhead, and the godhead is *esse*. At this depth we can no more know the existence of God than we can his nature. We apprehend this *esse divinum* only in terms of *esse commune*, the acts of existing the human mind observes in its environment and declares through the *est* of a judgment.[21]

9. Nevertheless *esse* is the noblest term a philosopher can use. No wonder, then, that scholastic theologians give the fullest ontological meaning to the phenomenological passage in Scripture; *When I come unto the children of Israel, Moses said, and shall say to them, The God of your fathers hath sent me unto you, and they shall say to me, What is his name? What shall I say unto them? And God said unto Moses,* I AM THAT I AM, *then shalt thou say unto the children of Israel,* I AM *hath sent me unto you.*[22] St Thomas, who hears the echo in our Lord's answer to the Jews, *Amen, amen I say unto you, Before Abraham was* I AM,[23] finds that of all names QUI EST is proper to God.[24] For 'God' is a general term, a *nomen naturæ*, but this lies deeper:[25] so the sacred name of revelation becomes the proper name for philosophical theology.

The language of later Scholastics who discuss the *constitutivum metaphysicum* of the divine nature may seem out of place, but their thought, while not striking the same awe, is faithful to the Scriptures when they see at the root of all perfection and infinity God's being of himself, *esse a se, esse subsistens,* or his 'a-seity', *aseitas*. There the *quinque viæ* mount together, for the quiet principle of motion, the uncaused cause of causation, the being necessary of itself, the perfect being, and the end of desire are all without composition at the depths of being, and all are one because pure *esse* cannot be divided or multiplied. On the other hand it is when beings hold a composition of really distinct 'parts' within themselves that they exist only as caused: this indeed is the constitutive of their creatureliness.[26]

10. So we are led to the consideration of God's unity. Though we have

---

[18]Ia. 50, 2 ad 3 [19]Ia. 7, 1; 8, 1 [20]e.g. Ia. 4, 1 ad 3
[21]Ia. 3, 4 ad 1, 2 [22]*Exodus* 3, 13–14 [23]*John* 8, 58. *In Joann.* 8, *lect.* 8
[24]Ia. 13, 11 [25]Ia. 5, 2. cf Ia. 13, 8 [26]*CG* II, 15

to use numerical terms when things are at all identified or distinguished, the unity a philosopher is looking for is not being that can be counted. Unity that is identical with being, *unum quod convertitur cum ente*, and is applied to being as being and to unquantified beings is not a mathematical term, and differs from the unit which is the principle of numeration, *unum quod est principium numeri*. You say that a being is one because it is undivided, and you are contrasting it with a condition of division; when you say of a thing that it is numerically one you are contrasting it with a plurality, *multitudo*, of like objects.[27]

God, then, is not numerically one, yet his is the supreme unity not only of being undivided but also of being indivisible, unlike composite things which can break up and lose their identity.[28] Nor can the divine nature be multiplied in many things, like human nature in many individuals where the principle of being this man is not the same as the principle of being man; the subsisting God is the godhead, and therefore, Cajetan says simply, *formaliter est Deus et hic*, indeed precisely as God he is also 'this',[29] yet not if 'this' is a limiting term, since he is sheer existence to which no differences can be added and into which no divisions can be introduced.[30]

11. St Thomas's terminology will be sharpened to an even keener edge when he comes to discuss the mystery of the Trinity, an open question to the philosopher—yet one that has wonderfully multiplied and polished the tools of his trade. There number directly relating to quantity can have only a metaphorical sense, as when we speak of divine breadth or height. Yet three Persons are confessed, and it will be the effort of the theologian to show how relations within the godhead sets up a trinity of distinct persons without separation, division, diversity, or difference.[31] On the other hand with reference to divine unity, St Thomas would not have us speak of God as sole, solitary, singular, or unique.[32]

T. G.

---

[27] Ia. 11, 1, c. & ad 1; 2
[28] Ia. 11, 1, 3. *Quodl.* X, 5, 1
[29] In Iam. 11, 3. cf Ia. 3, 3
[30] Ia. 11, 4
[31] Ia. 30, 1, c. & ad 3, 4; 3; 31, 1
[32] Ia. 31, 2, 3, 4

Appendix 13

PERFECTION AND GOODNESS
(1a. 4–6)

1. THE TERM 'perfect', which leaves its etymology from *perficere* behind when applied to God, since there can be no suggestion of his being accomplished or achieved, stands for what is actual and flawless.[1] 'Imperfection' is applied to all creatures, though it is good for them to be limited and strictly speaking a thing is called imperfect only when a potentiality there is not realized; it is none the worse for not possessing a positive quality which is not appropriate to its particular nature, the absence of which is purely negative: thus pigs are not adversely criticized because they cannot fly. The lack, however, of what could and should be present is privative, and to that extent a thing is called imperfect or bad:[2] thus pigs suffering from swine fever.

Accustomed to judge perfection by comparing this with that in particular respects, as at agricultural shows, and so relating things even of different classes, as when we find that dogs have better noses than men for hunting and men have better noses than dogs for drinking wine, we are less familiar than the medievals were with the neo-Platonic conception of 'perfections' taken in a more absolute and abstract sense, and more solemnly than by Socrates when he was teasing Critobolus in the *Symposium*; we hesitate to reckon that a man is a higher or better being in himself than a dog, and if we do, then it is with an ethical or æsthetic reference, not always in our favour, in the light of circumstances, not metaphysics.

2. In St Thomas's argumentation perfection is read in the light of being itself, that is of *esse* as the comprehensive form and actuality of reality. God is all this, and therefore his is the plenitude of perfection. He is not a sort of thing which may be equably be allowed not to possess the perfection of another sort of thing. In some sense he must have the perfections of all things, a conclusion that is inferred from his universal efficient causality and from his unlimited existing, that is by extending the *secunda via* and the *quarta via*.[3] Recall, from previous appendices, the vigour of *esse* in the *Summa*; in this sense the phrase from St Paul's speech on the Areopagus rises to a climax in declaring that in God *we live and move and have our being*.[4]

At this stage it will be useful to introduce a distinction and conclusion drawn by the Scholastics. Perfections fall into two classes, pure, *simpliciter simplices*, and mixed. The first involve no limitation or exclusion in their

---

[1] 1a. 4, 1 ad 1   [2] 1a. 48, 3
[3] 1a. 4, 2. For degrees of perfection, cf Appendix 9 (2, 3)   [4] *Acts* 17, 28

meaning, and any being, says St Anselm in effect, is the better for their presence:[5] thus intelligence and will. The second involve limitation, for though they exemplify the first they are keyed to a particular mode of being: thus sensation and emotion. The first are formally attributed to God, though in a heightened sense (*formaliter eminenter*) leaving behind all creaturely implications: thus his understanding is his being, not a quality distinct from substance, as with us, nor is it reasoned out. The second are not so attributed, since their very make-up is particular, yet they come from God's power, *virtus*, and are there contained like effects in a higher cause (*virtualiter eminenter*).[6]

3. 'Because a thing inasmuch as it is perfect is called good',[7] good indicating the final completeness of evoking love, *ens appetibile*, St Thomas then devotes two questions to the idea of goodness itself and to the goodness of God.[8] Here we find the sources for a full understanding of the *quinta via*.[9] God possesses every turn of goodness of himself, *per essentiam*—and in that sense God alone is good[10] and if other things are good then it is only by his goodness as by their 'first exemplar, efficient, and final principle'.

All the same we do not live in a world of shams; as creatures are real so are they denominated good by their own intrinsic forms, which are likenesses of God—and in this sense there is one goodness for all things, yet also many goodnesses.[11] St Thomas will develop this doctrine later when he discusses the creation and diversity of real beings or substances;[12] our present interest is not whether there are many goods in the universe, but whether perfections are manifold in God. On this account we anticipate the inquiry, are the terms we attribute to God all synonymous?[13]

4. The apparatus assembled by the Scholastics, which is more delicate than will appear from this brief description, is their tribute to a lively question for devotion. Their technicalities take up the protest of the Eleatic stranger; 'Oh heavens!' he exclaimed, 'can we imagine Being to be devoid of life and mind, an everlasting fixture?'[14] Does the complete self-identity of pure and active being entail sameness, as it were, all the way through? In that case not only will divinity be unutterable by the human mind, which it is,[15] but nothing that we can think or say about God will be really relevant; it will hold no interest for and in the loving reason, though speech of course will relieve our own feelings. The Scholastics, then, should be judged with sympathy, or at least granted their share of the burden laid on the Prophet: *And I said, ah, ah, ah, Lord God, behold, I cannot speak for I am a child. And the Lord said unto me, Say not, I am a child, for thou shalt go to all that I shall send thee, and whatsoever I command thee, thou shalt say.*[16]

---

[5]*Monologium* 15
[7]Ia. 4, *Prol.* Ia. 5, 1, 2
[9]Notably Ia. 5, 4; 6, 4
[11]Ia. 6, 4
[13]Ia. 13, 4. Vol. 3
[15]Ia. 12, 2

[6]I *Sent.* 2, 1, 2 & 3. cf Ia. 3, 5; 4, 3; 13, 1, 3, 5, 6
[8]Ia. 6 & 7
[10]Ia. 6, 3
[12]Ia. 45, 2, 3, 4; 47, 1, 2
[14]*Sophist* 249
[16]*Jeremiah* 1, 6–7

If human beings are to think and speak they have to articulate, to use 'words' of the mind and of the mouth. Their experience is not meant to be left a blur, their language not to go beyond onomatopœia. Truth, which consists in judgment, requires there an 'intention' or real relation to the object, not a real containing or comprehending.[17] Now God gives his truth to us ultimately that we may be possessed by him as he is, not as he can be represented, but in the meantime for us to hold by faith, the darkness of which the glitter of concepts does little to dispel. But Providence has ordained that we are meant to hold to him as he is, and also as we are. As he is in himself, not by sight, but by a judgment cleaving to him beyond all the rational evidence; as we are because we can signify him only in a human manner according the present conditions of human life. His truth is translated in our minds, and until translated it cannot be communicated to others by apostolic preaching. This is our bearing of the Word, and our witness to the Word.[18]

Hence the need of *sacra doctrina*,[19] prepared to be as expository as the subject allows and to tackle all the difficulties arising from the constitution of the human mind in its encounter with God's revelation.[20] Grace and nature are not in separate spheres; consequently faith seeking understanding meditates on its own proper truths quite unaffectedly in the truths of reason which are their setting. Both involve mysteries, about which the mind can be truthful so long as they are acknowledged and neither cried too soon nor mistakenly described. The mystery we are about to touch on belongs to philosophical theology, not directly to Christian theology.

5. It is the profound antinomy, God is absolutely simple, God contains within himself a plurality of perfections.[21] How can distinction exist within complete identity?

The problem is approached by defining what we mean by distinction, a question acutely examined by the Scholastics, themselves much given to the drawing of fine distinctions. To distinguish, *distinguere*, διαστίζω, is to mark an otherness. There are various types of distinction; when between distinct things it is called *diversity*, thus between Peter and Paul, when between distinct elements it is called *difference* if specific be contrasted with generic, thus in the differentiation by 'rational' of 'animal', and *real distinction* if referring to the real composition of partial principles within one complete whole, thus of matter and form in bodily things, and of substance and accidents in all created things.[22] None of the above types of distinction applies to God.

The human mind, however, draws distinctions about things which are not diverse in themselves, which contain no differences, and which of themselves exhibit no such composition. This happens whenever it judges one thing in the terms of subject and predicate, joining or splitting them,

---

[17]Ia. 12, 7; 16. 2   [18]2a2æ. 1, 2, 6; 2, 5; 3, 1 ad 3; 2 ad 1, 2
[19]Ia. 1, 1   [20]Ia. 1, 8   [21]*CG* 1, 31
[22]Ia. 3, 7 enumerates the kinds of real composition. See Appendix 12 (4)

componendo et dividendo, or reasons about the thing and forms a third judgment, or conclusion, from two premises. There is no falsification here, because the mind knows what it is doing, or should, and makes the appropriate correction.[23] This type of distinction is called a mental distinction, *distinctio rationis*.

A mental distinction may be purely logical or alternatively what is called a *virtual* distinction. A purely logical distinction, *distinctio rationis ratiocinantis*, is found when one and the same reality is differently construed according to a system extrinsic to it (or affected by an extrinsic denomination, as they say in the schools), which system may be formed by the concepts of formal logic or by a vocabulary. Thus 'man' can be considered as the major term or the minor term of a syllogism, and this position in an argument sets up no composition in him. Similarly we may speak of a man or a human being where the distinction is purely nominal; tautologies too can be useful for emphasis and for carrying overtones. But the object itself does not offer a distinction of logical entities or of words, which therefore is, as they say, *sine fundamento in re*.

On the other hand a mental distinction may be invited by the situation. The real object, though wholly simple in itself, may be so rich that a mind from a lower and more fragmented order of being can begin to represent it only by a variety of concepts. These concepts do not express purely logical constructions, but real forms discovered in the world, each expressed with a distinctive note. Such concepts as 'alive', 'wise', 'good' neither immediately imply nor exclude one another, and they can be represented apart from one another by the mind; that is where the actual distinction lies. Yet since the object does yield the grounds for the distinction it is said to be *cum fundamento in re*, and since the virtue of the object's single perfection is such as to call forth a manifold response from a mind at a lesser degree of being the distinction is said to be virtual. This, also called a *distinctio rationis ratiocinatae*, is much used at the heights of speculation, and not with error when the mind appreciates the conditions and does not coarsen distinctiveness into division.

6. In this manner a plurality of perfections is attributed to God while his supreme simplicity is simultaneously acknowledged. Furthermore, while in creatures distinct perfections either tend to cancel out, thus grave and gay, or perhaps to be strangers, thus good theory and good practice, in God all are identified at their peak in pure existence. Every poem springs from the eternal begetting of the Word and breathing of Love, every shimmer is a reflection of God's beauty. All things are like him, and less than him.[24] His is infinite variety because he is simple and one, full activity because he is still, perfect freedom because he is purely happy.[25] Dialectical but not analytical opposites come together and are resolved in synthesis, in the

---

[23]Ia. 85, I ad I; 3 ad 4; 5 ad 3. cf Ia. 16, I & 2
[24]Ia. 4, 3
[25]Ia. 19, 3

manner of Zeno's paradoxes, but at greater depth. Thus divine justice and divine mercy are not left as a dilemma, or rendered as one the rule and the other the exception, for mercy at the first root of things quickens all the works which show God's justice, and is more intense than the justice in them, *sicut causa primaria vehementius influit quam secunda.*[26]

T. G.

---

[26]Ia. 21, 4. cf 2a2æ. 120, 2

Appendix 14

TRANSCENDENCE
(1a. 7)

1. THE CONCLUSION that things are good by their own goodness as well as by God's goodness[1] bears on the discussion about how God surpasses all creation, for it disabuses us of the notion of an Infinite so enveloping that nothing else can stand up, a notion that appeared in the objection to God's existence, that his goodness would blot out all evil, since of two contraries if one be infinite the other must be completely excluded.[2] The objection was not met squarely at the time, and St Thomas was content to hint at a fuller reply which is developed later: God's infinite goodness is not the inclusive All intolerant of other particular goods—and evils, but surmounts our frame of reference altogether.[3] Nor is his being the Everything, but the pure and subsisting being transcending the host of particular beings and outside any series, finite or infinite, over which they may stretch. The 'all' composed of these can produce neither itself nor any of its parts in their very being; we have to look beyond the *esse commune* to the *esse divinum* which alone has the power, because existence is its own to communicate, to be the cause of other existences.[4]

It is the One who is the cause of the Many, and though ineffably exceeding our minds, its infinity is not that at which the imagination boggles so that the mind can scarcely entertain the thought. It threatens no nightmare of endless repetitions in boundless space by numberless multitudes, and is not so absolute as to repel relations; its stare is not blank, but full of intelligence. This in effect is what St Thomas is going to say, though not in the same terms. Remark in passing that he never suggests that a finite mind must be stunned by the infinite, and rarely refers to infinity as the reason why we cannot explain God's ways with man.

2. One of the first philosophers, the Ionian Anaximander, held that the primary element, ἀρχή, was an eternal and ageless substance, the Boundless, τό ἄπειρον, out of which all things come by an eternal motion of separating out, ἀπόκρισις, like sifting in a sieve. Since definite things are what we know, or think we know, it was later supposed that the infinite background from which objects appear is unintelligible, or at best to be presented by a question mark. St Thomas briskly addresses himself to this difficulty.[5] Drawing a distinction between negative and positive infinity, he admits that the first, or indefinite limitlessness is in itself unintelligible, for it is an amorphous sprawl, like shapeless matter undefined by form. On the other hand the

---

[1]1a. 6, 4   [2]1a. 2, 3 obj. 1   [3]cf 1a. 48, 4; 49, 2
[4]1a. 44, 1; 45, 1. cf Appendix 12 (4)
[5]1a. 7, 1; 86, 2. cf *In Meta.* XII, *lect.* 2

absence of limits because a form is not contracted within matter offers no
barrier to intelligence, indeed of all reality pure form unconfined by matter
is the most lucid and evident, though not appearing so to human minds
which in their present condition can only signify or infer it from things more
evident to them.[6] Throughout this section of the *Summa* as in his theory of
knowledge, St Thomas treats the human mind as a faculty of being, adequate
to refer truthfully to the entire range of things, though unable to encompass
or comprehend them.[7]

3. Infinity, an abstract notion represented negatively (*in-finitus*, non-
terminated),[8] is taken in the first place from quantity and then applied to
substance, as the meaning of *amplitudo* is transferred from width or size to
grandeur or importance. We have noticed that the term may refer either to
the boundlessly potential, the infinity of matter ever liable to suffer another
change, never completely 'realized' by a form,[9] or to the boundlessly actual,
the infinity of form unconfined or unparticularized by matter.

Since *esse* is the 'most form' of all forms, and God is pure existence or
actuality uncombined with potentiality, *non esse receptum, sed ipsum suum
esse subsistens*, it is clear that his is the infinity of form.[10]

4. St Thomas next introduces a subdistinction between relative, *secundum quid*, and absolute, *simpliciter*, infinity of form. The speculations of Neo-
Platonists and Arabic Aristoteleans in association with Rabbinic pneumato-
logy had produced the doctrine of a world of pure spirits each of which
possessed a form unmixed with matter. Such a form, like a Platonic universal,
would manifest the unbounded meaning of the idea and be itself the complete
species without particularization by another and individualizing principle,[11]
and therefore could be allowed the relative infinity of an unqualified form.
Since, however, a spiritual substance exists not of itself but by a cause, its
essence is not identical with its existence,[12] and therefore is without the
absolute infinity of subsisting *esse* which belongs to God alone.[13]

5. These distinctions, between the indefinite and the infinite, and between
the infinity of an idea and of an existent, run through the discussion of
questions taken from Avicenna and Algazel as to whether there can be
unlimited sizes or numbers.[14]

T. G.

[6]cf Ia. 2, 1; 12, 1 ad 2. For God's knowledge of infinities see Ia. 14, 12
[7]*Intellectus possibilis est quod est omnia fieri*, Ia. 79, 7. *In De anima* III, *lect.* 13
[8]Ia. 10, 1 ad 1
[9]cf Ia, 66, 2; 75, 6
[10]Ia. 7, 1
[11]cf Ia. 50, 2, 4
[12]Ia. 50, 5 ad 3
[13]Ia. 7, 2
[14]Ia. 7, 3 & 4. The *locus classicus* for St Thomas on the infinite is *In Physic.* III, *lect.*
6–13

Appendix 15

IMMANENCE
(1a. 8)

1. UP TILL now divine transcendence has been more stressed than the closeness of God's presence within things. A passage in Aristotle's *Metaphysics*[1] asks in which of two ways the universe involves the 'highest good'. Is it something separate and independent or is it the order of the parts in the whole. 'Probably both,' he answers, 'as in the case of an army; its fighting trim consists partly in its organization, partly in the general, but chiefly in the latter.' Yet he does not teach that God exists in both these ways, and in view of his oft-repeated doctrine of the priority of substance, the first cause, or God, must be for him a substance and not in immanent order of things which is an arrangement of substances.

2. St Thomas's more developed and comprehensive metaphysics of existence and causality disposes of any ambiguity. We have already noticed how the first mover immediately moves all things in motion, not merely a 'first heaven',[2] how the first cause is closer to the effect than any previous intermediate cause at one remove,[3] and how God is the immediate exemplar, efficient, and final cause of all things.[4] And so his first discussion on God's omnipresence goes straight to the point: nothing is closer to a thing than its own existence, and this is the direct and immediate effect of the sustaining causality of *ipsum esse per essentiam*.[5]

God causes being as such, totally and without restriction, whereas creatures are causes only of this or that form of being.[6] Hence he alone is everywhere, giving all things their existence and powers and activities, and filling all places, not however like a body displacing other bodies.[7] *Whither shall I go from thy spirit? and whither shall I flee from thy presence? If I ascend up to heaven, thou art there; if I make my bed in hell, behold thou art there.*[8]

3. The divine attribute of *immensitas* signifies this causal presence which fashions all things *back and front*.[9] Its distribution under the three headings, by essence, presence, and power, is traditional; St Thomas takes it from St Gregory the Great and explains it with his customary reverence for an authority and discovery of deeper reasons than were first intended.[10]

4. *Immensitas* is not his term, nor is *ubiquitas*, to signify God's being everywhere. Presence in a place can be by bodily contact through dimensive

---

[1]XII, 10. 1075a11–15. *In Meta.* XII, *lect.* 12
[2]cf 1a. 22, 3; 103, 6. Appendix 6 (6)
[3]cf Appendix 7 (4)   [4]1a. 6, 4. cf Appendix 11 (5, 6)
[5]1a. 8, 1   [6]cf *CG* III, 70   [7]1a. 8, 2 & 4
[8]*Psalm* 138 (139), 7–8   [9]ibid 5
[10]1a. 8, 2

quantity (*circumscriptive*), as water is in a bucket, by interior quickening of a thing in place (*per informationem*), as the soul is in the body, and by operating in a place (*definitive*), as when a spirit operates at a certain spot. The first two do not apply to God since he is neither body nor soul, and the third does not apply because his action does not tie him down and he is everywhere.[11] Yet not everywhere like a universal idea which is indifferent to the here and now, for he is here and now, actively present and yet uncommitted, in and yet beyond every place and moment of time.[12]

5. An additional manner in which God is present to rational creatures is somewhat cursorily touched on,[13] namely in a 'family manner' through grace, *familiari modo per gratiam*: the phrase is St Gregory's. It will be discussed later, when St Thomas considers the indwelling of the blessed Persons of the Trinity in those who live in divine friendship.[14] He calls it a *singularis modus*, which brings out the personal quality of the abiding, in contrast with the *communis modus* of causality. The presence is constituted by grace considered less as an effect than for its content, in which God opens out to us as the object of our knowing and loving. Mystical theologians understandably have seized on this teaching and have given various interpretations; here it is enough to apprehend that our living with God means our entering into the inner life of God where causal dependence is absent,[15] and that the relationships of knower and known, lover and beloved, are not to be resolved into the relationship of cause and effect. *Henceforth I call you not servants, for the servant knoweth not what his lord doeth, but I have called you friends.*[16]

T. G.

---

[11]Ia. 8, 4; 52, 1, 2
[12]Ia. 16, 7 ad 2
[13]Ia. 8, 3, sed contra, c. & ad 3, 4
[14]Ia. 43, 3, 6. Ia2æ. 109, 1, 2
[15]cf Ia. 33, 1 ad 1 for Greek and Latin usage of 'cause'
[16]*John* 15, 15

Appendix 16

ETERNITY
(1a. 9 & 10)

1. ETERNITY FOLLOWS deductively from God's immutability, discovered along the *prima via* and now dwelt on in the light of the preceding questions, especially of the one on simplicity.[1] Permanence and transience are considered in terms first of motion, and next of duration. The preference shown by Greek and medieval Latin philosophers for stability over change has been misrepresented. They did not try to capture living processes only to freeze them. Remember that the *immobile, ἀκίνητον,* is also the *movens, κινητικόν.* What is denied of the first cause is the imperfection of potentiality, what is affirmed is the fulness of life.[2] When God is called steadfast like a rock, the metaphor implies no petrification, or when he is said to come to us it does not mean that he passes from one place to another.[3] The complete identity of essence, existence, and activity is the reason why God is wholly immutable, and it belongs to him alone.[4]

2. Mutability is commonly observed by us in the growth and decay of things, their birth and dying away, happening in successive stages, which often can be timed. 'I know what time is,' says St Augustine, 'if nobody asks me, but I know not when I wish to explain it.'[5] St Thomas's working definition is from Aristotle; time is the measure of movement according to before and after, *ἀριθμὸς κινήσεως κατὰ τὸ πρότερον καὶ ὕστερον.*[6] Underlying this succession is continuous existence, or duration.

Three types of existence are set out and to each a type of duration is assigned:[7] 1. wholly unchanging existence, the duration of which is called eternity; 2. substantially unchanging existence accompanied and affected by changes of accident according to place and quality, the duration of which is called *ævum, αἰών,* a condition of being 'evermore', indicated later by the abstract term *æviternitas,* or everlastingness; 3. existence in a subject with transmutable matter and quantity. Only the specialist student of Greek and medieval cosmology need delay on the second, which refers to a world of purely spiritual substances and to a hypothetical order of indestructible heavenly bodies, which though closer than our temporal world to the condition of eternity do not of their natures possess it, for true and proper eternity is God's alone.[8] Take the *prima via* and continue, and you will reach the conclusion that all other things at core are *mobilia.*

3. The eternal, a notion which negatively represents the non-negative in

---

[1]1a. 3. cf Appendix 12   [2]Appendix 13   [3]cf 1a. 9, 1 ad 1, 2, 3
[4]1a. 8, 1, 2   [5]*Confessions* XI, 14   [6]*Physics* IV, 11. 219b1
[7]1a. 10, 4 & 5   [8]1a. 10, 2 & 3

our mind, should be distinguished from the perpetual or everlasting.[9] It is not found in an unending line or series of points, but dwells outside though enfolding all space and time. St Thomas, as we have seen, allows for the possibility of time never starting or stopping; what he is speaking of is another dimension altogether.[10] We cannot do better than to translate the passage from Boëthius which inspired him and his contemporaries.[11]

'Let us therefore consider what eternity is, for this declares to us both the divine nature and knowledge. Eternity then is the perfect possession altogether and all at once of boundless life, *interminabilis vitæ tota simul et perfecta possessio.* This is made more manifest by a comparison with temporal things.'

'For whatsoever lives in time is in the present and proceeding from the past to the future, and there is nothing placed in time which can embrace the whole space of its life at once. It has not yet attained tomorrow, and has lost yesterday; you live no longer in this day's life than in one changing and transitory moment.'

'Whatsoever suffers the condition of time, even though, as Aristotle thought of the world, it never began or were ever to end, and were its life to endure for interminable time, it is not such as to be deemed eternal. For it does not hold and embrace all the space of its life together, for it does not possess the future which is yet to come.'

'That then which grasps and holds the fulness of boundless life all together, from which nothing future is absent and from nothing past has escaped, is worthy to be accounted eternal. This must ever stand at and fully possess in an abiding present the infinity of changing time.'

'Hence they are deceived who, hearing that it seemed to Plato that this world had neither entrance nor would go out in time, think that thereby the world is co-eternal with its author. For it is one thing to be carried through an endless life, which Plato attributed to the world, another thing to embrace the present wholeness of endless life, which is manifestly proper to the divine mind.'

'Neither should God be represented as more ancient than created things in length of time, but rather as before them by the simplicity of his nature. For the infinite process of temporal things copies the state of the present in changeless life, though falling from immobility into motion, and decreasing from the simplicity of the present into infinite stretches of past and future since it is unable to reproduce or equal this state. Because it cannot possess the fulness of its life all at once, by never ceasing to be it seems to emulate in part that which it cannot fully obtain and express, for committing itself to this short and swift moment, which bears some likeness to that ever-abiding present, there is bestowed some semblance of existing. Unable to rest it took the interminable road of time, so that it continues a life by going whose

---

[9]Ia. 10, 1 ad 1. cf Ia. 11, 2 ad 4; 3 ad 2
[10]Ia. 10, 1
[11]*Consolationis philosophiæ* v, 6

fulness it could not clasp by staying. Therefore if we are minded to give things their right names, let us follow Plato and say that God is eternal and the world perpetual.'

4. St Thomas is without the homilist's scorn for the temporal. He sees duration in succession sustained by eternal duration as the *mobile* by the *immobile*, and, enlarging from the *prima via* to the other causal ways, he unconsciously echoes the *Timæus* on time as the moving image of eternity. He never escapes from his starting principle, that we come to know eternity through time.[12] What matters is the present, and it is the 'now' of time, the *nunc fluens*, that shows us the 'now' of eternity, the *nunc stans*.[13] Our unrest in time is due to our pursuit of the whole, for commenting by anticipation on Keats' last sonnet, St Thomas notes the eternity that lies at the heart of delight and is engaged from the beginning; for we desire to know things whole and perfect, and so take pleasure in their ever-changing face as one perfection follows another, and in this manner the whole is somehow felt.[14] Is not this the burden of all song and dance?

T. G.

---

[12]1a. 10, 1
[13]1a. 10, 2 ad 1
[14]1a2æ. 32, 2

Glossary

WHEN COMPOSING a glossary we may forget the different ways in which words have meaning and regard all words as names. When the words are technical we may even be tempted to believe in a corresponding world of technical objects existing within or behind the objects which ordinary words name. We must therefore make here two preliminary disclaimers.

First, even if the words in this glossary named objects, they would do so only because they expressed certain ways of conceiving these objects. The technicality of the words is not intended to indicate a new world of technical objects, but to express a technical way of thinking about ordinary objects. Sometimes this way of thinking results from a projection of the structure of our thought into the ordinary world, as for example the way of thinking implicit in such words as 'genus', 'species', and 'individual'. At other times it results from the cautious expression of analogies in structure between ordinary objects themselves. Thus, if a man is seen swimming, we can say in a sense that both the man and the swimming exist, but that the sense of 'existence' is different in both cases: man exists-as-that-which but the swimming exists-as-the-action-of. The analogy here, though expressed in words, is a real analogy of the man and the swimming; its technical expression, however, will involve us necessarily in such words as 'substance' and 'accident'.

Secondly, we can accept the words 'object' and 'naming' as themselves analogical in the sense just mentioned. And then it becomes true that every word in this glossary names an object, but now this will not predetermine in what sense that object exists.

Words italicized in the definitions are themselves defined elsewhere in the glossary.

accident: that which pertains to something but is not *essential* to it, either
   a. because it does not belong to the *substance* of the thing (what is called the *predicamental* accident), or *b.* because it does not belong to the thing necessarily (the *predicable* accident). A predicamental accident is anything the very *existence* of which consists in pertaining-to or existing-in a substance; thus any one of the nine *categories* of *being* other than substance. A predicable accident is contra-distinguished against a *property* in the strict sense: what a thing is can be conceived without considering its properties, yet it cannot be conceived as existing without those properties, whereas the thing can both be known and can exist without its predicable accidents. See also pp. 38–9, note *a.*

action: one of the categories of *being*: a deed, or better, the doing of the deed. Any *change* when regarded as being some *agent's* doing, or as being from some agent. Contrast *passion.*

actuality: any mode of being actual, of actually *being*, of really *existing* in the now. Often used to mean the fulfilment or realization of some prior *potentiality.*

æon: the measure of duration of non-*material* creatures, as *time* measures the duration of material creatures, and *eternity* that of the Creator.

agent: that which acts, anything regarded as initiating an *action.* See also *cause.*

analogy: an agreement or correspondence in certain respects between things which are simply-speaking diverse. A word is said to be used analogically if it is used in two or more senses which are nevertheless interdependent. 'Analogy' is most frequently used for that *transcendental* correspondence between the ultimate *genera* of things which enables each genus to be called a *category* of *being*.

being: that which is. Anything can be said to be, and each thing *is* in a sense peculiar to itself: thus what it is to be a carbohydrate requirement differs from what it is to be sauerkraut, and both these differ from what it is to be impoliteness. Nevertheless the senses of 'being' constitute a graded sequence of *analogical* senses, in which the sense of being-a-*substance* acts as a kind of paradigm case for the others. The best summary of the varying senses of 'being' is to be found in Aristotle's *Metaphysics*, v, 7 (1017a7–b9). See also *substance, existence, essence.*

categories: the ultimate *genera* of things which *exist*, hence the irreducibly different modes of existence, and consequently of *predication*. This use of the word is Aristotelian, and differs from the Kantian use. Aristotle listed the following modes or categories of *being*: being a *substance* (e.g. a baboon), being *quantified* (large), being *qualified* (black), being *related* to (leader of the troop), being in *action* (scratching), being acted upon or *passion* (being scratched), being in *place* (on the mountain), being in *time* (yesterday afternoon), being in an attitude (doubled up), and being in possession of something (having pyjamas on).

cause: that because of which something *exists*, a *principle* upon which the existence of something depends. Aristotle distinguishes four related senses of the word 'cause': i. that out of which, as out of material, something comes into existence (e.g. twigs and other bits and pieces), ii. the form which this material assumes, and which gives *definition* to the emergent thing (e.g. the structure and shape of the nest), iii. that by the *action* of which the material assumes its form (e.g. the bird), and iv. that for the sake of which the action is done, and the material is made to assume its form (e.g. to lay eggs in). These are usually referred to as the four causes: *matter, form, agent* and *end*; but it would perhaps be better to refer to them as the four factors involved in causation.

change: passage from one state to another, the process leading from *potentiality* to *actuality*, that fulfilling of potentiality which is not yet the final fulfilment. Change regarded as being from an *agent* is *action*; the same change regarded as being in the thing changed is *passion*.

definition: determination. The expression in words of a thing's determinate unity or *species*, as though it were a determination (*differentiation*) of some relatively indeterminate notion of the thing (*genus*): e.g. a human is a reasoning animal. The declaration of the *essence* of a thing.

demonstration: making a truth obvious and certain, making clear the connection of some *predicate* with some *subject* by exposing the intermediate predicate or predicates which make a necessary link between the two.

difference: the characteristic distinguishing one *species* from others in the same *genus*, e.g. reasoning distinguishes human animals from all others.

effect: the product of *action*.

end: that for the sake of which an *agent* acts, the determinate goal of an *action*. See also *good*.

essence: some unifying significance which can be discovered to bind together certain phenomena, so that what *exists* in and through them is manifested. That which makes a thing the sort of thing it is; its distinctive nature.

eternity: that which corresponds to duration and *time* in our apprehension of the unchangeable; the instantaneously whole and perfect possession of unending life. cf p. 135 ff.

existence: the most fundamental meaning of *actuality*. Since the idea of existing is the most primitive of all ideas, and is contained in all other ideas (cf 1a. 3, 4, p. 33 and 1a. 5, 1, p. 65), it cannot be *defined* in terms of some more primitive idea; one arrives at it by a sort of extrapolation from other less primitive ideas, such as *action* or possession. Thus to conceive of a thing as existing is to conceive all the particular doings the thing does as expressing one single unifying doing; or to conceive all the particular properties the thing possesses as expressing one single unifying having. Existence is the act of having meaningful identity, of actually possessing *essence*. See also *substance, being, categories*.

form: that which brings determination to *matter*; the *definiteness* and intelligible 'shape' of a thing. Also see p. 24, note *a* and p. 26, note *c*.

genus: a *universal* idea comprehending several *species*, a relatively indeterminate conception of what a thing is. Also see *definition*.

good: that which suits and attracts; that which, because it is *actual* and *perfect*, is to be aimed at; the general character of *ends*.

individual: that which can share *actuality* in common but cannot itself be shared in common. Contrast *universal*. Thus, the character of being a punctuation-mark when considered in the abstract is a universal; but in the concrete the punctuation-mark at the end of this sentence, and the being a punctuation-mark of *that* punctuation-mark, are individual.

matter: that out of which something comes to *exist*, the *potentiality* of new *forms* present in any *substance* subject to *change*. Also see p. 24, note *a*.

nature: often, *essence*. Sometimes, essence regarded not only as a *principle* of a thing's *existence*, but also further of its activity (*action*) and passivity (*passion*).

232

participation: sharing a property or mode of *being* which belongs primarily to something else; partaking such a property not to the fullest extent to which that property can *exist.* Also see p. 26, note *b.* Used especially to refer to Plato's theory that the existence of material things is a striving to conform to immaterial ideals; beautiful things, for example, are participations of Beauty Itself. Also see 1a. 6, 4, pp. 91–3.

passion: one of the *categories* of *being*: a being acted upon; any *change* when regarded as belonging to the thing in which it occurs. Contrast *action.*

perfect: not lacking *actuality*; that in which nothing required by a thing's particular mode of *existence* fails to exist.

place: one of the *categories* of *being*: the *definiteness* or determinateness of something in relation to other bodies in space; the immediate environment. Compare *time.*

potentiality: being capable of *actualization.* Active potentiality (or *power*) is capability of *acting* upon another thing; passive potentiality is capability of *passion*, of being acted upon by another thing.

power: potentiality of *action.*

predicable: one of five types of *universal* ideas, viz *genus, species* or *definition, difference, property* and *accident*; one of five ways, therefore, in which *predicates* can be related to a *subject.*

predicament: another name for a *category* of *being.*

predicate: that which is predicated, where 'to predicate' means 'to say something about something'. Also see Appendix 1.

principle: any starting-point, be it spatial, temporal, and whether it initiate *action, being* or *understanding.* Also see *cause.*

property: that which belongs to something. Often used more strictly to mean that which, while not belonging to a thing's *substance* or *essence*, nevertheless belongs to the thing necessarily. Thus, for example, a sense of humour is a property of the human animal, for whereas it does not *define* him, yet it is a necessary consequence of the rationality which does define him. See also *accident* and p. 38, note *a.*

quality: one of the *categories* of *being*: any modification of a *substance* inherent in that substance. Less frequently used to describe the specific *difference* which *defines* a thing by modifying some more universal generic idea.

quantity: one of the *categories* of *being*: the property of being divisible into parts without *qualitative* change, and yet being actually undivided.

relation: one of the *categories* of *being*: an inherent property of a *substance*, which does not modify the substance in itself, but only as compared to some other substance. Relations are necessarily founded on some more primary modification of one or both of the substances involved, either *quantitative*, or resulting from *action* and *passion.*

species: a *universal* idea comprehending several *individuals* of identical *form.* Also see *genus, difference.*

subject: that about which something is *predicated,* to which some property is attached.

substance: the most primary sense (or *category*) of *being*: that which *exists* without existing-in another thing. Hence contrasted with predicamental *accidents.* The word 'substance' is often used as equivalent to *essence,* a use which Aristotle called 'second substance' in contrast with 'first substance' defined as above.

time: one of the *categories* of *being*: the *definiteness* or determinateness of an occurrence in relation to other occurrences before or after. Compare *place.* Hence a measure of *change* and *existence* according to before and after.

transcendental: a mode of *being* which is present in every *genus* of things, and is therefore common to all beings by *analogy.* Examples are being *good* and being one.

universal: that which is common to many *individuals* and can be *predicated* of all of them.

Index

(Numbers refer to pages, italics to notes and appendices)

A

2—R

P

Q

R

S

Made in United States
North Haven, CT
25 January 2023